TRADITIONAL
JEWISH
COOKING

Also by
BETTY S. GOLDBERG

Chinese Banquet, Goldberg Style
Chinese Cooking, Goldberg Style
Chinese Kosher Cooking
International Cooking for the Kosher Home

TRADITIONAL
JEWISH
COOKING

Betty S. Goldberg

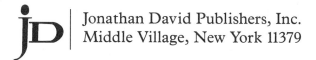

Jonathan David Publishers, Inc.
Middle Village, New York 11379

TRADITIONAL JEWISH COOKING

Jonathan David Publishers, Inc.
68-22 Eliot Avenue
Middle Village, New York 11379

2 4 6 8 9 7 5 3

Library of Congress Cataloging-in-Publication Data

Goldberg, Betty S.
    Traditional Jewish cooking / by Betty S. Goldberg.
        p.   cm.
    Includes index.
    ISBN 0-8246-0405-9
    1. Cookery, Jewish.   I. Title.
TX724.G6527   1994
641.5'676-dc20

93-44920
CIP

Book design by Jennifer Vignone
Printed in the United States of America

For my children-in-law

ACKNOWLEDGEMENTS

I could not have enjoyed writing this book without the help of the following:

My publisher, Alfred J. Kolatch, who set an example through three of his own books; my editor, David Kolatch, who gave me the focus through his patient, painstaking, and thorough direction; Nina Müller, for her early encouragement; Bernice Sisson for her honesty; Joyce and Avram Hellerman, who answered my every question with thoughtfulness and frequent humor; Rita Bush and Eleanor Feldman, Yiddish mavens; my mother, Edith Schultz, who shared the memories; my grandmothers, Lillie Sarnoff and Jane Schultz, who were with me in a special way throughout the cooking and writing; my husband, Josh, who gave me first dibs on the computer; our children, Aaron, Michael, Benjamin, and Nancy, who allowed me to teach them what I know about cooking, and then surpassed the master; and many others who contributed in various ways. I thank you all.

CONTENTS

A GRAND HERITAGE

"Ooooo, this is just like my mother used to make it!" These were magical words in our household, for they meant that my parents would be glowing—Mom because she had succeeded in duplicating her mother-in-law's dish, Dad because of a happy link to his past. For my parents, the special foods that are part of our heritage were a source of satisfaction and connection.

My food traditions come from an Ashkenazic heritage, for while my grandmothers, my parents, and my sister and I were all born in New York City, my roots go back to Russia and Poland, Germany and Hungary. I grew up with the foods of Eastern Europe: *blintzes, latkes, holishkes, knishes,* pastrami, corned beef on Jewish rye bread, chopped liver. In the late 1970s, when I was introduced to traditional Sephardic preparations by an Israeli friend, a marvelous new world of Jewish foods was opened up to me, and I was enjoying *hummus,* date *charoset,* and garlicky eggplant salad long before these foods became commonplace in parts of the United States.

When I began to gather ideas and test recipes for this cookbook, long forgotten images flashed into my mind, bringing unanticipated pleasure as glimpses of my past unfolded. As I talked with my mother about her own recollections, I wondered how many of today's Jewish mothers will remember how their grandmothers cooked, how many stories will be passed down, how many recipes. We are missing a piece of our culture when we lose touch with our traditional Jewish foods, the ones all our grandmothers used to cook by feel, by look, by taste. We're missing a grand opportunity to pass along a vital part of what makes us Jewish.

We are living in an age of change and intermarriage. Traditional Jewish cooking provides a delicious pathway for a non-Jewish partner or recent convert to Judaism to understand the connections between Jewish holidays and Jewish foods, to learn how to cook traditional foods, and to appreciate what may be new food tastes and ideas.

And so I am presenting here the *kugels,* the *blintzes,* the *kreplach,* the *knaidlach,* trying to duplicate tastes of the past while making the recipes manageable for today's cooks. I, too, cook by feel, look and taste, and in preparing this book and converting my estimates to ounces, tablespoons and cups, I know I am connecting my past with generations of the future. I hope you will find your own links to the past in happy memories as you taste your way through, and I hope you will pass them along to your children and theirs. And if you are just beginning to learn about Jewish foods, join me in a sumptuous exploration of the tastes and traditions of Judaism.

Betty S. Goldberg
Woodbridge, Connecticut

A BRIEF HISTORY OF JEWISH MIGRATIONS

Jewish civilization began in what we now call the Middle East. Babylonia (now Iraq) was for many centuries the foremost center of Jewish life. Jews also inhabited Egypt, Palestine, Persia (now Iran), Syria, and Yemen, and vibrant Jewish communities existed as far east as Bombay, India, and in the city of Kaifeng, in China's Henan province.

Over hundreds of years many Jews followed the trade routes and migrated west, settling in large numbers in Spain, and also in Portugal. The Jews of the Iberian Peninsula became known as "Sephardim" (Sepharad is Hebrew for Spain). Other Jews traveled to Italy, France, and to the Germanic countries of Eastern Europe, going as far east as what is now Russia and Ukraine. Most of these migrants settled in Germany, therefore these Jews became known as "Ashkenazim" (Ashkenaz is Hebrew for Germany).

Following the expulsion of the Jews from Spain in 1492 and from Portugal in 1497, large numbers of Sephardim were welcomed by the Ottoman Empire into Turkey and Greece, and others settled in North African countries. While the term "Sephardic" technically refers only to the Sepharads, or Jews of Spain and their descendants who migrated to other parts of Europe and North Africa, cookbook authors broaden the definition to include Jews of the Orient and the Mediterranean.

The first permanent Jewish settlers in North America arrived in New Amsterdam (now Lower Manhattan) in the fall of 1654 from Recife, a Dutch colony in Brazil, where they had fled from Spain and then Portugal during the Inquisition. When Portugal recaptured Recife, the safety of the Jews was again threatened, and twenty-three of them left for America. Other Jews left from the Netherlands or from England to settle in New York, and by 1733 there were Jewish settlements in Rhode Island, Pennsylvania, South Carolina, and

Georgia. But the biggest waves of Jewish immigration to America were from Germany and Austria in the late 1840s and 1850s, and from the countries we now know as Poland, Hungary, the Czech Republic and the Slovak Republic, Russia, and Ukraine in the early 1900s up to 1918. Therefore, until recently, it was from the Ashkenazim that most American Jewish cooking developed. However, since the birth of the State of Israel in 1948, American Jews have been increasingly aware of the delights of Sephardic cooking. The best of both the Ashkenazic and Sephardic traditions are presented in this cookbook.

WHAT IS JEWISH CUISINE?

The cuisine we know as Jewish cooking is multinational, a blend of the cooking of the countries in which Jews have lived modified by special dietary laws and the ingredients available as migration has occurred. In the United States, Jewish cooking is broadly divided into Ashkenazic (Eastern and Central European) and Sephardic (Middle Eastern and Mediterranean). With these two culinary heritages, traditional Jewish cooking is varied and versatile.

What makes foods Jewish? The foods of any culture, adopted and adapted by Jewish cooks to meet the laws of *kashrut* (the dietary laws as spelled out in the Book of Leviticus) and served repeatedly in Jewish households, become Jewish foods to us. *Borscht* is of Russian origin, to be sure, but it is known also as a Jewish preparation because it is served in Jewish households all over the United States by Americans who are not necessarily of Russian background.

Some traditional Jewish foods have developed around religious rituals. *Charoset* (a fruit-and-nut mixture) and horseradish, for example, are an integral part of the Passover *Seder*, serving respectively as a reminder of the mortar used when the Israelites were slaves in Egypt, and of the bitterness of slavery. Other dishes—*matzo brei* (a matzo-and-egg preparation) and flourless cakes and cookies—come from the biblical commandment to eat only unleavened bread for seven days during Passover. Some Jewish foods celebrate historic events. While *latkes* (pancakes) can be cooked any time during the year, potato latkes fried in oil during Chanukah serve as a reminder of the miracle when one day's worth of oil burned for eight. The *hamantashen* (triangular-filled pastries) enjoyed at Purim are very specifically tied to the holiday in which evil Haman is destroyed by Queen Esther and her cousin, Mordecai.

An imposing variety of *kugels* (puddings) made with noodles, rice, matzo, potatoes, carrots, or other vegetables is available in the repertoire of a traditional Jewish cook, for whenever there is a crowd to be fed there will be at least one kugel on the table. Kugels may have originated as a way to amply provide for a big family get-together without spending a lot of time or going to great expense. Main dish, side, and dessert kugels that can be prepared in advance and are reasonably inexpensive and transportable account for their popularity at synagogue events all over the United States. Who doesn't say yes when asked to bring a kugel?

Many Jewish foods are a tribute to the resourcefulness and ingenuity of cooks with limited financial means who made the most of affordable ingredients. The skin of the chicken neck stuffed with a mixture of flour, seasonings, and *schmaltz* (rendered chicken fat) is as tasty as it is filling. A few chicken livers, barely a mouthful for one person, can be enjoyed by several people when the cooked livers are chopped with a hard-cooked egg and some onion. Meat *tsimmes* offers a scrumptious blend of vegetables and potatoes or other starch, with just a small amount of meat sufficing to give the preparation a meaty flavor.

The Bible prohibits the consumption of blood. Because of the difficulty in removing all blood vessels from the hindquarter of an otherwise kosher animal, most kosher butchers sell only the forequarter. Therefore, kosher cooks have learned to use all permissible meats, sometimes making unusual dishes such as *p'tcha,* or calves' foot jelly. Some of the least tender cuts of beef, fresh brisket for one, are turned into savory preparations for holiday meals and other family gatherings. Leftover brisket is used to make *kreplach* (triangular meat-filled pockets of dough), reinforcing the identification of brisket as a Jewish food. Flanken (short ribs that are cut across the bone) has a place in Jewish cuisine because it can be cooked for long hours without drying out in the Sabbath preparation known as *cholent.*

Through repetition, enjoyment, association with happy memories, celebration of holidays, and the comfort of the familiar, special foods are passed along from one generation to the next. In other words, the foods become traditional Jewish foods. In keeping with tradition, all the recipes in this cookbook are kosher, and no *ersatz* ingredients are used to make them such. With chicken fat to use in meat meals, butter in dairy, vegetable or olive oil in either, we continue to prepare tempting Jewish foods with natural ingredients, the way all Jewish grandmothers once did.

WHAT DOES IT MEAN TO BE KOSHER?

The Jewish dietary laws are set forth in the Bible, primarily in the Book of Leviticus. They were instituted as a way to help Israel become a holy nation, separate from its idol-worshipping neighbors. Adherence to the laws in modern times—at once an expression of solidarity with the Jewish community and separateness from non-Jewish neighbors—provides a powerful way of passing down a sense of Jewishness from one generation to the next.

Kosher, in Hebrew *kasher,* means "ritually correct or ritually fit." The Bible lists the characteristics of a kosher animal: it must have genuine split hooves and it must chew its cud. Cows, goats, and sheep are some kosher animals; pigs, horses, and hares are among those prohibited. Kosher fish must have fins and scales; therefore, no shellfish are kosher. While permissible birds are not specifically mentioned in the Bible, any "clean" bird is fit for consumption. Chicken, ducks, geese, and pigeons are among the birds traditionally accepted as kosher. Nonkosher wild birds and birds of prey, including the hawk and the owl, are listed in the Bible.

A kosher animal must be ritually slaughtered by a well-trained *shochet* (ritual slaughterer). The purpose of ritual slaughtering is to drain off as much blood as possible from the animal, because blood, considered to be the essence of life, should not be consumed. Ritually slaughtered meat must then be koshered in a soaking and salting procedure designed to draw off as much of the remaining blood as possible. Although the koshering of meat is still done by some people at home, many kosher butchers sell meat already koshered. If the meat is prepackaged, it will often be labeled "koshered."

Liver contains so much blood that it cannot be koshered by soaking and salting. Instead, liver is broiled on a rack under an open flame in the oven or over hot coals. Fish, on the other hand, contain a small amount of blood and need not be koshered.

Observant Jews do not mix meat and dairy products when preparing food or when serving a meal. Separate dishes, cookware, and flatware are used in preparing and eating meat and dairy products. A waiting period is required between eating meat and dairy foods, and between eating dairy and meat preparations, but the intervals are not specified in the Bible or the Talmud. Therefore, the waiting periods have traditionally varied from community to community, depending on the rulings of local rabbinic authorities. Because of the prohibition against mixing meat and milk products, Orthodox law does not permit the consumption of cheeses made with rennet, which comes from the lining of an animal's stomach. Therefore, some cheeses are not considered to be kosher.

Foods that are considered neither meat nor dairy are called *pareve*, the Yiddish word for neutral. All plant life is both kosher and pareve. While fish are pareve, in some communities fish and meat courses must be separated by bread or soup; some do not combine fish and meat in the same preparation; and some do not serve fish during a meal in which dairy products are consumed.

Foods that are manufactured under rabbinic supervision and are certified as kosher have an identifying symbol printed on the box or package label. There are more than fifty *kashrut*-certifying entities in the United States, each with its own identifying symbol. The largest certifying agency, the Union of Orthodox Jewish Congregations, uses the Ⓤ symbol. A "κ" on a package indicates that the product is under rabbinic supervision, but one must write to the manufacturer for the name of the certifying agent.

For a complete discussion of the dietary laws, *The Jewish Home Advisor,* by Alfred J. Kolatch (Jonathan David Publishers, Inc.), is recommended.

JEWISH HOLIDAYS
AND FOOD TRADITIONS

THE SABBATH

The Sabbath, *Shabbat* in Hebrew, is a weekly holy day that is set aside as a day of rest and spiritual renewal. It is a weekly reminder of Creation. After creating the world in six days, God rested on the seventh. In Jewish tradition, the Sabbath is ushered in at sundown on Friday night with the lighting of the candles, and ends after sunset on Saturday evening when the *Havdalah* (Hebrew for separation or division) candle is extinguished.

A tradition of eating three meals during the Sabbath stems from a verse in Exodus in which Moses uses the word "today"—referring to the Sabbath—three times in telling the people to eat the manna in the desert. The first of the three traditional Sabbath meals is a lavish, leisurely repast enjoyed on Friday nights. The meal begins with the recitation of the *Kiddush* ("Sanctification") prayer over wine. A blessing is then recited over two *challot* (plural of *challah*), the traditional braided Sabbath bread. The bread is cut or broken and a small piece is distributed and eaten by each person present. Often, the first course of the Friday night meal is *gefilte* fish, a preparation which in earlier times was seen as an inexpensive way to extend a small amount of fish to feed a whole family. The first course is followed by soup—perhaps chicken soup with matzo balls or *kreplach*. The centerpiece might be a golden brown roast chicken, a savory brisket, a succulent stuffed veal breast, or—if the first course was not fish—a festive fish preparation. The main course is always accompanied by several appealing side dishes, frequently a potato or noodle kugel and at least one vegetable preparation. The traditional Friday night meal concludes with dessert and coffee or tea, following which the Grace After Meals is recited.

The Bible prohibits the kindling of a fire on the Sabbath. While precooked foods can be kept warm, no new cooking may begin. At the same time, in most communities it is traditional to eat a hot midday meal on Saturday. The solution to the apparent contradiction is a number of delicious preparations that can be cooked prior to the Sabbath, then held at a very low temperature all night, to be enjoyed at noon the next day. *Cholent* (pronounced *tsc*holent), *hamin,* and *tsimmes* are among the tasty traditional Jewish dishes that lend themselves to this kind of cooking.

Seuda Shelishit (literally, "Third Meal") is a light meal eaten late in the afternoon in the synagogue or at home. Challah, pickled herring or herring salad, hard-cooked eggs, and a plain cake might be served.

A FRIDAY NIGHT SABBATH MEAL

Challah (page 300)
Gefilte Fish (page 190)
Chicken Soup (page 80) with Chicken Kreplach (page 88)
Stuffed Breast of Veal (page 161)
Spätzle (page 262)
Applesauce (page 236)
Peas with Sautéed Mushrooms
Lemon-Orange Sponge Cake (page 336)
Fresh Melon and Strawberries or Fresh Citrus Fruit Cup

ROSH HASHANAH

Rosh Hashanah, literally "Head of the Year," is celebrated in September on the first two days of the Hebrew month of Tishri, which is actually the seventh month of the Jewish calendar. (Some Reform congregations observe Rosh Hashanah for only one day as prescribed in the Bible.) In ancient Palestine the new year coincided with the agricultural cycle. It was in Tishri that the final harvest was completed, and a new annual cycle was about to begin.

In modern times, Rosh Hashanah begins a ten-day period of prayer and introspection known as the Days of Awe or Days of Repentance. In Jewish tradition, during this ten-day period God passes judgment over every individual, with final judgment rendered on Yom Kippur. The traditional Rosh Hashanah greeting is *Le-shana tova tikatevu*, "May you be inscribed for a good year."

Many of the foods associated with Rosh Hashanah symbolize the hope for sweetness and prosperity in the New Year. Round challot are served as an expression of the hope that the coming year will be full, well rounded, and wholesome, uninterrupted by tragedy. Carrots are cut into rounds to represent gold coins. Pomegranates, popular since biblical times as a fruit identified with fertility and prosperity because of the hundreds of seeds they contain, are also eaten during the Rosh Hashanah holiday. Fish, another symbol of fertility, are served with the head on (or, fish heads are served), indicating the hope that the people partaking of the meal will assume leadership roles in the coming year. During the Middle Ages, a sheep's head was displayed or consumed in many communities, a reminder of the substitution of the ram for Isaac.

Honey, a favorite Rosh Hashanah food, is described in the Talmud as one of "seven healing substances." Pieces of apple or challah are dipped into honey to symbolize the expectation of a sweet and healthy New Year. *Lekach* (honey cake) and *taiglach* (a mound of balls of dough that are baked, then cooked in honey) are enjoyed during the holiday as well.

Other food traditions are reminders of the agricultural origin of this important holiday. Rosh Hashanah is ushered in after sundown with a lavish meal that is served at home and enjoyed with family and friends. This festive dinner contains an abundance of delicious foods, including fresh fruits and vegetables, an omen for a plentiful harvest as well as a wish for a full, successful year. It is traditional on Rosh Hashanah to serve the first fruits of the new season, including apples, figs, and grapes, in recognition of the beginning of the harvest season.

A ROSH HASHANAH MENU

**Round Challah (page 303) with honey available for dipping
Whole Gefilte Fish (page 192)
Chicken Soup (page 80) with Brisket Kreplach (page 88)
Oven-braised Brisket (page 142)
Roast Potatoes or Potato Kugel (page 286)
Honeyed Carrots (page 238)
Steamed Green Beans with Toasted Slivered Almonds
Applesauce (page 236)
Honey Cake (page 343) and/or Taiglach (page 390)
A Bowl of Fresh Fruit**

YOM KIPPUR

Yom Kippur, the Day of Atonement, concludes the Ten Days of Repentance that begin with Rosh Hashanah. This day of fasting begins before sunset on the evening of the tenth day of Tishri, which generally falls in late September or early October. Although Jews observe complete abstinence from food and drink for twenty-four hours on Yom Kippur, there are food traditions connected with the holy day. (The Yom Kippur fast actually extends for approximately twenty-five hours when one takes into account that it begins before sunset and concludes after nightfall the following day.)

A substantial pre-fast meal similar to a Sabbath or holiday meal is eaten before the family leaves for the synagogue for the *Kol Nidre* service on Yom

Kippur eve. In many Ashkenazic homes, kreplach are eaten because the chopped filling is a reminder of the flogging (chopping) to which Jews subjected themselves as atonement for their sins in earlier times. While the meal itself is plentiful and festive, the occasion is solemn.

The meal must be concluded before sundown. As a practical matter, it is wise to keep the salt and the spice content of the pre-fast meal to a minimum, and it is also a good idea to drink ample fluids before the fast begins.

For the break-the-fast meal after Yom Kippur, it is traditional to serve herring or another salty fish to encourage the consumption of water, replenishing fluids lost during the fast. A spread including bagels and lox, pickled herring, and smoked whitefish will be welcomed by the hungry family.

A Pre-Fast Yom Kippur Menu

Round Challah (page 303)
Gefilte Fish (page 190)
Chicken Soup (page 80) with Chicken Kreplach (page 88)
Roast Chicken (page 170)
Applesauce (page 236)
Rice Kugel (page 276)
Steamed Broccoli sprinkled with Lemon Juice
Tossed Salad
Orange-flavor Marble Cake (page 335)
Compote of Dried Fruit (page 329) or a Bowl of Fresh Fruit

SUKKOT

The seven-day holiday of Sukkot, which begins five days after Yom Kippur, is known both as the Festival of Ingathering and the Festival of Booths. Sukkot was originally an agricultural festival in which farmers came to Jerusalem by foot to visit the Temple, bringing gifts of their first fall crops to the Priests. It is popularly known as the holiday that commemorates the forty-year journey that brought the Israelites from slavery in Egypt to the Promised Land. During their wanderings in the desert, they built temporary living structures called *sukkot* (plural of the Hebrew *sukkah,* meaning "booth" or "hut"), which offered them protection from the elements.

The Bible presents both aspects of the holiday in Leviticus, Chapter 23. Verse 39 of that chapter states: "...on the fifteenth day of the seventh month, when ye have gathered in the fruits of the land, ye shall keep the feast of the Lord seven days." Verses 42 and 43 state: "Ye shall dwell in booths seven days...that your generations may know that I made the Children of Israel to dwell in booths when I brought them out of the Land of Egypt."

The coincidence of the agricultural pilgrimage with the building of sukkot is celebrated as one holiday by Jews who—immediately after Yom Kippur—begin building a temporary outdoor dwelling (sukkah) in which the family will eat and sometimes sleep during the holiday. The sukkah is adorned with fresh fruits and flowers, and meals featuring an abundance of vegetables and fruits, reminders of a bountiful harvest, are enjoyed in the sukkah throughout the holiday.

During Sukkot, it is traditional among Ashkenazim to serve stuffed cabbage (*holishkes*), symbolic of abundance. Stuffed vegetables and fruit-stuffed pastries are enjoyed by Sephardim. Vegetable-rich soups and stews, fruit-stuffed poultry, and fruity desserts are served during the holiday as well. As a practical consideration, one-dish meals are easy to carry out to the sukkah and will remain warm in a covered casserole on a cold October evening. A tsimmes overflowing with fruits and vegetables is a good choice during Sukkot. Or, try the following menu, which features Sephardic delicacies.

A Sukkot Menu

Lamb-and-Spinach Stuffed Pastry (page 56)
Rich Lentil Soup (page 112)

Spice-and-Nut Stuffed Mackerel (page 201)
Wheat Pilaf (page 272)
Apple Strudel with Phyllo (page 355)

HOSHANA RABBA

The final day of Sukkot, Hoshana Rabba ("Great Hosanna"), marks the end of the awesome holiday period that begins with Rosh Hashanah. According to Jewish tradition, while Yom Kippur is the day on which one's fate is decided, Hoshana Rabba represents the final opportunity to reverse an unfavorable decree. Willows are beaten on Hoshana Rabba to represent the flogging ritual to which Jews once subjected themselves on Yom Kippur. As is customary on Yom Kippur, kreplach filled with chopped (beaten) ingredients are traditionally eaten on the last day of Sukkot.

CHANUKAH

Chanukah, which means "dedication," is rooted in a historical event marked by the successful rebellion of the Jews of Palestine against the oppression of the Syrian-Greeks in the second century B.C.E. In an effort to impose the Hellenistic way of life upon the inhabitants of Palestine, King Antiochus IV of Syria prohibited the observance of sacred Jewish practices, and converted the Temple in Jerusalem into a pagan shrine. In 165 B.C.E., a revolt led by Judah "the Maccabee" and his brothers, members of the Hasmonean family of Mattathias the Priest, succeeded in routing the Syrian-Greeks from Palestine. The Temple was cleansed, restored, and rededicated.

According to the Talmud, when the Syrian-Greeks captured the Temple, they desecrated nearly all the jugs of oil that the High Priest had prepared for lighting the Temple *menorah* (Hebrew for candelabrum). When the Temple was rededicated by the Jews, only one small undefiled jug of oil could be found, barely enough oil to burn in the menorah for one day. The High Priest kindled the menorah, and a miracle happened—the flame continued to burn for eight days.

Chanukah is observed as an eight-day holiday beginning on the twenty-fifth day of the Hebrew month Kislev, which usually falls in December. In celebration of the miracle of the oil, Jewish families light special nine-branched *menorot* (plural of menorah) beginning with one candle or oil cup the first night, two the second, until eight have been kindled on the last night. The ninth branch is the *shamash,* or servant, which functions to light the other candles.

The story of Chanukah is recounted in the Book of Maccabees, one of the fourteen books of the Apocrypha. Because it is not mandated by the Torah, Chanukah is considered to be a minor holiday in Jewish tradition. In practice, in the United States Chanukah is celebrated in ways that exceed its traditional importance, particularly in the area of gift-giving.

Most of the Chanukah food traditions that have developed center around the miracle of the oil. Potato *latkes* (pancakes) fried in oil are a favorite Chanukah food among Ashkenazim, and Chanukah parties that feature latkes are common. Sweets fried in oil are popular among Sephardic Jews. In Israel, fried doughnuts are a favorite Chanukah treat.

Less well known is the tradition of serving goose on Chanukah. In earlier centuries the rendered fat of fowl was used to prepare holiday delicacies. It became traditional to serve goose on Chanukah and to reserve some of its rendered fat for use on Passover.

Although cheese is associated primarily with the holiday of Shavuot, there is a story in the Book of Judith, another book of the Apocrypha, linking cheese to Chanukah. According to legend, Nebuchadnezzar's army was about to destroy Israel when Judith, a member of the Hasmonean family, fed cheese to the general of the army. The cheese made the general thirsty, he became drunk upon consuming large amounts of wine, and he was beheaded by Judith, ensuring a Jewish victory. Cheese latkes and other cheese delicacies are served during Chanukah to commemorate the event.

A CHANUKAH MENU

Chicken Soup (page 80) with Mandlen (page 84)
Roast Goose (page 177) or Roast Duckling (page 174)
Applesauce (page 236)
Potato Latkes (page 288)
Steamed Carrots
Spinach-and-Mushroom Salad with
Lemon Juice and Olive Oil Dressing
Apple Cake (page 331)

PURIM

The holiday of Purim celebrates a historical event recounted in the Book of Esther, known popularly as "the Megillah" (*megillah* is Hebrew for scroll). In the fifth century B.C.E., Haman, the prime minister of King Ahasueros of Persia, was planning to annihilate the Jews. The date for the massacre, the thirteenth of Adar, was chosen by lots (*purim* in Persian). Haman's plot was foiled by his archenemy "Mordecai the Jew," as he was called by Haman, and Mordecai's cousin Esther, who had become the wife of the king by winning a beauty contest.

At great risk to herself, Queen Esther, who was not known by King Ahasueros to be Jewish, went before the king to plead for her people. Her efforts were successful, Haman's decree was nullified, Haman was executed in place of Mordecai, and the Jews were allowed to avenge themselves. Victory was complete on the fourteenth of Adar (usually falling in March), which is when Purim is observed by most Jews. (In Shushan, a walled city, the fighting continued for an extra day. Therefore, in walled cities it is customary to celebrate Purim a day later.)

The most well-known food associated with Purim is *hamantashen*, triangular-shaped pastries originally filled with poppy seeds or *mohn* (Hebrew for manna, described in Exodus 16:31). The pronunciation of mohn is similar to the Hebrew pronunciation of Haman, hence the connection between poppy seed pastries and Ha*man*. Although some say the shape of the pastries resembles the type of hat worn by Haman, the more traditional explanation for the three-cornered pastries is that Queen Esther derived her strength from her antecedents, and the shape represents the three patriarchs of Judaism: Abraham, Isaac, and Jacob. For this reason, triangular-shaped kreplach are also eaten on Purim.

From a culinary perspective, for many people the celebration of Purim is synonymous with hamantashen. As the fourteenth of Adar approaches, you know it is time to take out the poppy seeds. However, there are other important food customs associated with the holiday.

Because of the urgency of the moment, Queen Esther went before King Ahasueros without requesting prior permission, an act punishable by death. The Jews fasted to lend support to Esther, and the thirteenth of Adar continues to be observed as a fast day known as the Fast of Esther.

Although Purim is a minor holiday—while it appears in the part of the Bible known as the Holy Writings, it is not mandated by the Torah—it is esteemed in Jewish tradition and is celebrated with a festive meal on the afternoon of the holiday. Long challot are prepared as a reminder of the rope from which Haman was hanged on the gallows in place of Mordecai. In celebration of the great and unexpected victory, the wine flows even more freely than on other joyous occasions. According to the Talmud, on Purim a man must drink so much wine that he is no longer capable of distinguishing between the words "blessed is Mordecai" and "cursed is Haman."

In some communities, sweet-and-sour dishes are prepared to note the duality of the holiday—a day of mourning, fasting, and potential devastation turned into a day of joy and celebration. Another custom is to eat legumes on Purim because it is said that Esther did not want to eat nonkosher food and therefore ate only beans and peas. Another explanation of this tradition is the idea that eating legumes was a charm against the spirits.

The Book of Esther calls on Jews to show their joy and thankfulness for the outcome of the events by sending gifts to friends, neighbors, and relatives.

The Hebrew name for the custom, *misholach manot,* popularly known as *shalach-mones,* means "sending portions." It is traditional to send cookies, pastries, and other delicacies to friends and to donate charity to the poor. Because the plural form of the word "portions" is used, it is traditional to send at least two portions of food or two different kinds of goodies to friends, and to donate to at least two charities or two poor people, or to make a double donation to one charity or person.

A Purim Menu

Challah, long shape to resemble ropes (page 300)
Split Pea Soup with Flanken (page 108)
Sweet-and-Sour Salmon (page 197)
Fried Kreplach (page 90) with Kasha Filling (page 269)
Spinach Salad topped with Chickpeas
Hamantashen (page 383)

PASSOVER

Passover, a celebration of freedom commemorating the Exodus from Egypt, was originally two separate springtime holidays that were not related to the escape of the Children of Israel from bondage. The two holidays were a pastoral festival and an agricultural festival. The older of the two festivals, *Chag Hapesach,* the "Festival of the Pesach [paschal lamb]," was a celebration by nomadic shepherds of the advent of spring, when an animal sacrifice was offered. *Chag Hamatzot,* the "Festival of Unleavened Bread," was an agricultural festival during which farmers celebrated the beginning of the grain harvest. Before cutting the grain they discarded all sour dough, the fermented dough that was used instead of yeast for leavening bread. Each holiday was celebrated separately during the month of Nissan.

In time, the two festivals merged with another event that occurred in the springtime, the Exodus. The Festival of the Paschal Lamb became identified with the events preceding the Exodus when God "passed over" the houses of the Children of Israel, sparing the firstborn the tenth plague. *Pesach,* the Hebrew name for the Passover holiday, derives from the Hebrew root *pasach,* which means both "paschal lamb" and "pass over." The Festival of Unleavened Bread became linked with the hasty departure of the Jews from Egypt, when they "took their dough before it was leavened" (Exodus 12:34). The three holidays are now celebrated as one, beginning on the fifteenth of Nissan.

According to the Bible, Passover must be observed for seven days, and it is celebrated for seven days in Israel. However, in the Diaspora, since the exile from Palestine in 70 C.E., many people have observed Passover for eight days. The Jewish calendar is a lunar calendar based on the appearance of the New Moon, which was officially announced after witnesses testified to its arrival. But since errors could be made in transmitting this information from the source in Jerusalem to distant places in outlying areas, an extra day of observance was added to Passover (and Sukkot, Shavuot, and Rosh Hashanah as well) in order to ensure that everyone would be celebrating the festival on the correct day. Although in modern times the exact time of the appearance of the New Moon can be communicated worldwide almost instantly, the tradition remains. In many homes, a *Seder*—a family home service and meal—is held both the first and second evenings. The length of time Passover is celebrated becomes important because of the food restrictions that are so much a part of the holiday observance.

Passover is the most widely celebrated holiday in the Jewish calendar. It is no mere coincidence that Passover is also both the most food-oriented and the most family-oriented holiday in Jewish tradition, for the excitement of special foods and the memory of happy family gatherings make the holiday remarkably popular. Even "secular" Jews who do not follow other religious practices celebrate Passover with a Seder and a festive meal at home, and they eat matzo during the holiday.

The basic guidelines that distinguish prohibited from permitted foods during Passover are stated specifically in the Bible. The Book of Exodus (13:7) mandates that matzo, or unleavened bread, must be eaten, and prohibits all leaven. The word used for leaven in Hebrew is *chametz*, which literally means "sour" or "fermented." The prohibition is against fermented grains; therefore it is permissible during Passover to use baking soda, which is a leavening agent but not a fermenting agent.

In addition, during Passover the Bible prohibits the use of five grains—wheat, barley, spelt, rye, and oats—and anything made from them with the exception of matzo, which must be made from one of them. The moment water is added to one of the five grains for making matzo (traditionally wheat is used), the dough must be mixed, shaped, baked, and removed from the oven within eighteen minutes, so that it will not have had time to become fermented. Once the matzo is baked within the time limit, it can then be ground fine to make matzo meal or matzo cake flour, because the flour in the matzo is no longer subject to fermentation. Thus, while one may not make cakes from ordinary flour during Passover, it is permissible to make cakes from matzo flour.

Extending the prohibition against using the five grains listed in the Bible, Ashkenazic Jews do not eat rice or legumes during Passover, and many do not eat corn or corn products. While there are differing rules in different Sephardic communities, among the Sephardim rice, corn, and leguminous plants (peas and beans) are generally permitted. Peanut oil is permitted in many Jewish communities even among the Ashkenazim because the processing of peanut oil does not involve the manufacture of peanut flour. Rabbinical authorities differ on what is permissible, and observant Jews follow the dictates of their own rabbis or their particular communities.

During Passover, unless you live in a community where there is a very limited Jewish population, you will notice many packaged products labeled "kosher for Passover." Matzo and matzo products need to be "kosher for Passover" to ensure that no fermentation has taken place. You may wonder why a product such as Coca-Cola needs to be "kosher for Passover." During the year Coke is made with corn syrup, but during Passover sugar is used. The same is true for U-Bet Chocolate Syrup, various jellies and jams, and other products, and for Jews who do not consume corn syrup during Passover, the products would not be permissible if the corn syrup were not replaced. In addition, because not even a speck of chametz is permissible during Passover, there must be an inspection by a rabbinical authority of the plant facilities in which the soda, syrup, jam, etc., is produced to ensure that the equipment is cleaned of all leaven, and once cleaned, that there is no possibility that an employee might inadvertently drop a crumb from a sandwich or snack into the machinery or the product.

Passover begins in the home before the actual holiday, because a thorough cleaning is necessary to rid the home of all chametz. Any utensil that has come in contact with chametz is prohibited during Passover. Some articles can be koshered and used during Passover; others cannot. Observant families have special dishes, pots and pans, flatware, and utensils used only during Passover.

All foods and articles that one owns that are chametz are stored in an unused closet. The ownership is temporarily transferred when the items are symbolically "sold" to a non-Jew before Passover begins, with the understanding that the agreement is over when the holiday ends. The day before the first evening of Passover, a search is conducted for chametz. A small amount is purposely left to be found so that it can be burned the next morning in a special ceremony. The house will be rid of chametz, but matzo should not be eaten the day of the Seder either, so that the first taste of matzo at the Seder will be special.

The celebration of Passover begins at home on Passover eve with the Seder, a family home service that uses a *Haggadah,* or Passover prayerbook, to tell the story of the Exodus. The word *seder* means "order." Even though thousands of different *Haggadot* (plural of Haggadah) have been published, the recitation of the story, the ritual, and the special foods eaten as part of the service follow a prescribed order that is outlined in every Haggadah.

Every Seder table has three *matzot* (plural of matzo) placed in front of the leader, and a Seder tray consisting of ceremonial foods that will be discussed and—for some of the foods—eaten during the service. Four cups of wine are consumed during the course of the Seder. A grand, festive meal is enjoyed. Although a whole lamb was eaten when the holiday was a pastoral celebration in ancient days, in modern times many people do not serve lamb for the Seder for fear that it might be interpreted as an indication that Judaism still has a sacrificial system.

A Passover Seder Meal

The Ceremonial Foods

Matzo
Maror (Horseradish, page 72)
Charoset (page 75 or 76)
Karpas (a vegetable, often parsley)
Chazeret (a second, more bitter vegetable, such as radish or watercress)
Zero'a (roasted lamb shankbone)
Baytza (roasted egg)
Salt Water for Dipping
Wine

The Meal

Hard-cooked Eggs in Salt Water
Gefilte Fish (page 190)
Chicken Soup (page 80) with Knaidlach (page 91)
Short Rib Tsimmes (page 150)
Roast Chicken (page 170) with Roast Duckling Stuffing (page 175)
Potato Kugel made with matzo meal (page 286)
Applesauce (page 236)
Steamed Asparagus with Lemon Juice and Oil
Passover Nut Torte (page 341)
A Bowl of Fresh Fruit

SHAVUOT

Shavuot originated as an agricultural festival that celebrated the harvesting of the first wheat crop in late spring. Along with Passover and Sukkot, it is one of three major Pilgrim Festivals. The farmers who journeyed to Jerusalem on the sixth of Sivan (occurring in May or June) brought with them an offering of the first "fruits" of the wheat crop, hence the name Festival of First Fruits or Harvest Festival for Shavuot. The holiday is also known as the Feast of Weeks, because Shavuot—Hebrew for weeks—is celebrated seven weeks and one day after the second day of Passover. The days until Shavuot are counted with reference to Passover, and in the Talmud Shavuot is considered to be a concluding holiday to Passover.

In talmudic times the holiday became associated with the Revelation on Mount Sinai. The Rabbis noted that the agricultural celebration of Shavuot and the events at Mount Sinai occurred in the same season at about the same time, and the agricultural holiday became a time for Torah study and celebration of the Torah. In the third century C.E., Shavuot became known also as the Time of the Giving of the Torah.

Shavuot food traditions are primarily related to the celebration of the Torah. It is traditional to eat dairy foods during the holiday, a custom often explained by the phrase "honey and milk under thy lips" from the Song of Songs (4:11). These words are interpreted as meaning that the Torah is as sweet and nourishing to the spirit as honey and milk are to the body. Another explanation for the consumption of dairy dishes on Shavuot is that the Israelites had just learned about the laws of *kashrut* (the dietary laws) and did not have time to prepare meat dishes; therefore, they ate dairy.

Shavuot coincides with the season when grazing animals give birth and milk is plentiful. This would account for the emphasis on dairy products as traditional foods for the holiday.

In some communities it is customary to serve dishes that are symbolic reminders of the giving of the Torah. For example, challot are decorated with a ladder on top to represent the ascent of Moses to Mount Sinai to receive the Torah. Cheese blintzes are presented in groups of two, side by side, to represent the two tablets received by Moses. Cheese kreplach are served as well, representing the three parts of the Bible: Torah, Prophets, and Holy Writings. Cheese-filled triangular-shaped pastries made with phyllo leaves are popular among Sephardim.

In the Middle East, a favorite dairy lunch for Shavuot is raw vegetables with yogurt cheese. The Ashkenazic equivalent is a bowl of vegetables with cottage cheese and sour cream. For dinner, in some communities it is customary to serve a cheese dish first, then, after at least an hour's wait, a meat preparation. This is because some people take the biblical injunction in Exodus 23:19, "The choicest first-fruits shalt thou bring to the House of the Lord. Thou shalt not seethe a kid in its mother's milk," to mean that two main dishes are to be served at the Shavuot holiday meal, a dairy selection followed by a meat preparation.

The menu below features cream of potato soup and cheesecake for dessert; therefore, no meat is included. For dinner, small *bourekas* can be served as a side dish with the soup, and a noodle kugel presented as the main dish. For a lighter meal, make the pastries large and omit the kugel.

A Shavuot Menu

Challah with Ladder Decoration (page 303)
Cream of Potato Soup (page 117)
Cheese-and-Spinach Bourekas (page 253)
Fresh Fruit Salad
Cottage Cheese Cake (page 345)

Appetizers and Condiments

Overtures and Accompaniments

Appetizers and Condiments

Although appetizers (*forshpeis* in Yiddish) are defined as tidbits served before the main course to stimulate the appetite, in many Jewish homes it can be said that appetizers are used not to stimulate, but to temporarily satisfy the family's hunger pangs. After all, who needs stimulation when one can smell the brisket roasting in the oven, the stuffed cabbage (*holishkes)* simmering on the stove?

Two categories of appetizer are part of Jewish meals. A *nosh*—a little snack eaten at any time—is an appetizer when served informally shortly before dinner, while more formal appetizers are served at the dining table as the first course of a meal. Chopped liver is a nosh when spread on crackers but a first-course appetizer when presented at the dinner table on a bed of lettuce. Even the more formal appetizers are often meant for very casual eating. One is not expected to eat a fricassee of chicken wings with a knife and fork, but to pick up the wings and enjoy every last bit of gravy, even to the point of licking the fingers.

The distinction between appetizer and main dish is not always crystal clear in Jewish cuisine, because many traditional Jewish appetizers are small portions of what can also be served as the main course. For a complete listing of appetizers refer to the Index, where you will find main and side dishes that are also traditionally served as appetizers.

Traditional Jewish condiments turn out to be preparations that do indeed stimulate the appetite. When you enter a kosher deli, you are greeted by bowls of sour dill pickles and tomatoes. Don't those condiments conjure up a tantalizing picture of sandwiches piled high with thin-sliced corned beef, tongue, or pastrami? And who doesn't look forward to the gefilte fish when a dish of horseradish is placed on the table?

We begin with a recipe that is not exactly an appetizer or a condiment, but it is so much a part of traditional Jewish cooking that it deserves to be first.

SCHMALTZ

Makes ½ cup

It is fitting that *schmaltz,* when not referring to rendered chicken fat, is defined as sentimentality, because the taste of schmaltz is the taste of yesterday, when no one would dream of throwing away a flavorsome source of food energy. When people who eat traditional chopped liver (made with chicken fat) light up with, "Ah, real chopped liver," they are enjoying a memory as well as a delicious flavor, and both contribute to the appeal of the preparation.

Butter may not be used with meat in the kosher kitchen; therefore chicken fat has long been used in Ashkenazic Jewish households for cooking and flavoring. Nowadays pareve margarine is available for meat meals, but no margarine comes close to the taste of chicken fat. Mashed potatoes that have been topped with onions sautéed in salted chicken fat are much livelier than mashed potatoes that are dotted with margarine, and *knaidlach* (matzo balls) made with schmaltz are improved by the richness of the fat. People who do not want to use chicken fat in recipes can substitute vegetable oil, or olive oil when the oil does not need to be mild-tasting. Or, oil can be substituted for part of the chicken fat.

Duck fat, while used by European cooks for centuries, has a stronger flavor and heavier aftertaste than chicken fat, and it has not become popular in traditional Jewish cooking in the United States. In earlier centuries, goose (even more fatty than duck) was traditionally served on Chanukah, and the rendered fat was reserved for Passover preparations.

The chicken fat that rises to the top when homemade chicken soup is prepared can be spooned off and transferred to a container, then refrigerated or frozen for later use in any recipe calling for schmaltz. Or, render chicken fat from solid pieces of fat, as in this recipe, or from chicken fat and skin.

A given quantity of unrendered chicken fat will yield about half its volume when rendered. Uncooked pieces of skin do not yield as much schmaltz as the solid pieces of fat. *Gribenes,* the crisp pieces that remain after the solid chicken fat and skin have been rendered, are most appealing when fresh and warm.

INGREDIENTS:

**1 cup uncooked pieces of solid chicken fat, cut into
½-inch pieces**

DIRECTIONS:

1. In a skillet just large enough to accommodate the amount being rendered in a single layer, cook the fat over moderate heat until it begins to sizzle and barely brown. Reduce the heat to prevent smoking of the rendered fat and to ensure gradual browning. Turn the pieces of solid fat from time to time for even browning. The chicken fat will take about 10 minutes to become rendered, and all the solid pieces (gribenes) will be crisp and brown, with no pieces of yellow fat remaining.

2. Remove the gribenes with a slotted spoon, and drain well on paper towels. The gribenes lose their crispness if refrigerated, but they can be left at room temperature for a few hours for snacking.

3. Cool the rendered chicken fat slightly before transferring to a heavy plastic container. If you are using a glass container for refrigerator storage, allow the hot fat to cool to lukewarm before transferring it to the jar. The schmaltz will keep for at least a week in the refrigerator, and it freezes well. Freezing in glass is not recommended.

CHOPPED CHICKEN LIVERS

Serves 6

What may have begun as a mother's clever means of making the liver from one chicken stretch into a treat for the whole family, chopped liver (*gehakte laber* in Yiddish) has almost a mystique about it now. Huge mounds of this unsophisticated mixture are featured at Bar and Bat Mitzvah receptions, and one can expect to find a bowl of chopped liver at family gatherings, whether casual or festive. Perhaps it reminds people of all economic backgrounds of simpler days.

The ideal equipment for chopping liver and eggs to the right consistency was a big wooden chopping bowl with a special curved blade, as standard in yesterday's traditional kitchen as a food processor is in a modern household. The pieces can be chopped moderately coarse to fine—and if you are careful, you can use a food processor—but traditional chopped liver is not pâté and should not be made into a paste. The amount of egg is a matter of personal taste. The less egg, the stronger the taste of the liver and the darker the color of the finished preparation. For a very strong liver taste, substitute beef liver for the chicken livers. Although chicken fat imparts a distinctive flavor that contributes to the nostalgic effect of chopped liver, you can use up to half mayonnaise or a salad oil and still benefit from the taste of the chicken fat.

INGREDIENTS:

1 pound chicken livers
4 to 6 eggs (graded large), hard-cooked
4 tablespoons schmaltz (page 40), approximately
1 cup chopped onion
Salt and freshly ground black pepper

DIRECTIONS:

1. Remove the membranes and fat from the chicken livers, then broil the livers until no trace of redness remains, turning as necessary. (For beef liver, devein the liver after it has been broiled.)

2. Chop the livers into ¼-inch pieces. Add the hard-cooked eggs and continue to chop the livers and eggs until both are chopped medium-coarse to fine.

3. In a small skillet, melt the chicken fat over medium heat. Add the onion, cooking until lightly browned.

4. Mix the onion into the chopped liver and egg, and pour in enough melted chicken fat to bind the mixture together, mixing with a fork. Season with salt and pepper. Taste and correct the seasonings.

5. Serve with crackers as an informal appetizer, on a bed of lettuce to begin a sit-down meal. For a sandwich of note, spread chopped liver on a piece of rye bread, cover with onion rounds, some tomato slices, then the top piece of rye to hold everything together.

   Note: To process chopped liver in a food processor, cut the eggs into quarters and process using the pulse setting (on and off for a few seconds) until the pieces are evenly coarse to fine. Cut the livers into half-inch pieces, then add half the livers at a time. Process, again using the pulse setting, until the pieces are the same size as the eggs. Add the onion, chicken fat, and the seasonings. Process just until mixed. Transfer to a bowl; taste and correct the seasonings. If the food processor has a small capacity, chop the eggs and livers separately, then mix them together in a bowl. Add the cooked onion and chicken fat as in Step 4 above.

VEGETARIAN "CHOPPED LIVER"

Makes 2 cups

An accommodation to the Jewish dietary laws, this green bean-and-walnut spread has a taste reminiscent of chopped liver but may be served before dairy or meat meals. Serve chilled on crackers or on a bed of lettuce garnished with tomatoes, just as you would chopped liver.

INGREDIENTS:

> 1 pound fresh green beans
> 2 tablespoons vegetable oil
> 1 cup chopped onion
> 4 eggs (graded large or extra large), hard-cooked
> 1 cup chopped walnuts
> Salt and freshly ground black pepper

DIRECTIONS:

1. Wash the beans, remove the stem ends, then steam the beans until they are tender. Cool under running water.

2. In a small skillet, sauté the onion in the oil until the edges brown lightly.

3. Chop the beans coarsely, chop in the eggs, then the walnuts. Add the onion, scraping the oil into the mixture. Continue chopping until the mixture is fine (but not a paste). Season to taste with salt and pepper. Chill before serving on crackers or on a bed of lettuce with tomatoes as a garnish.

CHOPPED EGGS AND ONION

Serves 2

Long before there was commercial mayonnaise, there was schmaltz, and it may be that chopped eggs and onion moistened with chicken fat is the forerunner of egg salad with mayonnaise and celery. If you do not have rendered chicken fat on hand and are starting with pieces of chicken fat and skin to be melted down, add the fresh, crisp gribenes to the chopped eggs for a mild-tasting crunch that contrasts well with the sharp chopped onion. And if you do not like a sharp onion flavor and its aftertaste, brown the onion lightly in the chicken fat before mixing with the chopped eggs. Serve the chopped eggs and onion on a bed of lettuce, and garnish with chopped fresh parsley if you like.

INGREDIENTS:

4 eggs (graded large), hard-cooked
½ cup diced onion
¼ cup melted schmaltz (page 40), approximately
Salt and freshly ground black pepper

DIRECTIONS:

1. Using a wooden chopping bowl with a curved blade, chop the eggs until the pieces are evenly coarse to fine. Or, mash with a fork. To use a food processor, quarter the eggs, chop using the pulse setting (on and off for a few seconds), then transfer the chopped eggs to a mixing bowl.

2. Mix in the diced onion, then the melted chicken fat. Season well with salt and pepper. Serve immediately, or chill before serving. Refrigerate leftovers.

POTATO KNISHES

Makes sixteen 2½-inch knishes

Although *knishes* are most often described as a pastry related to the *piroshki* (little pies) of Russia, the knish may also have its antecedents in the potato dumplings of Germany. The tasty homemade knishes of this recipe, made of a well-seasoned potato mixture that forms a golden crust on the outside while remaining soft inside, are similar to baked dumplings. Here, the sautéed onion filling enlivens the knish, but the filling is secondary to the thick potato exterior. For knishes similar to the "Coney Island" type sold from pushcarts in New York City, see page 290.

Serve knishes as a snack, appetizer, soup accompaniment, or side dish in place of potatoes.

INGREDIENTS:

¼ cup schmaltz (page 40), or 2 tablespoons unsalted butter
and 2 tablespoons oil for dairy, or all oil for pareve

2 cups chopped onion

Salt and freshly ground black pepper

3 cups mashed potatoes

2 tablespoons soft or melted schmaltz (half butter
and half oil for dairy, all oil for pareve)

2 eggs (graded large or extra large)

⅔ cup unbleached white flour (stir the flour, spoon
gently into a dry-measure cup, then level with
the edge of a spatula)

¼ **cup minced onion**
Additional flour for kneading

DIRECTIONS:

1. In an 8-inch skillet, heat the chicken fat (or butter and/or oil) over moderately low heat. Cook the 2 cups of onion until light brown around the edges, stirring occasionally. Season to taste with salt and pepper. Remove from the heat. Set aside.

2. Preheat the oven to 375 degrees F.

3. Lightly grease or oil a large baking sheet with vegetable shortening, a tasteless salad oil, or a little chicken fat. Set aside.

4. In a large mixing bowl, use a wooden or large metal spoon to combine the potatoes, 2 tablespoons of chicken fat (or butter and/or oil), eggs, flour, and minced onion. Season to taste with salt and pepper.

5. Spread about ¼ cup of flour on a clean work surface. Turn the potato mixture out onto the flour. Knead for a minute, working in all the flour.

6. Divide the dough into 16 equal pieces. Shape each piece into a 2-inch ball. Place each ball of dough on the baking sheet, leaving space between each ball to flatten slightly. With a spoon (soup spoon size) make a deep indentation in the center of each ball of dough. Place a heaping teaspoon of the cooked onion in each indentation. Use your fingers to bring the dough around to cover the onion. Brush the balls of dough with any chicken fat (or butter/oil) remaining from the cooked onion.

7. Bake in the middle of the oven for 30 minutes or until golden. Serve hot.

HUMMUS

Makes 1½ cups

The many names for chickpeas—*garbanzo* beans in Spanish, *ceci* to Italians, *chana dal* in India, *nahit* (Yiddish for heartseed or heart-pea) in Jewish cuisine—attest to the popularity of this starchy, high-protein legume. Chickpeas can be stored almost indefinitely in their hard, dried state, and if not ground into flour, they must be soaked and boiled to be edible. Unlike dried split green and yellow peas, chickpeas retain their shape no matter how long they are cooked, remaining chewy. Chickpeas are central to the Sabbath stews of Spain *(cocido)* and Morocco *(couscous)*, and a staple in many African, Middle Eastern, and Western European cuisines. In their simplest form, cooked chickpeas seasoned only with salt, pepper, and sometimes garlic are eaten out of hand as a snack, like peanuts.

The Middle Eastern chickpea spread known as *hummus* has become as well known in Jewish American homes as it is in Israel and neighboring Arab countries. The preparation is liberally flavored with garlic, lemon juice, and olive oil, with a consistency that may vary from coarse to a smooth purée. The addition of *tahina,* or sesame seed paste, will give the hummus a somewhat nutty taste and will make the mixture smoother. Note that when the hummus is prepared hours in advance, the garlic and lemon juice flavors will be stronger than when the dish is eaten shortly after preparation.

As an all-natural, high-protein vegetarian product, purchased hummus has found favor among health food advocates and is widely available in health food stores and many supermarkets, but it is very easy to prepare at home. If you use chickpeas frequently and have a cup left over now and then, divide the recipe in half and have a healthy snack in five minutes. Hummus is traditionally served with wedges of the pocket bread known as *pita* (see page 310), and it is also popularly served as a dip with an assortment of cut-up raw vegetables.

INGREDIENTS:

2 cups cooked chickpeas (drain before measuring,
   reserve liquid)

2 teaspoons minced garlic

4 teaspoons freshly squeezed lemon juice,
   approximately

1 tablespoon olive oil, approximately

¼ cup tahina (optional)

Salt

Paprika

Additional lemon juice and olive oil

Chopped fresh parsley

Pita bread (page 310), cut into wedges

Carrot and celery sticks, red and green pepper strips,
   broccoli florets, cherry tomatoes, mushrooms (optional)

DIRECTIONS:

1. For a smooth hummus, purée the chickpeas in a food processor, using enough liquid from the drained chickpeas for smooth processing. Mix in the garlic, 4 teaspoons of lemon juice, 1 tablespoon of olive oil, the optional tahina, and salt to taste. Taste and adjust the seasonings. For a coarse preparation mash the chickpeas and garlic with an old-fashioned potato masher or a fork, then mix in the ingredients as above.

2. Transfer to a serving bowl. Cover and refrigerate if the spread will not be served within a few hours. Just before serving, sprinkle with paprika, drizzle with lemon juice and olive oil, then sprinkle with parsley.

3. Serve with wedges of pita and raw vegetables if desired.

Mediterranean Eggplant Spread

Makes about 3 cups

The eggplant originated in India, where its mild flavor combines well with virtually all of India's spices. At one time known as "poor man's meat," eggplant is now widely enjoyed in Europe, Asia, northern Africa, and the United States. The versatility of this vegetable can be attributed both to its texture and its relative blandness: eggplant can be fried crisp or cooked to a pulp; and having no strong competitive taste, it partners well with many vegetables, meats, and cheeses, along with a variety of herbs, spices, and seasonings. For Jews, only a few eggplant preparations (the eggplant, meat, cheese, and cream sauce of Greece's _moussaka,_ for example) are forbidden in the kosher home, and even those can be made kosher by omitting either the meat or the dairy products.

Eggplant, tomatoes, garlic, and olive oil are a starting point for many eggplant appetizers in Mediterranean countries (see the eggplant salad on page 239). An eggplant dish similar to the one in this recipe was first introduced to me years ago by a Moroccan Jewish couple, and the preparation is related to the _caponata_ of southern Italy. Here, a mélange of chopped vegetables blends into a slightly tangy spread in which the taste of tomatoes is made strong by the use of tomato paste. The consistency depends on how fine the vegetables are chopped: hand chopping usually results in more coarse pieces, whereas the food processor will chop fine. Pita, matzo, and any kind of cracker are appropriate to serve with the eggplant spread, although you might find that some people would be happy to have a small bowl and spoon and bypass the carbohydrate.

Note that while the eggplant itself does not have a strong flavor, an eggplant that has passed its prime before being picked will be seedy; one that is not fresh will be bitter. Select shiny, unblemished eggplants. Slice in half lengthwise. If the seeds are large and firm, remove them before proceeding.

INGREDIENTS:

1 eggplant (1 pound)

½ cup chopped onion

⅓ cup chopped green pepper

1 cup chopped fresh mushrooms

2 teaspoons minced garlic

⅓ cup olive oil

1 teaspoon salt

½ teaspoon freshly ground black pepper

1½ teaspoons fresh oregano leaves, chopped fine
   (or ½ teaspoon dried oregano)

1½ teaspoons granulated white sugar

¾ cup (6 ounces) tomato paste

¼ cup water

2 tablespoons red wine vinegar

DIRECTIONS:

1. Remove the stem, thoroughly wash the eggplant, and chop the unpeeled eggplant into ¼- to ⅛-inch pieces. For a food processor, cut the eggplant into 1-inch cubes and process using the pulse setting (on and off) until the pieces are fine but not a paste.

2. In a 10-inch skillet, mix together the eggplant, onion, green pepper, mushrooms, garlic, and olive oil. Cover and cook over moderate heat for 10 minutes, adjusting the heat as necessary to prevent burning.

3. Meanwhile, in a medium-size bowl mix together the remaining ingredients.

4. Stir the tomato paste mixture into the vegetables. Cover, adjust the heat so the mixture just barely boils, and cook for 25 minutes. Stir once or twice during cooking. The mixture will be soft and well blended. Chill before serving. Freezing is not recommended.

CHOPPED HERRING

Makes 2 cups

In Judaism, it is traditional for even the poor to serve fish on Friday evenings as part of the Sabbath meal. Both chopped herring and gefilte fish (page 190) originated as a way for the impoverished to make the most of a limited amount of fish by stretching it with other ingredients. Herring was the most widely available fish in Eastern Europe. Combining it with bread, eggs, and apple not only extended the fish but made the dish special. In modern times, many families chop herring with only a little vinegar and sugar and serve it as a spread with no extenders, but old-fashioned chopped herring remains popular.

Chopped herring is traditionally prepared with *schmaltz* herring—that is, herring caught just before spawning, when it has much fat. Today's cooks often find it practical to buy jars of herring fillets in wine sauce (see the first variation). If you would like to prepare herring the old-fashioned way, you will need to allow at least twelve hours to soak the fish in cold water (see Step One). This will reduce the saltiness of the herring.

INGREDIENTS:

1 schmaltz herring (about 12 ounces)
2 tablespoons distilled white vinegar
1 cup cubed challah or dark bread
2 tablespoons minced onion
2 eggs (graded large), hard-cooked
1 cup chopped peeled, cored apple
2 teaspoons granulated white sugar

DIRECTIONS:

1. Place the herring in a bowl, cover with cold water, cover with plastic wrap, and refrigerate the herring for a minimum of 12 hours. Change the water once during this period.

2. Open the herring out flat, then use your fingertips to reach under the flesh and pull out the spine and the small bones that are attached to it. Use a sharp knife to remove the outer layer of skin. Cut the fish into 1-inch pieces. Set aside.

3. In a small bowl, pour the vinegar over the bread. Mix lightly and set aside.

4. Using the fine blade of a grinder, chop the herring, then add the onion, eggs, and finally the apple. Or, use a wooden chopping bowl with a curved blade to chop the ingredients, mixing in each new ingredient while chopping.

5. Mix in the vinegared bread and the sugar. Continue chopping until the mixture is chopped fine and is well mixed. Taste and correct the seasonings (vinegar, sugar, a little salt if you like). Serve chopped herring as a spread with challah or crackers. Or, serve on a bed of lettuce, and garnish with tomatoes and olives.

VARIATIONS:

Chopped Herring Using Ready-to-Eat Herring

Omit Step 1. Substitute an 8-ounce jar of herring in wine sauce for the fresh herring. Drain the herring, rinse, and proceed with the recipe.

Chopped Herring for Passover

During Passover, substitute 1 square of matzo for the bread. Break the matzo into small pieces before soaking it in the vinegar.

FRICASSEE OF CHICKEN WINGS

Serves 4

In early times, *fricassee* was a general term used for a poultry or meat stew often made with vegetables, and some cooks still refer to any sauced chicken dish as a fricassee. The modern French fricassee describes a chicken that is browned in butter, then cooked in a white sauce, with lemon juice added toward the end of cooking. When German Jews adopted fricassee of chicken from their neighbors in France, they substituted chicken fat for the butter and broth for the cream, creating a tasty preparation with plenty of thick yellow-brown gravy to serve with their spätzle or other dumplings.

Family meals in Jewish homes are relaxed and informal, and a fricassee of chicken wings is perfect for those who just love to get their fingers messy when they eat. While the fricassee can be made with wings only, gizzards give the gravy a meaty flavor, and those who are too finicky to eat with their fingers will appreciate the gizzards. And for those who do not like gizzards, note the variation that uses meatballs.

INGREDIENTS:

1 cup unbleached white flour for coating

¼ teaspoon salt (optional)

¼ teaspoon each freshly ground black pepper and
   paprika

2 pounds chicken wings (remove and save the tips for soup)

1 pound chicken gizzards (optional)

3 tablespoons schmaltz (page 40) or vegetable oil,
   approximately

1 quart (4 cups) water
Optional thickener: 2 tablespoons additional
schmaltz or oil and 2 tablespoons additional
unbleached white flour

DIRECTIONS:

1. Place the flour, optional salt, the pepper, and paprika in a small paper bag (lunch-bag size). Coat the chicken wings (and gizzards) with the mixture by placing a few at a time in the bag and shaking the bag.

2. In a 10-inch skillet, heat 2 tablespoons of the chicken fat or oil over moderate heat. In two or three batches, brown the wings (and gizzards) all over, adding more of the chicken fat or oil if necessary. Transfer the browned wings (and gizzards) to a 4-quart pot.

3. When all the wings (and gizzards) have been browned and are in the 4-quart pot, add the quart of water. Bring to the boil over high heat, reduce to a gentle boil, cover the pot, and cook for about 45 minutes. If you are using gizzards, taste one at this point and continue cooking for a few minutes if it is not yet tender.

4. If the gravy needs thickening, in a 1-quart pot melt the 2 tablespoons of chicken fat or oil over moderate heat. Add the 2 tablespoons of flour. Cook and stir until the mixture is bubbly but not brown. Gradually stir in a cup of liquid from the fricassee. Boil for 1 minute, then add this liquid to the pot of fricassee, stirring all the while. Taste and correct the seasoning.

VARIATION:

Fricassee of Chicken Wings with Meatballs
Omit the gizzards. Prepare half a recipe of meatballs on page 129. From the meat mixture, shape 16 cocktail-size meatballs (each about an inch in diameter). Brown the meatballs in hot oil or chicken fat. With a slotted spoon, transfer the meatballs to the 4-quart pot during the last 15 minutes of cooking.

LAMB-AND-SPINACH STUFFED PASTRY

Makes two 14-inch logs; serves 6 to 8 as an appetizer

The influence of Turkish specialties on Sephardic cuisine is explained by the acceptance of the Jews into the Ottoman Empire following their expulsion from Spain in 1492. Large numbers of Jews settled in Turkey and Greece, and over a period of time Turkish delicacies became Jewish preparations as well. Thin sheets of oil-based phyllo dough were made into pastries by Turks and Greeks. The Spanish Jews, who already used olive oil in their cuisine, could enjoy meat- or cheese-filled phyllo pastries with no changes.

Prepared phyllo leaves are widely available today, but it is relatively easy to make a homemade phyllo that will produce a deliciously crisp pastry. While not as delicate as the packaged leaves, the thin, crisp covering of the homemade dough has more flavor than the prepared phyllo. Lamb or cheese with eggplant or spinach are popular filling combinations for phyllo, and vegetable fillings alone are enjoyed also. If the pastries were rolled up to make individual turnovers or small pies, they would be known as *bourekas* (see page 253).

Fresh spinach leaves are often sandy. To clean them, swish the leaves in a large bowl of cold water. Remove the leaves, rinse out the bowl, and repeat as often as necessary until the water remains clean. Shake the leaves to remove excess water, then use paper towels to pat them *completely* dry.

Serve one- to two-inch slices of this lamb-and-spinach pastry as cocktail hors d'oeuvres, larger portions as dinner-table appetizers. For a splendid informal meal, begin with a lentil soup (page 112) and present a substantial piece of the filled pastry as the main course. Serve a fruity dessert to complete the meal.

INGREDIENTS:

FOR THE FILLING:

> 2 tablespoons olive oil
> 2 cups diced onion
> 2 cups chopped or ground lamb
> 4 cups tightly packed minced fresh spinach leaves
> 2 teaspoons chopped fresh oregano leaves
> Salt and freshly ground black pepper

FOR THE DOUGH:

> ½ cup olive oil
> ½ cup water
> 2 cups unbleached white flour (stir the flour, spoon
>   gently into a dry-measure cup, then level with
>   the edge of a spatula)

DIRECTIONS:

1. For the filling, in a 10-inch skillet heat the oil over moderately low heat until it is warm. Olive oil burns easily and requires slow heating to prevent burning. Add the onion, raise the heat to moderate, and cook until the onion has wilted. Mix in the lamb. Continue cooking until the lamb is brown all over. Mix in the spinach leaves. Continue cooking for another 2 or 3 minutes, until the spinach loses its raw taste. Mix in the oregano. Season well with salt and pepper. Remove from the heat. The filling can be used as soon as the dough is ready, or it can be refrigerated for later use.

2. For the dough, in a 2-quart pot bring the olive oil and water to the boil. Add the flour all at once, stirring with a wooden spoon until the flour leaves the sides of the pan and forms a ball, which will take only a few seconds. Immediately remove from the heat.

3. Preheat the oven to 400 degrees F.

4. Lightly oil a large baking sheet in the areas where the pastry rolls will be placed.

5. Divide the dough in half. Keep one piece of the dough covered while working with the other piece. Roll out the dough between two sheets of wax paper to a 10 x 14-inch rectangle. From time to time, peel off the top sheet of wax paper and fold in the irregular edges of the dough. When the dough is the correct size, place half the filling an inch in from one long edge and ½ inch in from the sides. Roll up the dough tightly around the filling. Press the long edge of the dough against the filled roll. Place on the baking sheet seam side down, turning the ends under. Repeat with the remaining dough and filling.

6. Bake in the middle of the oven for 20 to 25 minutes, until the pastry is golden brown. Allow an extra 5 minutes if the filling has been refrigerated. Serve hot.

SWEETBREADS

Serves 3 to 4

Esteemed by Renaissance Italians, well known in classical and provincial French cooking, a delicacy in Hungary, and part of Germany's variety meat stews, sweetbreads were a familiar dish to the European Jews who immigrated to the United States. The sweetbread is the calf's thymus, a nonfibrous organ enjoyed for its delicate flavor and texture. The taste is mildly reminiscent of veal, with a very soft consistency unlike any other meat except brains, with which they are sometimes used interchangeably in recipes. In classic European cooking, it is desirable for sweetbreads to be white, and a period of soaking in cold water, a minimum of two hours, is said to whiten the meat.

Sweetbreads are traditionally served in Jewish homes as the first course of a large meal or as the main dish of a light one. Sometimes breaded and fried (see the recipe for calves' brains on page 61), often sautéed with mushrooms and seasoned lightly, sweetbreads are also served in a creamy sauce as they are here. As with all kosher "cream" sauces that are to be mixed with meat, no dairy products are used. Pieces of challah on the side are recommended for mopping up the delicious sauce. Or, serve over rice or spätzle (page 262). For those who think of Jewish cooking as starchy and heavy, try sweetbreads.

INGREDIENTS:

1 pound sweetbreads

2 tablespoons schmaltz (page 40) or vegetable oil

½ cup chopped onion

1 cup sliced small fresh mushrooms

2 tablespoons unbleached white flour

1 cup veal broth
1 tablespoon freshly squeezed lemon juice
Salt and white pepper

DIRECTIONS:

1. To whiten the sweetbreads, soak them in cold water for 2 hours.

2. Fill a 2-quart pot about halfway with water. Bring the water to the boil over high heat. Add the sweetbreads. When the water comes back to the boil, immediately remove the pot from the burner, cover, and let stand for 10 minutes.

3. Using a slotted spoon, transfer the sweetbreads to a bowl of cold water. When cool enough to handle, remove the sweetbreads from the water. Using a small, sharp knife and your fingers, cut and pull off the membranes and any bits of tube still attached. Dice the sweetbreads into $3/8$-inch cubes.

4. In a 10-inch skillet, heat the chicken fat or oil over moderately low heat. Cook the onion until it is wilted and golden.

5. Raise the heat to moderate, add the mushrooms, and cook until softened.

6. Stir in the sweetbreads, and continue cooking until the sweetbreads are white all over, stirring often.

7. Stir in the flour, then the broth. Bring to the boil, stirring all the while. Add the lemon juice. Reduce the heat to a very gentle boil, season to taste with the salt and pepper, and cook for another minute. Serve hot.

Fried Calves' Brains

Serves 4

If you are about to purchase this variety meat for the first time, you will quickly discover that it is not so easy to ask your butcher, "Do you have any brains today?" Although brains are fun to joke about, they can also be a culinary delight. Calves' brains are usually described as delicate, but this adjective doesn't really go far enough, for they dissolve almost immediately in the mouth, like cotton candy.

With little flavor of their own and a creamy texture that disintegrates when eaten, it is wise to either encrust brains, as in the first preparation below, or bathe them in the lemony herb dressing popular among Sephardim (see the variation). Note that brains are perishable and should be cooked within a day of purchase.

The use of matzo meal for coating the brains (or sweetbreads if you prefer) means that the preparation may be eaten during Passover.

INGREDIENTS:

1 quart (4 cups) cold water
1 tablespoon distilled white vinegar
1 pound calves' brains
1 cup matzo meal
Salt and freshly ground black pepper
1 egg (graded large), beaten
¼ cup schmaltz (page 40) or oil, approximately

DIRECTIONS:

1. Mix the cold water and vinegar in a medium-size bowl. Soak the brains for 1 hour. The water should cover the brains by about 2 inches. Add more water if necessary.

2. Drain the brains. Use your fingers to carefully remove any membranes, then scrape away and discard the soft white tissue.

3. Cut the brains into ½-inch slices that will be no more than 1 inch long in any direction. Season the matzo meal to taste with salt and pepper. Dip the brains into the beaten egg, covering completely, then into the seasoned matzo meal, again covering completely.

4. In a 10-inch skillet, melt the chicken fat over moderate heat. Add the coated brains. Cook until crisp and golden on one side, then turn and cook the other side. Add more schmaltz or oil if necessary. Drain on paper towels and serve hot.

VARIATION:

Marinated Calves' Brains, Sephardic Style

Omit the matzo meal, egg, and schmaltz. Prepare the brains as directed in Steps 1 and 2. Cut the brains into ¼- to ⅓-inch cubes. In a 10-inch skillet, heat 3 tablespoons of olive oil over moderately low heat. Do not allow the oil to smoke. Add the brains and cook for 3 to 5 minutes, stirring frequently, until they change color and are cooked through. Season to taste with salt and pepper. Sprinkle on 3 tablespoons of freshly squeezed lemon juice. Stir to mix. Remove from the heat. Stir in ¼ cup chopped fresh parsley and 2 tablespoons to ¼ cup chopped fresh dill. Refrigerate immediately until serving. Serve on a bed of shredded lettuce, garnished with tomato slices and olives.

P'TCHA
(Calves' Foot Jelly)

Serves 6 to 8

And if you think *p'tcha* is a strange name, in my family p'tcha was called "Calves' Foot Jelly Grandma Always Put Too Much Garlic in Hers." It is a dish of European Jewish peasantry, a taste of meat for those who could not afford meat, soul food in a sense. The use of calves' feet is also a direct reminder of the biblical injunction to eat only animals that have cloven hoofs (and chew the cud).

The original gelatin mold, p'tcha takes advantage of the high collagen content of calves' feet (it is the collagen in the bones and cartilage that makes the liquid gel). Although one can still buy calves' feet at the kosher butcher, p'tcha has all but disappeared in most modern Jewish communities, evolving into more popular gelatin molds filled with fruits and vegetables.

The cooked broth of calves' feet is bland, and while not traditional, the use of beef neck bones will produce a meatier taste. Much of the flavor of traditional p'tcha comes from garlic. Either a large quantity of garlic can be cooked with the broth or, for a much stronger garlic flavor, minced raw garlic can be mixed into the cooked broth (see the variation). How much garlic flavor is a matter of personal taste. Grandma always put—well, you know.

INGREDIENTS:

> 2 pounds calves' feet, cut into 2-inch pieces
> (or beef neck bones)
> 1½ quarts (6 cups) water
> 1 large onion, unpeeled, quartered
> 1 large carrot, unpeeled, cut in half

8 large cloves garlic, peeled and sliced
2 eggs (graded large), hard-cooked
Lettuce and tomatoes for garnish

DIRECTIONS:

1. In a 4-quart pot, place the calves' feet, water, onion, carrot, and the sliced garlic. Bring to the boil over high heat. Reduce the heat to a gentle boil, cover, and cook for 3 hours. The cartilage should pull from the bones very easily at this point.

2. Use a slotted spoon to remove the vegetables and the bones from the broth. Strain the broth through high-quality paper towels.

3. When cool enough to handle, cut off any meat and cartilage from the bones. Grind or mince almost to a paste. Spread on the bottom of a 2-quart casserole (7 x 12 inches, approximately).

4. Pour the strained broth into the casserole.

5. Slice the eggs into thin, even pieces, then carefully place them on top of the broth.

6. Refrigerate for a minimum of 6 hours, until the mixture gels. Just before serving, cut into squares. Serve on a bed of lettuce as an appetizer or a light lunch. Garnish with tomatoes if you like.

VARIATION:

P'tcha with Extra Garlic

Decrease the garlic in Step 1 to 2 cloves. In Step 3 mix a teaspoon of puréed fresh garlic with the meat and cartilage. Proceed as above.

KOSHER DILL PICKLES

For 2 pounds cucumbers (recipe can be increased many times)

When you prepare these pickles, your house will be filled with the aroma of an old-fashioned delicatessen, the kind with huge wooden barrels going down the center aisle. For some, the garlic and dill that permeate the kitchen when kosher dills are ripening may bring back memories of *bubba* (grandma) and her homemade pickles.

Although Jews enjoy eating fresh cucumbers in salads (page 212) and soups (page 97), a good crop during a growing season that has plenty of rain will produce more of the vegetable than one can eat, and the process of pickling is used as a means of preserving the cucumbers for later use. End-of-season cucumbers are plentiful at the same time that dill goes to seed, and this combination is used in preserving kosher dill pickles in a brine (salt) solution. Vinegar can be added to extend the keeping quality (and sharpen the taste of the pickle); mixed pickling spices will contribute the flavor of whatever spices are used (manufacturers have their own formulas and combinations of spices for pickling—allspice, mustard and coriander seeds, ginger, cinnamon, cloves, and black pepper are common ingredients); but the basic taste of the kosher dill pickle needs only the salted water, dill, and garlic used here. For a recipe that uses both vinegar and mixed pickling spices, see the variation.

Cucumbers steeped in brine ripen at room temperature and will become fully sour in about ten days. For crisp, bright green "new" pickles with little sour taste, the cucumbers require only a day or two in the brine; half-sour pickles will take three or four days. During a heat wave in a room without air conditioning, the pickling process will be shortened.

Kosher dill pickles are sometimes eaten whole and unsliced as an unusual snack, but more typically they are sliced lengthwise (never crosswise) and served alongside sandwiches. The fully ripened pickles are distinguished by a heavy taste of garlic, olive green color, crisp skin and soft inside, and the sour taste loved by Eastern European Jews. While "kosher dills" are no more or less kosher than other vegetable pickles, they always accompany the corned beef, pastrami, or tongue sandwiches in a Jewish deli—in fact, there is likely to be a bowl of dill pickles and pickled tomatoes on the table in a kosher delicatessen even before any food is ordered. By association with kosher Jewish foods, the pickles themselves have become known as kosher dill pickles.

INGREDIENTS:

> 2 pounds small pickling cucumbers (about 6 inches long)
> 3 cups water
> 1½ tablespoons salt
> 4 dill heads
> ¼ cup packed fresh dill leaves
> 4 large cloves garlic, peeled and sliced

DIRECTIONS:

1. Scrub the cucumbers thoroughly. Set aside.

2. In a 1-quart pot, bring the water and salt to the boil to dissolve the salt and to kill undesirable organisms. Cool to room temperature.

3. Scatter half the dill and half the garlic in the bottom of a ceramic crock or casserole that will be just big enough to hold the cucumbers and liquid. Place half the cucumbers over the dill and garlic, scatter the remaining dill and garlic over the cucumbers, and place the remaining cucumbers on top. Pour the cooled brine over the cucumbers. Place a plate or bowl on top of the cucumbers, and weigh down with a tightly sealed jar of water or a large clean stone.

4. Allow the cucumbers to stand at room temperature until they are soured to your satisfaction. Skim off any scum that forms.

5. Transfer the finished pickles to a sterilized jar, fill with the brine solution along with the garlic and dill, and store tightly covered in the refrigerator. If there is not enough liquid to cover the pickles, make up a new brine solution, cool, and fill the jars to cover the pickles.

Note: Should you find that your pickles spoil after a short time, next time rinse off the pickles before storing. Prepare a fresh brine solution with garlic, cool, and pour over the pickles. Refrigerate as above.

VARIATION:

Kosher Dills with Vinegar-and-Spice

Add $\frac{1}{4}$ cup of distilled white vinegar with the salt to the 3 cups of water before bringing to the boil. Scatter a total of 2 teaspoons of mixed pickling spices with the garlic and dill.

PICKLED TOMATOES

Makes about 2 quarts

Green tomatoes require about two weeks to become sour without softening, and unlike kosher dill pickles which are sometimes ripened for only a day or two, green tomatoes sit long enough in brine and vinegar to become lip-puckering sour. For those who like extra zip as well, add a small slice of a fresh hot red chili pepper to each quart of tomatoes. The addition of a 3-inch slice of celery (gardeners might enjoy the celery-like taste of lovage as an alternative) to each quart will add flavor. Select small (two-inch diameter is ideal), very firm, round, unblemished, even-sized green tomatoes that are just turning whitish, with no red color. Before beginning, sterilize two one-quart jars and lids by boiling them in water to cover for fifteen minutes. Leave the jars in the water until you are ready to use them.

Pickled tomatoes were eaten by Ashkenazim not merely to make use of end-of-season tomatoes. Sour foods were enjoyed as a way of spicing up a monotonous diet of cereal, bread, vegetable soups, and herring. Today, sour green tomatoes are typically served alongside kosher dill pickles as part of a condiment tray with thick delicatessen sandwiches.

INGREDIENTS:

3 pounds small, uniform-size, firm green tomatoes

3 tablespoons sliced peeled garlic

2 slices (3 inches each) celery (optional)

2 slices ($\frac{1}{4}$ x 1-inch strips) hot red chili peppers (optional)

$1\frac{1}{2}$ quarts (6 cups) water

¼ **cup salt**
½ **cup distilled white vinegar**

DIRECTIONS:

1. Scrub the tomatoes well.

2. Pack half the tomatoes, garlic, and optional celery and hot peppers in each sterilized jar, scattering the garlic as you pack in the tomatoes.

3. In a 2- or 3-quart pot, bring the water, salt, and vinegar to the boil. Boil for 2 minutes. Pour the boiling liquid over the tomatoes, filling the jars to over-flowing. Close the jars securely.

4. Allow the jars to stand at room temperature for 10 days to 2 weeks, or until the tomatoes are soured to your satisfaction, then refrigerate the packed jars. If the tomatoes have been prepared with the celery, serve this tasty pickled vegetable along with the tomatoes.

EINGEMACHTS
(Beet Preserves)

In the days when many Jews of Eastern Europe had little money to spend on food, they took advantage of any vegetables that grew abundantly in the areas they inhabited. Many more beets were grown than could be eaten during the growing season, and ways were found to preserve the beet roots (the leaves are edible as salad greens) for future consumption.

Eingemachts is not only a beet preparation that prevents spoilage: the thick, rich syrup conveys an impression of wealth rather than poverty. A small quantity of almonds goes a long way but makes the preserves special. The sweet-and-sour flavor characteristic of many Ashkenazic dishes is evident, along with a pronounced gingery taste. Eingemachts is served in small portions as a condiment rather than a vegetable and may accompany either meat or dairy foods.

It was the end of an era when Grandma Lillie stopped making her eingemachts for my family. Grandma's recipe was loose at best, representative of the way recipes were passed down from one generation to the next. As reported by my mother: "We used canned sliced beets (two cans), sugar to taste, and ground ginger from the spice shelf, sliced lemon and blanched almonds. Let it cook slowly for hours in its own juice and add almonds almost at the end. It should also be thick and clear. Sweet from the sugar and ginger to taste. Not too sharp."

This recipe reproduces the taste and texture of Grandma's eingemachts—sweet from the sugar, gingery but not too sharp, and a very thick syrup, but we begin with fresh beets, the way Grandma's grandmother did.

INGREDIENTS:

> 4 cups thin-sliced peeled fresh beets
> 1 quart (4 cups) water

3 cups granulated white sugar

1 medium-size lemon, seeded and cut crosswise
  into ¼-inch slices

2 tablespoons minced peeled fresh ginger root
  (substitute 2 teaspoons ground ginger)

1 cup whole blanched almonds

DIRECTIONS:

1. In a 2-quart pot, bring the beets and water to the boil over high heat. Reduce the heat and cook gently, covered, for 30 minutes or until tender. Stir in the sugar, lemon, and ginger.

2. Bring to the boil again, stir, then reduce the heat to a gentle boil. Cover and cook for 1 hour. At this point, taste the mixture and add a little more sugar, fresh lemon juice, or ginger as necessary.

3. Remove the cover from the pot and continue cooking the mixture over low heat until the liquid is very thick, syrupy, and glazed. This will take approximately 15 to 30 minutes, depending on how much liquid has boiled away and how much sugar has been added. Toward the end of the cooking, as the mixture thickens, it will come to a rolling boil. Stir down as necessary so the liquid doesn't boil over.

4. Add the almonds and cook for 5 minutes longer. Pack the preserves into small sterilized jars and top off with hot melted wax. Or, pack into jars with tight-fitting lids and refrigerate.

HORSERADISH

Makes about 2½ cups

A plant native to western Asia and Central Europe and cultivated for its pungent root, horseradish has found favor in Jewish cuisine as a zesty enhancement for relatively plain foods, including boiled beef and chilled poached fish. Horseradish (*chrain* in Yiddish) is virtually always served as a condiment with gefilte fish. It is traditionally the *maror* (bitter herbs) of the Passover Seder, symbolizing the bitter lot of the Israelites during their enslavement in Egypt.

Unlike hot chile peppers, which are caustic to the mouth, horseradish mainly affects the olfactory system, and a good whiff of freshly grated horseradish will clear out the sinuses and bring tears to one's eyes. To give horseradish more flavor and tone it down at the same time, grated beets are often added to the preparation.

In our home there is a ritual associated with horseradish that has become an unwritten part of our Passover Seder. When we serve the gefilte fish, it is accompanied with our friend Tom Bleek's "mild-as-a-child" homemade horseradish. Everyone is quiet. Tom breathes in slowly. The first brave soul takes a bite. Cough, sneeze, red face. Tom breathes out. Big smile. Success.

Tom, a chemist and horseradish aficionado, grows his own horseradish root so that he can harvest it at its best. He suggests using young, supple roots for maximum hotness and sharp bite. Older, thick roots may be rubbery or dried out.

For Tom's "BB/BP: before blenders/before processors" horseradish, he tells us to "fill small sterile glass jars three-quarters full of root grated on the fine side of a hand grater, then vinegar that has been mixed with salt (a teaspoon of salt mixed into two cups distilled white vinegar), enough to fully wet the root. Close the jar tightly, then refrigerate. Use several small jars instead of a large one to ensure keeping qualities. For example, four small jars will remain potent longer than one big jar that is exposed to the air repeatedly once opened."

Here, Tom's favorite recipe is modernized and uses a food processor for a smoother, more uniform texture than hand-grated horseradish. However, he notes that you should still prepare horseradish in a well-ventilated area: "Remember you still have to get the horseradish out of the food processor bowl." The recipe begins with soaking the root. Therefore, you will need to start the preparation at least a day before you plan to serve it. If the horseradish is to be enjoyed during Passover, make sure to use kosher for Passover vinegar and oil.

INGREDIENTS:

One 7- to 10-inch horseradish root ($^{3}/_{4}$ to 1 pound),
    young and supple, not woody
Water for soaking
1 cup boiled water, cooled to room temperature
1$^{1}/_{2}$ cups distilled white vinegar
1$^{1}/_{2}$ teaspoons salt
1$^{1}/_{2}$ tablespoons granulated white sugar
1$^{1}/_{2}$ tablespoons mild-tasting vegetable oil
$^{1}/_{2}$ cup finely grated peeled beets, uncooked
    (optional)

DIRECTIONS:

1. Find that perfect root and begin by washing it thoroughly. Soak the root for one to three days in fresh, clean water. The water should be changed each day. This allows the root to revitalize and brings out the hotness.

2. Peel the horseradish as you would a carrot, then slice it into 1-inch-thick rings under running water. Quarter the rings. Set aside in a bowl of cold water.

3. Mix the cup of cool boiled water with the vinegar, salt, and sugar.

4. Use the grating blade on the food processor to grate the root. Transfer the grated root to a bowl, remove the grating blade, and put in the chopping blade.

5. Feed about a quarter of the grated root into the chute, stopping to add a quarter of the vinegar mixture to improve consistency and aid in mixing. Add another quarter of the root and more of the vinegar mixture; then add the oil to prevent oxidation of the root. If you are using the beets, add half of the grated beets at this point. Continue adding root and liquid, just enough vinegar so that the blade spins freely and floats in the mixture. Add the remaining optional beets. Process until the root is chopped to a fine, uniform consistency.

6. Transfer the horseradish to small sterile jars, topping off with vinegar if the horseradish doesn't reach the top. Close tightly. Refrigerate, then celebrate.

SEPHARDIC DATE CHAROSET

Makes 2 cups

All Jews prepare *charoset* for the Passover Seder to symbolize the mortar made by the Israelites when they were enslaved in Egypt. To the Ashkenazic Jew, whose traditional charoset preparation is an apple-and-nut mixture, the Sephardic charoset based on dates and nuts is new and different. For the Sephardim living around the Mediterranean, however, the fruits available for charoset have been dates and figs since antiquity. To Sephardic Jews, therefore, it is the apple-and-nut mixture that is unusual.

In addition to its use during Passover, Sephardic charoset is a marvelous condiment for broiled, steamed, or poached fish year-round, and can even be used as a stuffing for baked fish. For variety, use a combination of dates with figs and/or dried apricots.

INGREDIENTS:

> 2 cups pitted dates (or dates, figs, and/or dried apricots)
> 1 cup almonds (whole or slivered, blanched or unblanched)
> Pinch to ¼ teaspoon ground cinnamon
> ½ cup orange juice

DIRECTIONS:

1. Chop the fruit and almonds together until the pieces are very small, almost a paste if you like.

2. Mix in the cinnamon to taste, then the orange juice. Refrigerate until serving.

ASHKENAZIC APPLE-NUT CHAROSET

Makes 2 cups

Here is the traditional Ashkenazic apple-and-nut charoset. The ingredients should be chopped into fine, uniform pieces. The consistency of the mixture must be fine enough to be reminiscent of mortar used in constructing buildings, but the taste must be sweet, for charoset is also used symbolically during the Passover Seder in combination with horseradish to lessen the bitterness of slavery.

This charoset makes a delicious snack on matzo, and will keep at least a week under good refrigeration if stored in small, tightly closed containers. With today's food processors, the recipe can be increased many times without much effort, enough to last the entire week of Passover. Process the nuts first, transfer to a mixing bowl, process one-inch pieces of apple, then mix with the other ingredients.

INGREDIENTS:

> 1 cup chopped walnuts
> 2 cups chopped peeled apple
> 1 tablespoon ground cinnamon
> 2 tablespoons sweet Passover wine

DIRECTIONS:

1. Mix together all of the ingredients.

2. Adjust cinnamon and wine to taste. Refrigerate until serving.

Soups, Garnishes, and Dumplings
Light to Substantial
Soups and Complements

Soups, Garnishes, and Dumplings

Golden, steaming, emitting a pleasing aroma that draws us into the kitchen to lift the cover off the pot and take in a deep breath—homemade chicken soup seems to have magical powers. Whether Grandma is Greek, Egyptian, German, Hungarian, or third-generation American, her chicken soup elicits memories of home and love.

Of course, traditional Jewish soups offer more than emotional comfort. Thick and nourishing cabbage, lentil, bean, or beet soups that are hearty with flavor sustained the impoverished in harsh times. Meat soups, a sign of wealth, might be served on the Sabbath, when even a small piece of meat added to the kettle contributed to the joy of Shabbat. These tasty and highly nutritious soups are part of the heritage of Jewish foods that are now savored more for taste than sustenance. While meals based on wholesome soups and coarse whole-grain breads are eaten today, a brimming bowl of hot split pea soup is more likely to be a first course than the main dish.

Sumptuous fruit soups of Eastern European communities might seem expensive to us today, but these preparations were developed in the days before refrigeration, when fruit that was abundant at harvest time needed to be consumed quickly. What better way to "take" vitamins and minerals than to eat a bowlful of concentrated, all-natural fruit soup?

With the ubiquitous chicken soup, vegetarian soups hearty enough to be main courses, and dairy soups that might be served as light meals, there is a broad range of delicious traditional Jewish soups to be enjoyed for any occasion. We begin the chapter with chicken soup and the dumplings and other enrichments traditionally served with it.

CHICKEN SOUP

Makes 3 quarts soup

She's old, she's fat, she's tough. But the stewing hen, sold also as "fowl," is the poultry traditionally used by Jewish cooks for a rich, tasty chicken soup that doesn't rely on cubes, powders, or additives for flavor. A bowl of hot clear chicken soup (*goldene yoich* in Yiddish) is soothing to those who are feeling under the weather, and satisfying but not filling when served as a light prelude to a meal.

The soup is best prepared a day ahead and refrigerated so that the fat that solidifies on top can easily be removed. The fat can be used in any recipe calling for schmaltz, and is likely to be richer than chicken fat rendered from solid pieces and skin alone.

The vegetables in the recipe below are used for flavoring the soup and are not necessarily eaten. If they are going to be served with the soup, peel them and cut them into even-sized pieces before cooking. Or, peel the vegetables before cooking, then purée them after the soup is cooked. The onions are un-peeled because the onion skins add a richer color to chicken soup. The onions can be peeled and the skins added separately.

Chicken necks, backbones, and uncooked bones saved from cutlets (see the variation) also make a flavorful soup when cooked with vegetables or veg-etable peelings and herbs. When skins are used as well, the taste will be even richer. The gizzards add a meaty taste and can be cut into small slices and en-joyed in the soup.

Chicken soup makes an enticing overture to any meat meal, especially when accompanied by any of the light dumplings that appear following this recipe. Cooked carrot rounds and pieces of celery and chopped fresh parsley are popular additions. For a heartier soup, serve the pieces of chicken meat in the soup. Or, reserve the cooked meat for chicken salad or chicken kreplach (page 88). The broth itself can be served plain, used as a base for a meat or vegetable soup, used in place of cream or milk to make "cream" sauces, or added to fricassee gravies for extra flavor.

INGREDIENTS:

> 1 stewing hen, about 6 pounds, cut into quarters
> 2½ quarts (10 cups) water
> 4 or 5 carrots, cut into halves or thirds
> 4 stalks celery with tops
> 3 small to medium-size onions, quartered
>   (unpeeled)
> 3 large cloves garlic, crushed with the back of a
>   large spoon (peeled or unpeeled)
> 4 or 5 sprigs parsley
> 2 or 3 sprigs dill (optional)
> Salt

DIRECTIONS:

1. In an 8-quart pot, place the chicken with the water. Bring to the boil over high heat, making sure the water doesn't boil over. Skim off any scum that rises to the surface. Reduce the heat to a gentle boil, cover the pot, and cook for 1½ hours.

2. Add the carrots, celery, and onions. Cover and cook for an additional hour, until the chicken is tender when pierced with a fork.

3. Now add the garlic, parsley, dill if desired, and salt to taste. Cook for an additional 10 minutes.

4. Use a slotted spoon to remove the vegetables. Unpeeled vegetables can be discarded. Vegetables that have been peeled can be served in the soup in chunks or slices or puréed. Remove the chicken and set aside.

5. Strain the soup through high-quality paper towels. While cheesecloth can be used, it is more porous than high-quality paper towels and will allow small particles and fat to pass through.

6. Return the chicken to the soup. Refrigerate overnight. Before reheating, skim off all the fat from the soup. Then remove and discard the skin and bones from the cold chicken. Serve the chicken in the hot soup or use in other recipes. To freeze the soup for later use, freeze in plastic containers, leaving an inch of headspace.

VARIATION:

Chicken Soup from Bones and Gizzards

Fill a 6-quart pot halfway with chicken bones, gizzards, necks, and skins. Add 3 cups of mixed chunks of carrot, celery, and onion. Fill the pot with enough water to just cover the vegetables. Bring to the boil over high heat. Skim off any scum that rises to the surface. Reduce to a gentle boil, cover, and cook for 1¼ hours. Add salt to taste, 2 teaspoons of chopped garlic, and 3 tablespoons each of chopped fresh parsley and dill. Cook for an additional 10 minutes. Remove from the heat. Cool in the pot for 30 minutes, then use a slotted spoon to remove the bones and vegetables. Strain the soup through paper towels. Serve hot, or refrigerate for use within two or three days. Freeze in plastic containers (leaving an inch of headspace) for longer storage.

EINLAUF
(*Egg Drops*)

Makes enough for 1 quart of soup

Einlauf thickens chicken soup while distributing very soft pieces of a flour-and-egg mixture throughout. For those who have little time, einlauf is an ideal enrichment for plain soup: the batter can be mixed in a matter of minutes; the cooking takes only a few minutes longer.

INGREDIENTS:

> 1 egg (graded large or extra large)
> ¼ cup water
> 3 tablespoons unbleached white flour, sifted after measuring
> ¼ teaspoon salt
> 1 quart (4 cups) chicken soup (page 80 or 82)
> Chopped fresh parsley for garnish

DIRECTIONS:

1. In a small mixing bowl or a 1-quart measuring cup, beat the egg with a fork, then stir in the water. Beat in the flour and salt until the mixture is smooth, beating rapidly so the flour does not form lumps. The batter will be thin.

2. Meanwhile, in a 2-quart pot bring the chicken soup to the boil.

3. In a slow, steady stream, pour the batter from the bowl into the boiling soup. When all the batter has been added, reduce the heat and cook gently for 2 or 3 minutes, stirring once or twice. Serve immediately, with parsley as a garnish and mandlen (see next recipe) if desired.

MANDLEN

Mandlen, the Yiddish word for almonds, are known also as "soup nuts." Although crisp like nuts, mandlen are not made from almonds but rather from a noodle dough. Because they are cut into small cubes then baked, not boiled, they will remind you more of croutons or small crackers than of noodles—a Jewish version of "oyster" crackers. Mandlen are traditionally served with chicken broth and are a fitting light accompaniment for any soup.

To keep mandlen crisp, serve them at room temperature—to be dropped into hot soup just before eating. The size of the cubes will depend on how much time and patience you have: the mandlen here are rolled and cut into half-inch pieces, but they can be made half the size. For smaller soup nuts, decrease the baking time. Mandlen store well at room temperature in a tightly closed container, or they can be frozen for later use. If they should lose their crispness, heat them in a 300-degree F. oven for a few minutes.

INGREDIENTS:

> 1½ cups unbleached white flour (stir the flour, spoon
>   gently into a dry-measure cup, then level with
>   the edge of a spatula)
> ½ teaspoon salt
> 2 eggs (graded large)
> 2 tablespoons mild-tasting vegetable oil

DIRECTIONS:

1. Preheat the oven to 375 degrees F.

2. Lightly grease a large baking sheet.

3. In a medium-size mixing bowl, place all the ingredients in the order listed. Use your fingers to mix everything together to form a stiff dough.

4. Divide the dough evenly into 8 pieces. Roll each piece into a log about 10 inches long and ½ inch in diameter. Using a sharp knife, cut each log into ½-inch pieces.

5. Place on the baking sheet. Bake in the middle of the oven for 20 minutes or until golden brown, shaking the pan after 10 minutes for more even browning.

6. Cool, then transfer to a covered container. Store at room temperature, or freeze for later use.

FARFEL

Makes 2 cups dried farfel

Another soup embellishment made from a noodle dough is *farfel*, also called egg barley. Farfel is made by grating a firm ball of dough into irregular pellets that are shaped much like little pieces of dried cracked corn. The dough is dried at room temperature or in the oven, then stored at room temperature until it is ready to be cooked. Farfel is cooked in liquid, swelling as it absorbs the liquid to become tender but somewhat chewy, similar to the consistency of barley.

Farfel is cooked in chicken soup to make a satisfying but not overly filling first course soup. It can also be prepared as a tasty side dish (page 282) or cooked with a tsimmes (page 228), picking up flavor from the other ingredients in the tsimmes while adding a slightly chewy texture. Note that the matzo farfel sold in packages during Passover is simply matzo broken up into small, irregular pieces.

INGREDIENTS:

1½ **cups unbleached white flour (stir the flour, spoon**
   gently into a dry-measure cup, then level with
   the edge of a spatula)
¼ **teaspoon salt**
2 **eggs (graded large)**
A few drops of water

DIRECTIONS:

1. Place the flour in a medium-size mixing bowl. Stir the salt into the flour. Add the eggs, stirring with a fork until the dough begins to hold together. Use your fingers to gather up the dough into a ball, sprinkling the dough with a little water if it is very dry. The dough should be very stiff.

2. Divide the dough in half and shape into 2 balls.

3. Using the coarse side of a hand grater, grate the dough onto a large baking sheet. If the dough is too soft to grate, allow it to dry at room temperature until it can be grated easily.

4. **To dry at room temperature,** spread out the pieces of dough on the baking sheet and allow the dough to dry for 24 hours, turning occasionally to expose all sides to the air. The farfel will become hard, and the pieces will separate.

   To dry quickly, place the baking sheet in a preheated 300-degree F. oven. Bake for 10 minutes, until the pieces dry out and begin to brown very lightly. Do not overbake. Remove from the oven, stir, and allow to cool on the baking sheet.

5. Store the dried farfel at room temperature in a tightly closed container.

6. To cook, add the farfel to boiling chicken soup and cook for about 5 minutes, until tender. Use about ½ cup dried farfel per quart of soup. If you like, sprinkle chopped fresh parsley on each bowl of soup.

KREPLACH

Makes 24 kreplach

Leftover meat or poultry fills triangular pockets of a homemade noodle dough in one of the most well-known preparations in Jewish cuisine. While the *wontons* of China and the *ravioli* in Italian cuisine are related to *kreplach*, the Jewish dumplings are more than a delicious food. They are linked by tradition with some of the Jewish holidays.

Kreplach filled with a mixture of chopped (beaten) meat and chopped onions are eaten on Yom Kippur eve, a reminder of the flogging, or beating, to which Jews once subjected themselves as atonement for their sins. They are eaten again on Hoshana Rabba, the last day of the seven-day Sukkot holiday, when willows are traditionally beaten on the floor or against a chair—a reminder of the practice of flogging as a sign of penitence. And kreplach filled with chopped (beaten) meat are served on Purim as well, symbolic of slapping or beating whatever object is handy when the name of the wicked Haman is mentioned during the reading of the Megillah.

The shape of kreplach, with its three sides, has been associated with the three patriarchs (Abraham, Isaac, and Jacob) and the three parts of the Bible (Torah, Prophets, and the Holy Writings). Kreplach are served on Shavuot because of the associations between the number three and events connected with the giving of the Torah (see page 256).

Kreplach are cooked in boiling salted water or directly in chicken soup, or they can be fried in oil and served separately as a soup accompaniment (see the variation). In place of the meat filling below, chopped liver (page 42) or cooked kasha and onions (page 269) can be used for the filling. Cheese kreplach, traditionally served on Shavuot, appear on page 256.

Note that kosher wonton wrappers and egg roll wrappers are available in some supermarkets and Asian groceries and can be used in place of homemade dough in preparing kreplach.

INGREDIENTS:

FOR THE FILLING:

> 1 cup finely chopped cooked brisket, chicken, or
> veal
> 2 tablespoons minced onion
> 1 egg (graded large)
> 1 tablespoon schmaltz (page 40), optional
> Salt and freshly ground black pepper, to taste

FOR THE DOUGH:

> 1½ cups unbleached white flour (stir the flour, spoon
> gently into a dry-measure cup, then level with
> the edge of a spatula)
> ½ teaspoon salt
> 2 eggs (graded large)
> 2 tablespoons water, as necessary

DIRECTIONS:

1. Mix together all of the ingredients for the filling. Refrigerate until ready to use.

2. For the dough, in a medium-size mixing bowl use a fork to mix together the flour and salt. Using a fork or your fingers, work in the eggs. Blend in the water a tablespoon at a time until the dough is soft but not sticky.

3. Turn out onto a lightly floured surface. Knead briefly, about 20 times. Cover the dough with the mixing bowl and let it rest for 15 to 20 minutes. This will make the dough easier to roll out.

4. Divide the dough in half. Work with one piece of dough at a time, keeping the other half covered. On a clean, lightly floured surface, roll out the dough into a 6 x 18-inch rectangle. Cut the dough in half lengthwise, then cut each rectangle into six 3-inch squares. There will be twelve 3-inch squares.

5. Using half the filling, place a heaping teaspoonful of filling slightly off-center on each square. Fold the dough over the filling to form a triangle, pressing the edges together securely. Set the triangles aside on a floured plate or work surface, and cover with a clean kitchen towel.

6. Repeat the process with the reserved piece of dough, filling and shaping 12 more kreplach.

7. In a 4-quart pot, bring 3 quarts of water or chicken soup to the boil. Carefully drop in the kreplach. Regulate the heat so that the water boils gently. Cook uncovered for 7 to 10 minutes, until the noodle dough is cooked through. The dough will become lighter in color and it will thicken as it absorbs water. Taste one of the kreplach to confirm that it has cooked enough. Serve hot. Reheat leftovers gently so that the kreplach do not fall apart.

VARIATION:

Fried Kreplach

Fry the uncooked kreplach in ¼ inch of oil over moderate heat, turning as needed until both sides are golden. Drain well on paper towels. Boiled kreplach can be fried when cold.

KNAIDLACH
(*Matzo Balls*)

Makes 10 to 12 knaidlach

The Sabbath is ushered in with a meal that both reflects caring and that is not ordinarily served on weeknights. While a plain broth might be eaten during the week, on Friday night the broth contains something special—kreplach (see previous recipe) or knaidlach, for example.

The word *knaidlach* is used for dumplings in general, including potato or liver dumplings, but the most well-known knaidlach are "matzo balls," so called because their basic ingredient is matzo meal. Knaidlach are traditionally served during Passover, when ordinary flour is not used except to make matzo, which may then be ground into matzo meal for use in cooking. Pareve knaidlach are made by using oil for the chicken fat and vegetable broth or water in place of the chicken soup.

When knaidlach are cooked in soup, the broth will cloud up a bit, but the knaidlach and the soup each enrich the taste of the other; therefore, cooking in soup is recommended. The matzo balls absorb a lot of liquid during cooking: plan ahead and have an extra quart of soup on hand for serving. The knaidlach here are rich and tender but more compact than some recipes. For fluffier knaidlach that are lower in fat, see the next recipe.

A friend's aunt who is in her seventies remembers to this day her first experience making knaidlach. Her mother measured everything by hand, and the matzo balls came out delicious every time. So when Aunt Tessie set up her own household, she tried Mother's knaidlach, having watched all those years. Unfortunately, Mother's hand was small and daughter's large, so Aunt Tessie ended up with a mixture she knew was too stiff. She added more eggs and liquid, and the mixture was too wet. She went back and forth with matzo meal and liquid until she had a mixture that seemed to be the correct consistency. However, instead of making ten matzo balls, she had enough mixture for forty-eight! Were they tender like Mother's? No, they were like rocks.

If your hand holds exactly half a cup of matzo meal, you can prepare the following recipe and have ten or twelve knaidlach that come out tender every time. If not, use a measuring cup. And if you do want forty-eight matzo balls, the recipe doubles, triples, and quadruples very well.

INGREDIENTS:

> 2 eggs (graded large)
> 2 tablespoons schmaltz (page 40), at room temperature, or oil
> ½ cup matzo meal
> ½ to 1 teaspoon salt
> 2 tablespoons chicken or vegetable broth, or water
> 2 tablespoons chopped fresh parsley (optional)
> 3 quarts chicken soup or water for cooking

DIRECTIONS:

1. In a small mixing bowl, use a fork to beat the eggs with the chicken fat or oil until they are well combined. Stir in the matzo meal and salt to taste, then the 2 tablespoons of liquid and the optional parsley. Cover the bowl and refrigerate for a minimum of 1 hour. The mixture will become firm.

2. In a 4-quart pot, bring 3 quarts of chicken soup or water to the boil. Add salt if desired. Using a heaping teaspoon as a rough measure, shape the mixture between wet hands into 10 or 12 balls, each approximately 1¼ inches in diameter. Drop into the boiling soup or water. When all the knaidlach have been added, reduce the heat to a gentle boil, partially cover the pot, and cook for about 40 minutes, until tender throughout. Serve hot in bowls of steaming chicken soup.

FLUFFY KNAIDLACH

Makes 10 to 12 knaidlach

Knaidlach made from matzo meal and eggs, with no fat added, become exceptionally fluffy when the eggs are separated, the egg whites beaten until stiff, and the matzo balls cooked as soon as the mixture is prepared. If the mixture is refrigerated for an hour, the egg whites lose some air, resulting in knaidlach that are still light but more firm.

For a completely fat-free matzo ball mixture, a well-seasoned vegetable broth can be substituted for the egg yolks (see the variation). The resulting knaidlach are exceptionally delicate in texture, and are tastiest when cooked and served in a well-seasoned vegetable broth.

INGREDIENTS:

> 3 quarts chicken soup, vegetable broth, or water for
>   cooking
> Salt (optional)
> 2 eggs (graded large), separated
> $\frac{1}{2}$ to 1 teaspoon salt
> $\frac{1}{2}$ cup matzo meal
> $\frac{1}{4}$ cup chicken soup, vegetable broth, or water

DIRECTIONS:

1. In a 4-quart pot, bring the 3 quarts of liquid to the boil. Add salt to the liquid if desired.

2. Meanwhile, in a small clean, dry mixing bowl use a clean, dry whisk or an electric mixer to beat the egg whites until they hold stiff peaks but are still moist.

3. Working quickly so the egg whites do not deflate, in another small mixing bowl use a fork to beat the egg yolks until slightly thickened. Beat in the salt. Stir in the matzo meal, then the ¼ cup of liquid. The mixture will be coarse but not crumbly.

4. Stir ¼ cup of the stiffly beaten egg whites into the matzo meal-egg yolk mixture to soften it a bit. Using a rubber spatula, gently fold and mix the remaining beaten whites into the matzo meal mixture. The whites should be evenly distributed into the matzo meal mixture, but the mixing must be gentle so that the beaten whites do not collapse.

5. Between wet hands, shape the mixture into 10 to 12 even-size balls, each approximately 1½ inches in diameter. Drop the matzo balls into the boiling liquid. When all the knaidlach have been added, reduce the heat to a gentle boil, partially cover the pot, and cook for about 40 minutes, until tender throughout. Serve in hot chicken soup or a vegetable broth.

Note: If a more firm texture is desired, refrigerate the mixture for an hour before shaping and cooking the knaidlach.

VARIATION:

Fat-free Knaidlach

Beat the egg whites as in Step 2 above. Omit the egg yolks in Step 3. Mix the matzo meal with ¼ cup of a well-seasoned vegetable broth. Add salt to taste. (You will not need to add salt if the broth is salty.) Mix the egg whites into the matzo meal as directed in Step 4. Chill for 30 to 60 minutes before cooking in vegetable broth.

HOT BORSCHT WITH BEETS, CABBAGE, AND FLANKEN

Makes 2½ quarts soup (plus bones)

Second only to chicken soup in its identification as a traditional Jewish soup, *borscht* is the national soup of Russia and Ukraine, as well as Poland. A soup well known to both the prosperous and the peasantry of those countries, borscht defies definition in much the same way that tsimmes (see page 228) as a food cannot be defined, for borscht can be a meaty soup with the strong flavors of beets and cabbage, full of chunks of potatoes and tomatoes; but borscht can also be a meatless beet soup or a cabbage-based soup with no beets at all.

The word *borscht* does not translate to "beets" or "beet soup," as an American Jewish person used to purchasing borscht in glass jars might expect. Rather, it refers to the preparation itself, which varies both according to one's nationality and one's personal preferences. Ask a recent Russian Jewish émigré what borscht is, and that person is likely to answer "cabbage soup." Ask a third-generation Ashkenazic Jew and you will probably hear "cold beet soup."

As a dish of Russia and Poland, borscht is cooked with ham, sausage, and other pork products forbidden in kosher Jewish cuisine. Why, then, its popularity as a traditional Jewish soup? For those for whom meat was a luxury, the issue of nonkosher meats did not arise in preparing borscht. In fact, the soup in Jewish cuisine was based on a European method of preserving beets by fermenting them in a meatless preparation known as beet *russell* (see the following recipe). Jews who could afford meat enjoyed their borscht with kosher meats including flanken, brisket, or beef bones. Borscht, then, is a soup that reminds Jews of their national and religious heritage at one and the same time.

INGREDIENTS:

3 pounds meaty beef neck bones and marrow bones

2 pounds flanken

2 quarts (8 cups) water

3 cups julienne-sliced peeled fresh beets

3 cups shredded green cabbage

1½ cups sliced onion

1 teaspoon minced garlic

2 cups cubed peeled potatoes (1-inch cubes), optional

1 pound coarsely chopped fresh or canned tomatoes,
   optional

2 tablespoons freshly squeezed lemon juice

Salt and freshly ground black pepper

DIRECTIONS:

1. In a 6-quart pot, bring the bones, flanken, and water to the boil over high heat. Boil for 2 or 3 minutes, skimming off any scum that rises to the top.

2. Add the beets, cabbage, onion, garlic, and the potatoes and/or tomatoes if desired. When the water comes back to the boil, reduce the heat to a gentle boil, cover the pot, and cook for 2 hours.

3. Add the lemon juice and salt and pepper to taste. Cook for an additional 15 minutes. Taste and correct the seasonings. Skim off the fat before serving. For a smooth soup, remove the bones and flanken, then rub the soup and vegetables through a food mill or a sieve. Or, purée the soup in a food processor. Return the bones and flanken to the soup.

CHILLED BEET BORSCHT

Makes 1 quart

Here is the homemade version of the simple beet borscht that is available year-round in the international section of supermarkets and groceries. Even in areas with small Jewish populations, borscht is typically displayed during the Jewish New Year and Passover.

In talmudic times (the first few centuries C.E.), beets were among the plants considered to have medicinal value. The tradition of eating beets on Rosh Hashanah dates back to the Talmud and the writings of the scholar Abaye, who said that at the beginning of the year a person should eat beets (among other vegetables), for they grow in abundance and are good omens. During Passover, when the Ashkenazim do not eat legumes, the soups one may eat are temporarily limited. But cold beet borscht is widely available and has become a popular luncheon soup or a first course at dinner during the holiday.

Cold beet borscht was originally made from fermented beet juice, the product of covering fresh beets with water and allowing them to stand for a month. It was a way of preserving beets for future use before refrigeration was available. Here, lemon juice is used to produce a sour taste. While this plain beet version of borscht can be served hot, it is most often served chilled. Traditional accompaniments to cold borscht are chopped cucumber; the thick, cultured sour cream well known in Russian cookery; and—incongruous though it may seem—hot boiled potatoes. The recipe itself is pareve. The addition of the sour cream will turn it into a dairy dish.

Note that the beautiful deep crimson color of raw beets will act as a dye. Take care when handling fresh beets: peel them with a vegetable peeler, slice the beets with a sharp knife, then immediately wash your hands to avoid staining your clothing.

INGREDIENTS:

3 cups shredded peeled fresh beets
1 quart (4 cups) water
¼ cup granulated white sugar
2 tablespoons freshly squeezed lemon juice
Salt
Accompaniments: peeled chopped cucumber; dollops
    of sour cream; small hot boiled potatoes, peeled
    but left whole, 2 per serving

DIRECTIONS:

1. In a 2- or 3-quart pot, bring the beets and water to the boil over high heat. Reduce the heat to a gentle boil, cover the pot, and cook for 30 minutes, until the beets are tender.

2. Stir in the sugar. Cook for a minute or so until the sugar dissolves.

3. Stir in the lemon juice. Add salt to taste. Chill before serving. Serve cold, with the traditional accompaniments, as a light lunch on a hot summer's day or as the first course of a dairy meal.

CABBAGE SOUP
WITH MARROW BONES

Makes 2½ quarts soup (plus bones)

Green cabbage, one of our most versatile vegetables, grows well in temperate climates throughout the world and is well known in Central and Eastern European cookery. Although this cruciferous vegetable is an excellent and inexpensive source of vitamin C and many minerals, cabbage was important in the diets of Ashkenazic Jews long before its health benefits were known. Individual leaves were softened and stuffed for savory holishkes (page 135); shredded cabbage was mixed with noodles (page 245), stuffed into strudels (page 247), and used in borscht (page 95) and other hearty vegetable soups.

While cabbage has a strong taste when cooked and can easily dominate a whole pot of soup, here the tomato sauce, fresh tomatoes, and ketchup balance the cabbage flavor. For a meatier soup, brown three pounds of flanken in oil before adding the soup bones and water.

I'm ten years old again when I eat this soup, transported to my grandparents' dinner table. Following informal appetizers in a small area outside the dining room, we chatted with Grandma and Grandpa in the living room until we heard the announcement, "Soup's on!" As we entered the dining room, steaming bowls of soup awaited us at the table. My bowl always had at least one marrow bone in it, and if I was lucky, a meaty neck bone as well. Grandma always said that mealtime was a time to relax and be happy, so it was okay to slurp, and it was okay to chew on the bones. Now, I like to serve this soup for informal dinners, when my guests can relax, be happy, slurp, and chew on the bones.

INGREDIENTS:

2½ pounds meaty beef neck bones

1 pound marrow bones

2 quarts (8 cups) water

2½ cups shredded green cabbage

1 cup tomato sauce

1½ cups diced fresh plum tomatoes

¾ cup chopped onion

¼ cup ketchup

2 tablespoons freshly squeezed lemon juice

2 tablespoons firmly packed brown sugar

Salt and freshly ground black pepper

DIRECTIONS:

1. In a 5-quart pot, bring the bones and water to the boil over high heat. Boil for 2 or 3 minutes, skimming off any scum from the top.

2. Add the cabbage, tomato sauce, tomatoes, onion, and ketchup. When the mixture comes back to the boil, reduce the heat to a gentle boil, cover the pot, and cook for 2½ hours.

3. Add the lemon juice, sugar, and salt and pepper to taste. Cook for another 15 minutes. Taste and correct the seasonings. Do not purée the soup. Skim off the fat before serving. Or, if you like, refrigerate the soup and remove and discard the fat that congeals on top before reheating.

4. For a formal meal, serve the soup as a first course without the bones. For informal occasions, serve the soup with the bones right in it, either as a first course or as a main dish along with a loaf of a hot crusty bread with a coarse crumb (pages 307 and 312).

VEGETARIAN CABBAGE SOUP

Makes about 2 quarts

Do you know the story of "nail soup"? Briefly, a hungry traveler stops at the cottage of a peasant who offers to prepare a big pot of delicious nail soup. He is incredulous, but nonetheless agrees to watch her prepare the soup. She begins by boiling a pot of water with one nail in it. "You know," she says, "this is coming along nicely, but it would be tastier if we had an onion in it." The man remembers having seen some wild onions not far from the cottage, and he offers to dig them up for the soup. "Ah, that's better," she says. "Now if we only had a carrot or two...." And, from his pocket, the traveler pulls some carrots that he had been saving for his journey.

Another traveler happens by and is invited to stay. "This soup smells good," says the traveler. "But I think it needs a tomato. Do you mind if I add one?" And so it goes with more passersby, who bring cabbage, potatoes, garlic, and wild herbs, until a delicious "nail soup" is ready.

A wholesome vegetarian cabbage soup is, in a way, nail soup, relying on a mixture of ordinary vegetables to provide flavor, substance, and nutrition. A dish of European peasantry, cabbage soup was eaten by people of various nationalities and religions, including Jews. As a Jewish preparation, it is a humble reminder of a heritage in which children did not go hungry, because Mama managed to gather whatever was available for a filling, vegetable-laden soup.

Here, the strong cabbage flavor is matched by the pronounced taste of caraway seeds. If the caraway seeds are omitted, the taste of cabbage will predominate. The tomato background and sweet-sour taste will remind you of traditional stuffed cabbage (page 135). Potatoes make the soup more filling and the broth somewhat thicker. Sliced carrots add color and flavor.

INGREDIENTS:

4 cups shredded green cabbage

2 tablespoons unbleached white flour

1 cup chopped onion

1 tablespoon vegetable oil

1 can (28 ounces) whole peeled tomatoes

½ teaspoon minced garlic

2 cups cubed peeled potatoes (½-inch cubes)

2 cups sliced peeled carrots

2 cups cold water

1 tablespoon caraway seeds (optional)

½ teaspoon salt

½ teaspoon freshly ground black pepper

2 tablespoons firmly packed brown sugar

3 tablespoons freshly squeezed lemon juice

DIRECTIONS:

1. Toss the cabbage with the flour. Set aside.

2. In a 3- or 4-quart pot, over moderate heat, cook the onion in the oil for about 5 minutes, until wilted but not brown.

3. Meanwhile, drain the tomatoes, reserving the juice. Chop the tomatoes coarsely.

4. Stir the garlic into the onion, then add the cabbage, the tomatoes with their juice, potatoes, carrots, and the water. Bring to the boil over high heat.

5. Stir in the optional caraway seeds, the salt and pepper, and the brown sugar. Reduce the heat to a gentle boil, cover the pot, and cook for 45 minutes to 1 hour, until the cabbage is very soft.

6. Stir in the lemon juice. Taste and correct the seasonings. Serve immediately, or refrigerate and reheat. Freeze in plastic containers (allowing an inch of headspace) for longer storage.

VARIATIONS:

Cabbage Soup with Flanken or Brisket

For a meat meal, after sautéing the onion, push the onion to the side, add a little more oil to the pot, then brown 2 pounds of flanken or the fatty top piece of a whole brisket on both sides. Proceed with the recipe, increasing the cooking time to 2 to 2½ hours, until the meat is tender. Skim the fat off the top before serving. To serve, cut the flanken into 2-inch pieces or the brisket into slices or small chunks, making sure to include some meat in each serving.

Cabbage-Chicken Soup

Substitute chicken soup (page 80 or 82) for the water.

Vegetarian Cabbage Soup with Dairy Accompaniments

For a dairy meal, prepare the pareve soup. Serve with a bowl of thick sour cream on the side, to be spooned on top of the soup by each diner. Pareve potato or kasha knishes (page 290 or 292) or cheese kreplach (page 256) make delicious accompaniments.

MUSHROOM AND BARLEY SOUP WITH MEAT

Makes 2 quarts soup (plus bones)

Barley has provided sustenance since ancient times as the grain originally used by the Israelites in making flour and breads. Until the finer-grained wheat replaced barley as the primary source of flour, barley was a staple in the diets of the Hebrews of biblical times. In fact, the Book of Deuteronomy lists barley as one of the seven foods with which the Land of Israel is blessed.

Plain but nourishing barley porridges evolved into tasty soups and substantial casseroles, sustaining the Jews of the Fertile Crescent as well as those who, in later years, migrated to Central and Eastern Europe, where barley also grew well. A bowl of barley soup made interesting by the addition of local vegetables was pleasing, and one could enjoy a meat flavor on the Sabbath by cooking barley in a beef, veal, or chicken broth among Ashkenazic Jews, lamb or chicken broth among Sephardim.

Barley is enjoyed by modern Jews in thick soups, main dishes (see cholent on page 154), and side-dish casseroles (refer to the Index for recipes). Today's meat barley soups are made with rich broth or chunks of meat, brimming with plenty of mushrooms, carrots, and celery.

Here, fresh mushrooms are supplemented with a small quantity of the European dried mushrooms that are well known in Ashkenazic cooking. The dried mushrooms give the soup a unique smoky flavor while darkening the broth. Look for them in a small container (one ounce) near canned mushrooms on grocery shelves. The soup will have a milder flavor if the dried mushrooms are omitted.

This recipe uses beef bones and marrow bones. For a meatier soup, brown three pounds of flanken in a little oil before adding the soup bones and water.

INGREDIENTS:

¼ cup dried mushrooms

Hot water for soaking

2 pounds beef bones and marrow bones

2 quarts (8 cups) water

1 cup chopped onion

1 cup chopped celery

1 cup chopped peeled carrots

4 cups sliced fresh mushrooms

1 cup pearl barley, picked through and rinsed

Salt and freshly ground black pepper

DIRECTIONS:

1. Soak the dried mushrooms in a cup of hot water for 10 minutes. Drain, squeeze out the water, then chop the mushrooms into ½-inch pieces.

2. In a 6-quart pot, bring the bones and 2 quarts of water to the boil over high heat. Boil for 2 or 3 minutes, skimming off any scum from the top.

3. Add the dried mushrooms, the onion, celery, carrots, fresh mushrooms, and the barley. When the water returns to the boil, add salt and pepper to taste. Reduce the heat to a gentle boil, cover the pot, and cook for 1 hour or until the barley is tender and meat begins to pull away from the bones.

4. Taste for seasoning, adding salt and pepper as necessary.

5. Skim off the fat before serving. Or, if you like, refrigerate the soup. Before reheating, remove and discard the fat that congeals on top.

6. For a formal meal, serve the soup as a first course without the bones. For informal occasions, serve the soup with the bones right in it either as a first course or as a main dish with a big tossed green salad on the side.

MUSHROOM AND BARLEY SOUP

Makes 1 quart

Although the pareve version of barley soup uses ingredients similar to the meat soup of the previous recipe, here, in the delicate broth, the tastes of the individual vegetables stand out more. The addition of a cup of milk or light cream in the dairy variation again emphasizes the broth, but both the individual textures and the tastes of the vegetables remain important to the preparation. The soup is thickened with flour which, for convenience, is added during the beginning of cooking.

A more traditional method of thickening with flour is to use an *einbren,* a paste of flour and fat. In a small skillet, heat the flour with oil or melted butter, stirring constantly until bubbly. Add about half a cup of liquid from the soup to the mixture, stirring until smooth. The thickened broth is then added back into the pot of soup.

INGREDIENTS:

1 tablespoon dried mushrooms

Hot water for soaking

1 tablespoon vegetable oil

1 cup chopped onion

1 cup sliced fresh mushrooms

2 tablespoons unbleached white flour

3 cups water

½ cup pearl barley, picked through and rinsed

1 cup thin-sliced peeled carrots

½ cup diced celery

1 teaspoon salt

A healthy dash of freshly ground black pepper

DIRECTIONS:

1. Soften the dried mushrooms in hot water for about 10 minutes. Slice them thin, then set aside the dried mushrooms.

2. In a 2-quart pot, place the oil, the onion, and the fresh mushrooms. Cook over moderate heat until the vegetables just begin to sizzle. Stir in the flour, stirring constantly for a minute.

3. Add the 3 cups of water. Bring to the boil over high heat, then add the remaining ingredients, including the dried mushrooms that have been soaked and sliced. Reduce the heat to a gentle boil, cover the pot, and cook for about 45 minutes, until the barley is tender. Serve hot as the first course of any meal or as the main dish of a light lunch with mandlen (page 84) or bread and a salad.

VARIATION:

Mushroom and Barley Soup, Dairy Version

When the barley is tender, add 1 cup of milk or light cream and 1 tablespoon of butter. Stir until the soup is hot and the butter has melted.

SPLIT PEA SOUP WITH FLANKEN

Makes 2½ quarts soup (plus bones)

Green split pea soup is appreciated in European and American households as one last meal in which to use up a ham bone. Of course, the use of any pork product is forbidden in kosher kitchens, but Jews enjoy delicious, nourishing split pea soups made with flanken and marrow bones. Flanken, a bony cut of beef that comes from cutting the short ribs across the bones, is especially well suited for long-simmering soups, adding a rich, meaty flavor without falling apart. As a relatively fatty meat, flanken was historically important to the Jews in the colder climates of Europe because it supplied calories along with good taste. It may be difficult for us to imagine *seeking* fats in our diets, but people with limited means needed to consume foods with high energy value.

Split pea soup is thick and filling. Serve small portions with mandlen (page 84) as a first course. For a hearty main dish, serve in big bowls along with a coarse, heavy bread (see pumpernickel bread, page 307). Potato or kasha knishes can be served on the side in place of the soup nuts or bread.

INGREDIENTS:

> 1 pound (2¼ cups) dried split green peas, picked
> through and rinsed
> Water for soaking the peas
> Vegetable oil for browning the meat
> 2 pounds flanken
> 1 pound marrow bones
> 1 cup each chopped onion and celery
> 1 cup each chopped peeled carrots and potato

2 quarts (8 cups) water
Salt

DIRECTIONS:

1. In a 4-quart pot, place the split peas with cold water to cover by 3 inches. Bring to the boil over high heat. Boil for 2 minutes then turn off the heat, leaving the pot on the turned-off burner. Cover the pot when the boiling subsides. Let stand for 1 hour.

2. Drain the soaked split peas, then rinse in cold water.

3. Coat a 6-quart pot with a thin layer of oil. Over moderate heat, brown the flanken in the oil. Add the drained split peas, the marrow bones, vegetables, and the 2 quarts of water. Bring to the boil over high heat. Skim off any scum that rises to the top. Reduce the heat to a gentle boil, stirring to make sure that no peas are sticking to the bottom.

4. Cover the pot and cook the soup for 2 hours or until both the split peas and flanken are tender. Stir occasionally. Add salt to taste, then cook for an additional 10 minutes.

5. If desired, purée all or part of the soup using a strainer, food mill, blender, or food processor. (First remove the flanken and the soup bones, setting both aside. Return the meat and bones to the puréed soup.)

6. Serve immediately, or refrigerate for later use. When the soup has chilled, discard the fat that congeals on top. Reheat the soup over low heat, stirring often so that the peas do not stick to the bottom of the pot and burn. Once the soup is warm, the heat can be raised to moderately low. Serve each bowl of soup with a piece of flanken and soup bones for those who enjoy them. To freeze, transfer to plastic containers, leaving an inch of headspace. If the contents of all the containers will not be heated up at once, be sure to put some flanken and marrow bones in each container.

VEGETARIAN SPLIT PEA SOUP

Makes 2½ quarts

The division of foods according to the kosher dietary laws into meat (*fleishig* in Yiddish), dairy (*milchig* in Yiddish), and *pareve* (neither meat nor dairy) gave the creative forebears of traditional Jewish cuisine a way to triple their soup repertoire. Soup of the day could vary each day for three days—all based on one set of ingredients.

Legumes have always been popular as the base for soups in Jewish cooking because they are inexpensive, highly nutritious, and versatile. Here, the dried split peas of the previous recipe become a hearty pareve soup textured by bits of vegetables. Herbs are added in the final stage of cooking so their flavors will remain strong. The addition of a cup of milk or cream for a dairy soup adds nutrients and changes the flavor of the soup.

While mandlen (page 84), bread and butter, or cheese kreplach (page 256) are all delicious accompaniments, note that serving butter or cheese with the pareve soup turns it into a dairy course.

INGREDIENTS:

1 pound (2¼ cups) dried split green peas, picked
   through and rinsed
Water for soaking the peas
1 cup chopped onion
1 cup diced celery
1 cup diced peeled carrots
1 cup diced peeled potato
2½ quarts (10 cups) water

2 teaspoons salt, or to taste

¼ teaspoon freshly ground black pepper

2 tablespoons chopped fresh parsley

2 tablespoons chopped fresh dill

1 cup warm milk or cream (optional)

DIRECTIONS:

1. In a 4-quart pot, place the split peas with cold water to cover by 3 inches. Bring to the boil over high heat. Boil for 2 minutes, then turn off the heat, leaving the pot on the turned-off burner. Cover the pot when the boiling subsides. Let stand for 1 hour.

2. Drain the soaked split peas, then rinse in cold water.

3. In a 6-quart pot, combine the drained split peas, the onion, celery, carrots, potato, and the 2½ quarts of cold water. Bring to the boil over high heat. Add the salt and pepper. Reduce the heat to a gentle boil, stirring to make sure no peas are sticking to the bottom.

4. Cover the pot and cook the soup for 1½ to 2 hours, until the split peas are tender. From time to time, stir to make sure the peas aren't sticking.

5. Add the fresh parsley and dill. Cook for an additional 5 minutes. Stir in the milk or cream if desired. Taste for seasoning, adding salt and pepper as necessary. Serve immediately, or refrigerate for later use. When reheating, take care to see that the peas do not stick to the bottom of the pot and burn.

6. To prepare the soup for freezing, do not add the herbs or the milk or cream. Freeze the soup in plastic containers, allowing an inch of headspace for expansion. To serve, reheat the soup over moderately low heat, stirring frequently to prevent sticking. Add the fresh parsley and dill to the warm soup. Add the milk or cream if desired. Cook for an additional 5 minutes.

RICH LENTIL SOUP

Makes about 1 quart; 6 small portions

Lentils, among the oldest cultivated plants known, were an important source of nourishment for the general population in biblical days. Lentils are thought to be the pottage for which Esau sold his birthright to Jacob, and they made up a substantial part of the diet of David's army. High in protein, this legume remains popular in the diets of Sephardic Jews of the Mediterranean and Middle Eastern countries in thick, tasty soups and well-seasoned main or side dishes.

While lentils can be boiled and served plain, they combine well with other vegetables and a variety of herbs and spices. The soup below is a superb blend of vegetables and seasonings, incorporating ingredients widely favored by Sephardic cooks: garlic, cumin, coriander, lemon juice, and olive oil in a tomato-and-lentil base. Although very ripe, fresh tomatoes are used in the Mediterranean, in order to make this a year-round preparation tomato juice (or ketchup and water) is suggested for a good tomato flavor. Using beef broth in place of the tomato juice (see variation) has the effect of making the lentil taste more pronounced. The soup is traditionally thick and rich, but not overly seasoned, surprisingly subtle despite the tablespoon of garlic. The taste of cumin and coriander are distinctive, however, and the spices can be adjusted according to personal taste.

Although the lentils in this preparation become very soft during cooking, they retain their shape. The soup can be served with the lentils whole for those who like a more pronounced lentil taste in a soup textured with small bits. Puréeing part of the soup, up to three-fourths, makes a smooth soup with some clearly identifiable whole lentils. For those who prefer a smooth, creamy blend, purée the entire preparation.

A marvelous way to begin any meal, but take care: this soup is exceptionally filling, so unless you plan to make a whole meal of it, limit the servings to three-fourths of a cup per person.

INGREDIENTS:

1 cup brown lentils, picked through and rinsed
2 cups water
1 tablespoon olive oil
1 cup chopped onion
1 tablespoon minced garlic
½ teaspoon ground cumin
½ teaspoon ground coriander
1 cup shredded carrot
3 cups tomato juice (substitute ¼ cup ketchup and
    2¾ cups water)
Salt and freshly ground black pepper
1 tablespoon freshly squeezed lemon juice
1 tablespoon olive oil (optional)
Optional garnishes: chopped fresh coriander leaves
    or chopped fresh parsley; chopped fresh red ripe
    tomatoes

DIRECTIONS:

1. In a 1-quart pot, bring the lentils and water to the boil. Turn off the heat, stir the lentils, cover the pot, and allow the lentils to stand for 15 minutes.

2. In a 2-quart pot, heat the olive oil, onion, and garlic over moderately low heat. Cook, stirring occasionally, for 5 minutes or until the onion has wilted. Do not allow the garlic to brown.

3. Stir in the cumin and coriander, then the carrot, next the tomato juice (or ketchup and water).

4. Drain the lentils and add them to the pot. Bring to the boil over high heat, stir once with a large spoon, reduce to a gentle boil, cover the pot, and cook for 45 minutes to an hour. Stir once or twice during cooking to make sure that the lentils are not sticking. The lentils should be soft, the soup very thick. If you prefer a thinner consistency, gradually thin with boiling water, adding a tablespoon at a time.

5. Season to taste with salt and pepper.

6. If desired, purée all or part of the soup in a blender or food processor. Or, pass through a strainer or food mill.

7. Return the soup to the pot. Stir in the lemon juice and the optional olive oil. Serve at once, garnished with the chopped fresh coriander or parsley and fresh tomatoes if you like. (Fresh coriander is acrid, so do make sure that it will be appreciated before sprinkling it on the soup.)

VARIATION:

Rich Lentil Soup with Beef Broth

In place of the tomato juice, substitute 2 cups of beef broth and 2 cups of chopped very ripe, red tomatoes. The soup will have a beefy taste, and the taste of the lentils will be stronger as well.

LIMA BEAN SOUP

Makes 2 quarts

The dried lima beans indigenous to South America were appreciated by the Ashkenazim of North America who recognized another source for a tasty, filling, nutritious soup that did not depend on meat for flavor. Lima beans and barley thicken the broth naturally, and the beans themselves have a pleasant starchy taste. This pareve soup is turned into a meat-based soup with the substitution of beef broth for the water, or a dairy soup when milk or cream is added instead.

INGREDIENTS:

1 cup dried lima beans

1 quart (4 cups) water for soaking the beans

1 cup chopped onion

1½ cups thin-sliced carrot rounds

1 cup chopped celery with leaves

1 cup sliced fresh mushrooms

6 tablespoons barley

1 quart (4 cups) cold water

1 teaspoon salt

½ teaspoon freshly ground black pepper

DIRECTIONS:

1. In a 2-quart pot, bring the lima beans and 1 quart of water to the boil. Boil for 1 minute, then turn off the heat. Cover the pot. Allow the limas to stand on the turned-off burner for 1 hour.

2. Drain the beans.

3. In a 4-quart pot, place the soaked lima beans with the onion, carrots, celery, mushrooms, barley, and 1 quart of water. Bring to the boil over high heat.

4. Stir in the salt and pepper, then reduce the heat to a gentle boil. Cover the pot and cook for 45 minutes to 1 hour, until the beans and barley are tender. Taste and correct the seasonings. Serve immediately, or refrigerate and re-heat.

VARIATIONS:

Lima Bean Soup with Meat Broth

For a meat soup, substitute beef or chicken broth for the 1 quart of cooking water in Step 1.

Lima Bean Soup, Dairy Version

For a dairy soup, prepare the soup as directed in the basic recipe. Just before serving, stir 1 cup of warm milk or light cream and a tablespoon of butter into the hot soup, melting the butter.

CREAM OF POTATO SOUP

Makes approximately 1 quart

Potatoes, which are native to South America, were introduced to Europe by explorers in the 1500s. A primary source of nourishment among the Jews of Eastern Europe, potatoes were later brought to North America by European immigrants. Each new wave of immigrants brought tastes of the homeland, including the inexpensive, unpretentious potato soups eaten in Jewish households in Germany and in the countries of the Austro-Hungarian Empire.

The basic traditional Jewish potato soup is simple and satisfying, a soup that can be quickly cooked from ingredients on hand to go with any meal. When prepared as a dairy soup and sprinkled with cheese, it makes a wholesome first course. Large portions can be served as a main dish along with a tossed green salad and a hearty bread.

INGREDIENTS:

2 cups diced peeled potatoes (1/4-inch dice)
1 cup diced celery
1 cup finely chopped onion
3 cups water
Salt and freshly ground black pepper
1/4 cup (1/2 stick) unsalted butter or vegetable oil
1/4 cup unbleached white flour
2 cups milk or light cream
Paprika
Shredded Cheddar, Swiss, Monterey Jack, or
    other cheese

DIRECTIONS:

1. In a 2-quart pot, bring the potatoes, celery, onion, and water to the boil over high heat. Reduce to a gentle boil, cover the pot, and cook for 30 minutes, until the vegetables are very soft. Add salt and pepper to taste. Set aside.

2. In a clean 2- or 3-quart pot, heat the butter or oil over moderately low heat. Stir in the flour, and cook for a minute. The mixture should be bubbly but not brown. Add the 2 cups of milk or light cream, stirring until the mixture comes to the boil and is smooth and thickened. Cook for an additional minute, then mix the cooked vegetables with all their liquid into the cream sauce.

3. If desired, rub through a food mill or sieve, or purée in a food processor or blender. Serve immediately, or refrigerate and reheat. Just before serving, sprinkle with paprika. Serve the soup hot, with shredded cheese for each diner to sprinkle on individually.

VARIATION:

Potato Soup, Pareve Version

Substitute water for the milk or cream in Step 2. In place of the shredded cheese, garnish each serving with chopped fresh parsley, dill, and chives.

SCHAV

Makes 2 cups

Sorrel, also called sour grass because of its natural sour taste, has been known since antiquity. As a wild herb native to Europe and Asia, sorrel was used by ancient gatherers in soups, salads, and vegetable preparations. As a cultivated plant, sorrel is known in Europe, Asia, and North America as a base for soups and as a sophisticated salad green.

As a soup in Jewish cuisine, sorrel is cooked in water with sugar and lemon juice to make a pleasantly tart soup known by Ashkenazim as *schav*. The egg thickener makes the soup creamy. Schav is a pareve preparation, but it is often served with a dollop of sour cream, making it an appropriate soup to serve in celebration of Shavuot, when dairy products are eaten (see pages 34 and 256). Schav is served cold, a refreshing soup on hot days. When fresh sorrel leaves are plentiful, double the recipe to make a quart.

Although spinach is almost invariably suggested as a substitute when sorrel is unavailable, kale is much closer in taste to sorrel and makes a better alternative.

INGREDIENTS:

2 cups loosely packed shredded sorrel leaves
    (substitute minced kale leaves)
2 cups water
1 tablespoon granulated white sugar
1 ½ teaspoons freshly squeezed lemon juice
1 egg (graded large)
Sour cream for garnish (optional)

DIRECTIONS:

1. In a 2-quart pot, bring the shredded sorrel leaves and water to the boil. Reduce to a gentle boil then cook, covered, for 10 minutes.

2. Add the sugar and lemon juice. Cook for an additional minute to dissolve the sugar. Remove from the heat.

3. In a medium-size mixing bowl, beat the egg very well. In a slow, steady stream pour the hot soup into the egg, stirring rapidly so that the egg does not curdle.

4. Chill before serving. For a dairy meal, have sour cream available at the table.

SOUR CHERRY SOUP

Makes 1 quart

Jews who emigrated from Germany, Hungary, and Austria to the United States discovered that the same sour cherries from which they made refreshing chilled soups, flaky strudels, and tasty dumplings in the Old Country were available in America. While it might be typically American to make cherry pie from sour cherries, to the Ashkenazim sour cherry soup was a taste of home. Sour cherries are juicy, fruity, and when cooked as soup, they will remind you of cherry pie—and of the Old Country.

INGREDIENTS:

> 2 cups pitted ripe sour cherries
> 2 cups water
> ¼ cup granulated white sugar
> ½ teaspoon ground cinnamon
> 2 tablespoons cornstarch dissolved in ¼ cup
>   cold water
> Sour cream (optional)

DIRECTIONS:

1. In a 2-quart pot over high heat, bring to the boil the cherries, water, sugar, and cinnamon. Stir occasionally. Reduce to a gentle boil, cover the pot, and cook for 10 minutes or until the cherries are very soft.

2. Stir together the cornstarch and water until smooth, then add the mixture to

the soup. Bring to the boil while stirring, cook for about 15 seconds, then remove from the heat.

3. Cool to room temperature in the pot, then transfer to a covered container and chill.

4. Serve cold, with a dollop of sour cream if desired. The soup is usually served as an appetizer or as the main dish for a light lunch, but it can be served as dessert as well.

FRUIT SOUP

Makes about 2 quarts

The three major festivals ordained in the Bible—Passover, Shavuot, and Sukkot—began as agricultural holidays celebrating the beginning of the grain harvest, the harvesting of the new wheat crop, and the ingathering from the fields, respectively. The preparation and consumption of fruit soups among Jews of European ancestry parallels the celebration of the ingathering, for although fruit soups are not specifically linked with Jewish holidays, they are a celebration of nature's bounty.

It would have been unthinkable to waste any of the fruits of a successful harvest. Rich, flavorful, tasty fruit soups gave an aura of extravagance but were actually a way to enjoy the taste of fresh fruit without any waste. Although refrigeration has lengthened the life of fresh fruit in modern times, fresh fruit soup remains a delicious link with Jewish tradition.

Pears, blueberries, strawberries, and sour cherries also make appealing fruit soups in varying combinations. While an additional cup of blueberries, strawberries, or cherries will not change the flavor of the basic fruit soup dramatically, pears tend to dominate other tastes in fruit soups and fruit sauces and should be used cautiously. For a taste of pure fruit, no spices are added. If a gentle cinnamon taste is desired, cook the fruit with a piece of cinnamon stick.

INGREDIENTS:

3 pounds mixed fresh peaches, plums, and apricots
1 quart (4 cups) water
1 piece (2 inches) cinnamon stick (optional)

¼ cup granulated white sugar (optional)
1 tablespoon cornstarch dissolved in 2 tablespoons
    cold water (optional)
Sour cream (optional)

DIRECTIONS:

1. Wash and slice the unpeeled fruit, discarding the stones.

2. In a 3- or 4-quart pot, bring the fruit, water, and the optional cinnamon stick to the boil. Reduce the heat to a gentle boil, cover, and cook for 15 minutes or until the fruit is tender. If you do not want to add sugar or the cornstarch thickener, skip to Step 5.

3. Taste and add sugar if desired. Continue cooking for a few more minutes if necessary to dissolve any sugar.

4. If desired, thicken the soup with cornstarch. Stir together the cornstarch and water until smooth, then add the mixture to the soup. Bring to the boil while stirring, cook for about 15 seconds, then remove from the heat.

5. Remove the cinnamon stick. Rub the fruit through a food mill or a sieve, or purée in a food processor or blender, then chill.

6. Serve cold, with a dollop of sour cream if desired. As with the cherry soup of the previous recipe, fruit soup is usually served as an appetizer or as the main dish for a light lunch, but it can be served as dessert as well.

Meat Main Dishes

Beef, Lamb, Veal, and Poultry

Meat Main Dishes

In biblical times, Jews (then called Israelites or Hebrews) were basically a vegetarian people. The consumption of animals was reserved for the Sabbath, holidays, and other special occasions. Most people did not have the resources to obtain meat, and once an animal was butchered, it had to be consumed quickly to prevent spoilage.

The long tradition of enjoying meat on festive occasions has continued to the present day. The Friday night Sabbath meal often centers around a large piece of brisket or a whole chicken; many holidays are celebrated with elaborate meat-based meals; and lavish wedding and Bar and Bat Mitzvah dinners feature not just one but two, even three main dish meat choices.

Before beef, veal, and lamb became affordable to the general population, Jewish cooks found inventive ways of flavoring large vegetable, legume, or grain casseroles with small amounts of meat. Some traditional Jewish dishes rely on the full flavor of meaty bones. For example, veal breast overflowing with a delectable stuffing is rich and tasty.

The biblical prohibition against consuming blood in effect limits the cuts of meat available in traditional kosher cooking. While technically all the arteries and veins can be removed from the blood-rich hindquarter, the procedure is so time-consuming that most kosher butchers choose not to sell beef, veal, or lamb from the hindquarter. Some Jews consider it impossible to remove all of the blood vessels from the hindquarter, and therefore they will not use meat from this part of the animal under any circumstances.

Despite the limitations of the kosher dietary laws, there is no shortage of tasty meat dishes in Jewish cooking. Drawing on a culinary experience that stretches across continents, classic Jewish cuisine uses many cuts of beef, lamb, and veal to create a wide and tempting array of preparations.

Before the sixteenth century, meat pies were favored as a Sabbath food. Home-raised chickens became popular in the sixteenth and seventeenth centuries. Today, of course, a variety of poultry—chicken, duck, goose, turkey, Cornish hen—is well known in the Jewish household. In a different era, fatty birds such as the duck and goose were prized not only for their meat but for their fat, which was saved and used in preparing other foods. While today's cooks do not savor poultry fat to the degree that their forebears did, many traditional Jewish preparations rely on the flavor of schmaltz.

Many nutrition experts suggest limiting the amount of meat consumed. With this in mind, the serving sizes suggested in this chapter are generally moderate, and most recipes can be increased for those who enjoy large servings of meat. In a few recipes, generous portions of meat are indicated. Traditional Jewish meals often feature satisfying side dishes, and the quantity of meat eaten in one meal will depend on what else is being served.

This chapter presents a range of beef, veal, lamb, and poultry preparations that are traditional in Jewish cooking. For additional meat dishes, refer to the appetizers and soups chapters as well as the Index.

A WORD ABOUT SALT IN MEAT RECIPES

Because salt is used in the koshering process to draw off as much blood as possible from the ritually slaughtered animal, kosher meat is generally more salty than its nonkosher counterpart. It is typical these days for the kosher butcher to wash, soak, salt, and rinse meat for the customer. The amount of salt used by butchers varies, and so does the saltiness of kosher meat. Therefore, in most beef, veal, lamb, and poultry recipes in this cookbook, salt is optional.

MEATBALLS

Serves 6 as an appetizer, 3 to 4 as a main course

Economic hardship and severe winters suffered by Eastern European Jews made scraps of beef—sometimes heavy with fat—attractive for chopped meat. When well seasoned and shaped into meatballs, the meat could go a long way in a large family. Bread or matzo meal was used not only to extend the beef, but actually to retain the fat! In an era before labor-saving devices, when people worked hard physically and leisure time was at a minimum, food energy (the calorie) was important as sustenance.

Ground beef, or chopped meat as it is still called by older generations, is also a way of tenderizing tough cuts of meat by shortening the fibers. In modern times, people of all economic means enjoy ground beef, whether as meatballs, meatloaf, hamburgers, or in meat sauces. Today, ground beef with a very low fat content is at a premium, but the meat is still mixed with breadcrumbs or matzo meal to make light meatballs. Here, the meatballs are lightly seasoned with onion, garlic, and parsley. In place of milk and cheese often mixed into meatballs by nonkosher cooks, beef broth is used.

To serve the meatballs as an hors d'oeuvre, spear them with toothpicks and pass them with a condiment such as mustard or ketchup. Enjoy them with a fricassee of chicken wings (page 54), or make potted meatballs with gravy and serve them as a main dish with mashed potatoes (page 264) and a hot vegetable.

INGREDIENTS:

2 tablespoons matzo meal or breadcrumbs
3 tablespoons beef broth
1 pound ground beef (lean or extra lean)

      1 tablespoon minced fresh parsley

      2 to 3 tablespoons grated onion, to taste

      $\frac{1}{2}$ to 1 teaspoon minced garlic, to taste

      $\frac{1}{2}$ to 1 teaspoon salt (optional)

      $\frac{1}{4}$ teaspoon freshly ground black pepper

      $\frac{1}{4}$ teaspoon paprika

      1 egg (graded large)

      2 tablespoons schmaltz (page 40), olive oil,
         or vegetable oil

DIRECTIONS:

1. In a medium-size mixing bowl, soak the matzo meal or breadcrumbs in the broth. (If beef broth is unavailable, substitute chicken broth or water.) When the liquid has been absorbed, mix in the meat with your hands. Add the remaining ingredients except for the chicken fat or oil. Mix lightly with your hands until everything is combined well.

2. Shape firmly into about two dozen $1\frac{1}{4}$-inch meatballs.

3. In a 10-inch skillet, heat the chicken fat or oil over moderate heat. Add the meatballs. Brown well all over, shaking the pan to keep the meatballs from sticking. If the meatballs stick, gently turn them with a large spoon or a pancake turner. After the meatballs have browned (about 5 minutes), reduce the heat to low and cook uncovered for about 5 minutes longer, until they are cooked through.

   For potted meatballs, transfer the browned meatballs to a bowl, pour off any accumulated fat, then add 1 cup of beef broth to the skillet. Bring to the boil over high heat, scraping up any bits of meat that may be sticking to the bottom. Place the meatballs back in the skillet, reduce the heat so the liquid just barely boils, then cover and cook for 10 minutes longer.

SWEET-AND-SOUR MEATBALLS

Serves 4

Meatballs are known in many cuisines as tasty morsels that may be spicy, sweet, plain, stuffed, skewered, speared with toothpicks to be dipped into a savory condiment, or bathed in sauce. In the Middle East, the meatballs are likely to be made of lamb, perhaps mixed with cracked wheat and sauced with a lemony mixture; in China, the meatballs are made of pork, the sauce sometimes of fruit and rice vinegar; for Italian Americans, the meat is likely to be a mixture of beef and pork, the sauce tomato-based; and for Ashkenazic Jews, meatballs are made of beef or veal, and are often served in a flavorsome sweet-and-sour sauce.

Sweet-and-sour meatballs can be served as an appetizer or as the main course for dinner. As with many other meat preparations in traditional Jewish cuisine, the sauce is a way of stretching the meat and flavoring the dish. Whether the meatballs are served with rice, noodles, potatoes, or kasha, the sweet-sour sauce makes the starch extra delicious. Raisins are popular in Eastern European cuisine, a sweet but nutritious addition to sweet-and-sour preparations.

INGREDIENTS:

> 1½ **pounds ground beef (lean or extra lean) or veal**
> ¼ **cup minced or grated onion**
> 2 **tablespoons breadcrumbs**
> 1 **egg (graded large)**
> ½ **teaspoon salt (optional)**
> ¼ **teaspoon freshly ground black pepper, or to taste**
> 1 **tablespoon vegetable oil**

1 cup water or beef broth

3 tablespoons freshly squeezed lemon juice

2 tablespoons granulated white sugar

½ cup dark raisins

1 tablespoon vegetable oil

1 tablespoon unbleached white flour

DIRECTIONS:

1. On a clean work surface or in a medium-size mixing bowl, mix the ground beef or veal, onion, breadcrumbs, egg, salt, and pepper. Mix lightly with your fingers. Shape into 1½-inch balls, making about 20 meatballs.

2. In a 10-inch skillet, heat the tablespoon of oil over moderate heat. Add the meatballs and brown well all over, shaking the pan to keep the meat from sticking. Use a slotted spoon to transfer the meatballs to a bowl.

3. Pour off all the accumulated fat from the skillet. Add the water or beef broth, lemon juice, sugar, and raisins. Stir to distribute the ingredients, then add the meatballs. Bring to the boil over high heat, then immediately reduce the heat so that the liquid boils gently. Cook for 20 minutes.

4. To thicken the gravy, in a small skillet heat the remaining tablespoon of oil over moderate heat until it is hot but not yet smoking. Stir in the flour. Cook until bubbly but not browned. Reduce the heat and cook for about half a minute. Push the meatballs to one side of the skillet, or transfer them temporarily to a bowl, then blend the flour-and-oil mixture into the meatball gravy. Cook half a minute longer. Return the meatballs to the skillet. Serve over rice, cooked farfel (page 86), mashed potatoes (page 264), noodles, kasha (page 268), or any starch desired.

CARNATZLACH
(*Romanian Sausages*)

Serves 4

When Romania was under the rule of the Ottoman Empire, a vibrant Jewish population existed. While maintaining their own identity, the Jewish people adopted two of the most popular Romanian dishes as their own—a cornmeal preparation called *mamaliga* (page 315) and a favorite sausage called *carnatzlach* in Yiddish.

Like the spicy *koftas* of India, the herbed ground lamb *kebobs* of the Middle East, the *wursts* of Germany, and Polish sausage, carnatzlach is identified by its seasonings, namely the heavy use of garlic and ground black pepper. In some families it is traditional to add small quantities of spices (often allspice and cloves) and larger amounts of herbs (including oregano and parsley), but the basic sausage is a garlicky, peppery ground beef mixture that is shaped into small frankfurter-like cylinders and broiled. In the Romanian tradition, they are served with a cooked white bean mashed with liberal amounts of garlic.

Enjoy carnatzlach as an hors d'oeuvre, or serve them as a main course with cooked beans as suggested above. Pickled cucumbers or tomatoes (pages 65 and 68) or a spicy onion relish, mamaliga (page 315), and a tossed green salad are appropriate accompaniments.

The variety and quantities of seasonings used are a matter of personal taste. A good way to test any ground meat mixture is to begin with a small quantity, shape and cook one meatball in a skillet or a microwave oven, and adjust the seasonings.

INGREDIENTS:

1½ pounds lean ground beef

1 to 2 tablespoons minced garlic

¾ to 1 teaspoon freshly ground black pepper

Salt to taste

Optional spices: dash to ¼ teaspoon allspice, cloves,
cumin, coriander, or other spices

Optional herbs: 1 to 2 tablespoons chopped fresh
parsley; ¼ to ½ teaspoon chopped fresh
oregano, thyme, or other herbs

DIRECTIONS:

1. Mix the ground beef with the garlic, pepper and salt, and the spices and herbs desired. Knead with your hands for 3 or 4 minutes. This will mix the ingredients evenly and will also prevent the sausage from falling apart when it is cooked. Cook a small piece of the meat mixture and adjust the seasonings. To allow the seasonings to permeate the meat, let the mixture stand at room temperature for half an hour before cooking.

2. Shape the meat into small cylinders about 1 inch in diameter and 3 inches long. Broil a few inches from the heat, turning as necessary to cook all over.

STUFFED CABBAGE

(*Holishkes*)

Makes 12 cabbage rolls

Cabbage, one of the sustaining vegetables during the cold winters in Eastern Europe, was made into a main course when stuffed with rice and meat by the cooks of Hungary, Poland, and Russia. While the general population of those countries stuffed their cabbage leaves with a pork filling and thickened the sauce with sour cream, the Jews adapted the idea to meet the laws of *kashrut*. Stuffed cabbage is also related to the stuffed vine leaves of the Middle East.

In the classic Jewish preparation known as *holishkes,* tender cabbage leaves are filled with a chopped beef-and-rice mixture, then cooked in a delectable sauce sweetened with sugar and raisins, touched with the piquant flavor of lemon juice. Originally a dish of the peasantry, holishkes continue to be served at home for family gatherings. But stuffed cabbage also has a place in more luxurious settings.

Catered Bar and Bat Mitzvahs are likely to feature huge warming trays filled with holishkes as one of many appetizers, along with more expensive fare such as smoked whitefish and smoked salmon. Stuffed cabbage is typically on the menu of Jewish delicatessens and restaurants that serve a Jewish clientele.

The cabbage leaves give the appearance of being generously stuffed. That, coupled with the rich taste, conveys a feeling of bounteousness. It is therefore appropriate to serve them at Sukkot, which originally celebrated a bountiful harvest that would last the winter. When you make holishkes, you may want to double or even triple the recipe. You never know who might want to take some home to enjoy another day.

Select a pot that will be plenty big for the cabbage rolls and the remaining ingredients. Transfer them to a serving casserole if you wish to line them up "for show." Incidentally, stuffed cabbage benefits from being prepared in advance and reheated. And, should there be leftovers, it freezes well.

INGREDIENTS:

½ cup long-grain white rice

1 cup cold water

1 head green cabbage (2½ to 3 pounds)

Boiling water for the cabbage leaves

1 pound lean ground beef

¼ teaspoon salt (optional)

¼ teaspoon freshly ground black pepper

¼ cup finely chopped onion

1 egg (graded large or extra large)

1 can (28 ounces) whole peeled tomatoes, cut up
    (reserve the juice)

1 cup chopped onion

⅓ cup freshly squeezed lemon juice

¼ cup firmly packed dark brown sugar

½ cup dark raisins

Additional salt, freshly ground black pepper,
    lemon juice, brown sugar to taste

DIRECTIONS:

1. In a 1-quart pot, bring the rice and 1 cup of water to the boil. Reduce the heat just enough so the water keeps boiling, and cook uncovered for 10 minutes. The water should be absorbed but the rice will not be quite tender. Set aside to cool.

2. To soften the cabbage leaves, plunge the whole head of cabbage into a pot of boiling water large enough to accommodate the head completely. The whole head of cabbage must be covered by the water. Turn off the heat. Allow the cabbage to sit for 5 minutes. Remove the cabbage, cut out the core, and carefully peel off 12 leaves. (Note that the head of cabbage can also be

softened by being placed in the freezer overnight, or microwaved on high for a minute.)

3. Shred the remaining cabbage and set aside.

4. For the filling, use your hands to mix together the ground beef, partially cooked rice, optional salt, pepper, ¼ cup onion, and egg. If you like, cook a small amount of the mixture so that you can taste and correct the seasoning.

5. Divide the meat mixture into 12 even-size mounds. Shape each mound into an oblong and place it in the center of each cabbage leaf. Fold over the top and bottom, then overlap the sides, making a tight package. Cut out the tough ribs as necessary to make the leaves fold easily.

6. Place the shredded cabbage, tomatoes with their juice, the cup of chopped onion, lemon juice, brown sugar, and raisins in an 8-quart pot. Mix gently. Set the cabbage rolls, flap side down, on top of the mixture.

7. Bring to the boil over moderate heat. Reduce to a gentle boil, cover the pot, and cook for 1 to 1½ hours. The cabbage leaves around the meat and the cabbage in the sauce should be very tender. Taste the sauce and correct the seasonings (salt, pepper, lemon juice, brown sugar).

8. To blend the flavors, turn off the heat and allow the stuffed cabbage to rest for about 15 minutes before serving. To serve holishkes as a buffet dish, pour some sauce in the bottom of a serving casserole. Arrange the cabbages on top of the sauce, then spoon a little more sauce on top of the cabbage rolls. For an appetizer, allow one or two stuffed cabbages per serving. To serve stuffed cabbage as a main dish, begin the meal with a clear chicken soup and mandlen (page 84) or farfel (page 86), or chicken soup thickened with einlauf (page 83). Allow three holishkes per person as a main course, four for very hungry people. Pass extra white rice for the sauce.

BEEF STEW WITH VEGETABLES

Serves 4 heartily

Although the meat preferred by Hungarians has always been pork, with sour cream-and-meat mixtures very popular, the Jews of Hungary adapted the soup-like stew known as *gulyas* (goulash) to meet the dietary laws, and thus enjoyed beef stew. In its simplest form, beef stew among those with an Ashkenazic heritage is a slowly simmered meat dish with onions and paprika and the taste of tomatoes in the sauce.

In the more elaborate preparation here, a generous amount of vegetables is added. The gravy is thin as in traditional goulash. For a thickened gravy, roll the meat in flour after seasoning the cubes in Step One. If you like, omit the potatoes and serve the stew over spätzle (page 262) or noodles.

INGREDIENTS:

2 pounds stewing beef, cut into 1-inch cubes

Salt (optional), freshly ground black pepper, paprika

2 tablespoons vegetable oil

1 cup coarsely chopped onion

2 teaspoons minced garlic

½ teaspoon additional paprika (optional)

2 cups beef broth or water

2 tablespoons ketchup

1 pound carrots, peeled and sliced into 1-inch rounds

1 pound potatoes, peeled and cut into 1-inch chunks

2 cups fresh or frozen green peas

DIRECTIONS:

1. Sprinkle the meat with the optional salt, the pepper, and the paprika.

2. In a 3- or 4-quart pot, heat the oil over moderately low heat. Sauté the onion until it is golden but not brown. With a slotted spoon, transfer the onion to a bowl.

3. Increase the heat to moderate and brown the meat (in several batches if necessary). Add a little more oil as needed. When all the meat has been browned, return all of the meat and the sautéed onion to the pot. Stir in the garlic, the optional paprika, the beef broth or water, and the ketchup. Bring the liquid to the boil, reduce to a gentle boil, cover the pot, and cook for 1 hour.

4. Add the carrots and potatoes, and more broth or water if necessary to cover the vegetables. Continue cooking for about an hour longer, until the meat is tender.

5. Mix in the peas and cook for a few minutes longer, until the peas are tender. Taste and correct the seasonings. Serve in shallow bowls. To absorb some of the delicious gravy, either offer bread on the side or suggest that the diners mash the potatoes in the bowl. Beef stew is especially tasty when prepared a day ahead and refrigerated, and it freezes well.

VARIATION:

Lamb Stew

Rub 3 pounds of meaty lamb neck bones with garlic, then proceed with the recipe, substituting the lamb for the stewing beef. In Step 3, reduce the initial cooking time of the lamb to 30 minutes.

BRISKET
(Pot-roasted)

Serves 4 to 6

For many years, our neighborhood mascot was a dog named Biscuit. However, some of the children called him what they were far more familiar with—namely, Brisket. For what Jewish child has not grown up with one of the tastiest cuts of meat, fresh brisket of beef, made tender through long, slow, moist cooking?

Fresh brisket is *the* pot roast of Jewish cuisine. While most beef that is pot-roasted is cut from the hindquarter (round and rump roasts) and is therefore not usually available in kosher butcher shops, brisket is cut from the forequarter. The oven-braised brisket of the next recipe uses a more modern cooking method.

Many of the beef preparations traditional in Jewish cooking are designed to stretch a small piece of meat to feed a large number of people. Not so for brisket, which is eaten in slices that can be thin or moderately thick. Even when served with applesauce and a kugel or kasha on the side, the brisket is the important part of the meal. Notwithstanding the luxury status of brisket, a few slices of leftover meat can be stretched into two dozen delicious kreplach (page 88).

INGREDIENTS:

1 flat cut fresh brisket of beef (3 to 4 pounds),
   trimmed but with a little fat on top
Salt (optional), freshly ground black pepper, paprika
2 cups chopped onion
2 tablespoons vegetable oil
2 cups water
1 pound carrots, peeled and cut into rounds or chunks
2 pounds potatoes, peeled and cut into chunks

DIRECTIONS:

1. Rub the brisket with the optional salt, the pepper, and the paprika.

2. In a 5- or 6-quart pot, lightly brown the onion (first without oil) over moderately low heat, then add the oil. Cook for 5 minutes longer, stirring occasionally.

3. Push the onion toward the sides of the pot. Brown the brisket, fat side down first. Turn to brown the other side. It is important to brown the meat well for maximum flavor in the gravy.

4. Add the water to the pot. Bring to the boil over high heat, immediately reduce to a gentle boil, then cover the pot and cook for approximately 2½ hours, until the meat is very tender. Turn the brisket occasionally.

5. Toward the end of the cooking time, cook the carrots and potatoes in boiling (salted if desired) water until tender. Add to the cooked meat and cook in the gravy for another 10 minutes. To serve, cut the meat into slices. Return the meat to the gravy along with the carrots and potatoes. Serve with a dish of applesauce (page 236) on the side. Note that because it is easier to slice brisket if the meat is cold, cooking a day in advance is recommended.

VARIATION:

Brisket with Fruit

Add 12 ounces of mixed dried fruit (apricots, prunes, peaches, and pears) during the last 45 minutes of cooking.

BRISKET
(Oven-braised)

Serves 6 generously, with leftovers

"The holidays are so early this year, I'm not ready. I haven't even bought my brisket yet." Even the most spiritual and introspective holy days have a practical side in Jewish life, and fresh brisket of beef is often the center attraction for Rosh Hashanah dinner.

A whole brisket is best for oven-braising. Even when part of the top piece is used for cholent (see page 154), the remaining well-marbled piece keeps the oven-cooked brisket moist and adds a rich flavor to the gravy. If only the meaty, thin cut is used, do not trim all the fat for oven-braising, or the meat will be too dry. Once the brisket is cooked and has cooled, any fat can be skimmed off.

Brisket slices best when cold, so it is wise to cook the meat a day ahead. Use the oven-braised top piece for a tasty kreplach filling (page 88). And if you should have leftovers, pile thin slices of steamed brisket between two slices of rye bread for a superb sandwich.

INGREDIENTS:

1 whole trimmed fresh brisket of beef (8 pounds
    trimmed weight)
Salt (optional) and paprika
3 cups chopped onions
2 tablespoons vegetable oil
2 pounds potatoes, peeled and cut into chunks
1 pound carrots, peeled and cut into 2- to 3-inch
    chunks
3 cups hot water

DIRECTIONS:

1. Preheat the oven to 325 degrees F.

2. Sprinkle the brisket all over with salt if you like, and with lots of paprika. Rub the seasonings into the meat.

3. Scatter the onions in a large stoveproof roasting pan. Place over 2 adjacent burners over moderate heat. First brown the onions lightly without any oil, then add the oil and sauté them for another 5 minutes.

4. Push the onions to the sides of the pan. Cook the brisket, fat side down, until well browned. Turn to brown the other side.

5. Scatter the potatoes and carrots around the meat, pour in the water, then cover the roasting pan well with foil. Use several pieces of foil if necessary, overlapping the edges. Crimp the edges around the pan.

6. Cook in the oven for 2½ hours. Remove the roasting pan from the oven. Carefully take off the foil, pulling it away from you so you don't get a steam burn. Pierce the meat with a large kitchen fork. If it is not tender, recover the roasting pan and return the brisket to the oven for 30 minutes longer.

7. Skim off any fat. To make the gravy thick and light in color, purée the gravy and onion in a blender or food processor.

8. Slice the meat and serve immediately, or cool and chill overnight in the gravy, then slice while the meat is still cold. Remove and discard any solidified fat, then heat the meat in the gravy or steam the sliced meat for a few minutes. Fresh brisket is delicious as a cold meat. Serve cold brisket with horseradish (page 72) and applesauce (page 236) on the side.

   If you like, omit the potatoes and serve hot brisket and gravy with a traditional accompaniment: kasha (page 268), kasha varnishkes (page 270), noodles, or potato kugel (page 286). Mashed potatoes (page 264) are especially good when covered with brisket gravy.

PASTRAMI

Makes enough for 4 to 6 sandwiches

Pastrami, from the Romanian word *pastra,* "to preserve," is a garlicky, peppery, smoked brisket of beef that originated as a way of preserving beef before refrigeration was standard. One of the few very spicy foods in traditional Ashkenazic Jewish cuisine, pastrami is rarely cured at home from a fresh brisket. More often it is eaten in a deli, brought home as sandwiches, or purchased sliced to be steamed at home and piled on rye bread.

If you do preserve the meat at home, you will wonder at first how this spicy meat can be made from a fresh brisket. However, as soon as you begin cooking the marinated meat and the aroma pervades the kitchen, you will say, "Aha! Pastrami." In the old-fashioned method, the meat is smoked in a smokehouse. Here, marinated brisket is steamed, then smoked using brown sugar. If you have a smoker, follow the manufacturer's directions.

INGREDIENTS:

> 3 tablespoons crushed garlic
> 3 tablespoons whole coriander seeds
> 3 tablespoons whole black peppercorns
> 1 tablespoon salt
> 2 teaspoons saltpeter to keep the meat pink
>   (optional)
> 1 flat cut fresh brisket of beef (3 pounds), trimmed
>   but with a little fat on top
> ½ cup mild-tasting vegetable oil
> 3 tablespoons firmly packed brown sugar

½ **cup distilled white vinegar**
1½ **teaspoons ground allspice**
1 **cup firmly packed brown sugar for smoking**

DIRECTIONS:

1. Using a mortar and pestle, coarsely crush the garlic, coriander, pepper-corns, salt, and the optional saltpeter. Rub the mixture into the brisket, then place the meat in a ceramic container just large enough to accommodate it. Cover with a tight-fitting lid or with foil. Refrigerate for 24 hours.

2. In a small bowl mix together the oil, 3 tablespoons of brown sugar, the vine-gar, and the allspice. Pour the mixture over the meat. Marinate in the refrigerator for another 24 hours, turning once.

3. Place the meat on a steamer tray set into a steamer with enough water to steam the meat for 2½ hours. Pour the marinade over the meat. Some or most of the marinade will drip down into the water below. Bring the water to the boil, then reduce the heat so that the water boils constantly to create steam but doesn't boil up and over. Cover the pot tightly with a lid or with foil. Steam for about 2½ hours, until the meat is tender but not falling apart.

4. Turn off the heat. Remove the steamer tray with the meat from the steamer. Clean the steamer pot. Line the bottom and about an inch up the sides with aluminum foil. Place 1 cup of brown sugar on the foil. Return the steamer tray with the meat to the steamer, cover, and adjust the heat to medium. When you begin to smell the brown sugar smoking, reduce the heat so that the sugar continues to smoke without burning. Smoke the meat for 15 min-utes, then turn off the heat and leave the steamer on the turned-off burner until cool.

5. Slice the meat thin, pile onto rye bread spread with mustard, and don't for-get the kosher dills (page 65). Steam the meat to reheat.

CORNED BEEF

Makes enough for 4 to 6 sandwiches

In the previous recipe, smoking is used for preserving beef. Another method of preventing the spoilage of meat is corning, or preserving with salt. The term "corned" beef derives from the fact that the beef was once preserved by a salt-curing method that used corn-size pieces of salt. For more even distribution, the coarse salt used for koshering meat is used here in place of the larger pieces once used.

The corned beef popular in Irish cookery and New England boiled dinners can come from the round or the brisket, but the corned beef of Jewish cuisine always begins with a fresh brisket of beef. If you do not want to corn the brisket yourself, skip right to Step Four.

INGREDIENTS:

2 quarts (8 cups) cold water

¾ cup coarse (kosher) salt

1½ teaspoons crushed garlic

1½ teaspoons crushed bay leaves

1½ teaspoons whole black peppercorns

1½ teaspoons coriander seeds

1½ teaspoons yellow mustard seeds

1 teaspoon saltpeter to keep the meat pink
(optional)

1 flat cut fresh brisket of beef (3 pounds), trimmed
but with a little fat on top

DIRECTIONS:

1. In a 3-quart pot, combine all the ingredients except the brisket. Bring to the boil over high heat. Partially cover the pot, and boil briskly for about 5 minutes to dissolve the salt. Cool completely.

2. Place the brisket in a ceramic bowl just large enough to accommodate the meat and the pickling solution. Ideally, the meat will be wedged in so that it won't rise to the top when the liquid is added. Add the liquid with all the spices to the ceramic bowl. If the brisket does not remain on the bottom, weight it down with a plate or a bowl.

3. Cover the ceramic bowl with cheesecloth or wax paper. Do not cover too tightly. Refrigerate for 2 weeks.

4. To cook the corned beef, remove from the liquid and rinse well. In a 5-quart pot, bring 4 quarts of water to the boil. Add the corned beef. As soon as the water comes back to the boil, reduce the heat to a gentle boil, cover the pot, and cook for 2½ to 3 hours, until the meat is very tender.

5. For deli-like sandwiches, chill the meat thoroughly before attempting to slice very thin. The meat can be reheated briefly in a steamer. Serve corned beef sandwiches on rye bread with mustard, accompanied by pickled tomatoes (page 68) and kosher dill pickles (page 65), and cole slaw and potato salad on the side.

   Note: To reduce the saltiness of the meat somewhat, cook for 1 hour, then discard the water. Rinse the pot and begin again with a fresh pot of cold water. Cook for another 1½ to 2 hours, until the meat is tender.

TONGUE WITH RAISIN SAUCE

Serves 6

Tongue, one of the most tender of all meats, is another favorite on the menu in Jewish delis. More delicate in taste than either corned beef or pastrami, it makes a splendid sandwich when sliced thin and heaped between two pieces of fresh rye bread. In earlier times, tongue was more often cut into thicker slices, covered with a rich sweet-and-sour sauce, and served as an appetizer at weddings or for a main course at home.

Raisins and gingersnaps are common in the sweet-sour sauces of Ashkenazim. The raisins are a natural sweetener and are used to add a textural interest. The molasses and spice of the cookies enhance the sweet-and-sour taste, and as the gingersnaps dissolve, they thicken the sauce, eliminating the need for a separate flour thickener.

INGREDIENTS:

1 smoked beef tongue (3 to 4 pounds), rinsed
Water
6 gingersnaps
½ cup firmly packed dark brown sugar
¼ cup distilled white vinegar
1 cup hot water or water from cooking the tongue
1 lemon, sliced, ends and seeds removed
⅓ cup golden or dark raisins

DIRECTIONS:

1. In a 6-quart pot, place the tongue with water to cover by an inch. Bring to the boil over high heat, then reduce the heat to a gentle boil and cover the pot. Cook for 2½ to 3 hours, turning the tongue occasionally, until it is tender when pierced with a fork. To decrease the saltiness, change the water after the tongue has cooked for 30 minutes.

2. For the sauce, just before the tongue is done, break up the gingersnaps between your fingers. Place in a 1- or 2-quart pot with the remaining ingredients. Bring to the boil over moderate heat, stirring frequently. Boil for about a minute. Keep warm over low heat.

3. Remove the skin from the tongue while it is still warm. Slice into pieces about ¼ inch thick. Spoon a little sauce over each serving. Don't waste a drop of the delicious sauce—serve noodles or mashed potatoes (page 264) and pass the rest of the sauce separately.

Short Rib Tsimmes

Serves 4 as a main dish, 6 to 8 as a side dish

When distance separates you from your family, you may find yourself creating familial traditions with nearby friends. Thus it is with the Goldsholls, a family with whom we have shared Passover for the last sixteen years. Kathy Goldsholl's short rib tsimmes, which comes to her by way of her mother-in-law, Naomi, is a must on Passover, regardless of how many other foods we set on the table.

A *tsimmes* is a special kind of stew that can be made of vegetables alone, vegetables and fruit, or vegetables, fruit, and meat. This is a very meaty tsimmes, made with short ribs, one of the tastiest of all cuts of beef. The bones of the short ribs contribute to the rich flavor of the gravy. The carrots, sweet potatoes, dried fruit, and the brown sugar make it a very sweet dish. The white potatoes contrast with the sweetness of the other ingredients. On Rosh Hashanah, when it is traditional to usher in a sweet New Year with apples and honey, substitute honey for the brown sugar, and add apple wedges from two peeled and cored Golden Delicious apples during the last five minutes of cooking.

The knaidlach (my addition to the Goldsholl recipe) cook right in with the vegetables, absorbing the delicious gravy. Tsimmes reheats well—some people think it is even better the second day because the flavors have had a chance to blend. You might want to double the recipe so that you do have leftovers. And don't just save tsimmes for the holidays—enjoy it as a buffet dish for a gathering or as a main dish at any time. Scrumptious!

INGREDIENTS:

3 pounds lean short ribs
Salt (optional), freshly ground black pepper, paprika
1 tablespoon vegetable oil

1 cup hot water

1 pound carrots, peeled and cut into 1-inch rounds

1 pound yams or sweet potatoes, peeled and cut into
  chunks

1 pound white potatoes, peeled and cut into chunks

$\frac{1}{4}$ cup firmly packed dark brown sugar

2 cups boiling water

1 recipe Knaidlach (page 91), uncooked

$\frac{1}{4}$ cup firmly packed dark brown sugar, again

$1\frac{1}{2}$ cups pitted prunes and dried apricots

DIRECTIONS:

1. Sprinkle the meat all over with the optional salt, the pepper, and the paprika.

2. In a 4-quart pot, heat the oil. Brown the meat well all over in the oil, in two or three batches if necessary.

3. Add the cup of water. Bring to the boil over high heat, immediately reduce the heat to a gentle boil, cover the pot, and cook over low heat for 1 hour.

4. Add the carrots, sweet potatoes, and white potatoes. Sprinkle $\frac{1}{4}$ cup of brown sugar over the meat and vegetables. Add the 2 cups of boiling water. Regulate the heat to a moderate boil, cover the pot, and cook for 20 minutes.

5. Shape the knaidlach mixture into 12 balls. Scatter the matzo balls in the liquid, adding a little boiling water if necessary to keep the knaidlach at least half covered by liquid. Cook for 15 minutes, then turn over the knaidlach. Sprinkle the remaining $\frac{1}{4}$ cup of brown sugar into the pot and cook for another 15 minutes. Scatter the prunes and apricots and cook 15 minutes longer, until everything is tender.

BRISKET TSIMMES

Serves 6 to 8

Imagine spending a little over half an hour in the kitchen in the morning, going out for the day, then coming home to the most tantalizing aroma and an ambrosial fully-cooked meal! This recipe takes advantage of the long, slow, moist cooking needed to tenderize fresh brisket of beef. A symphony of meat, vegetables, fruit, and dumplings cooks all day in a very low oven, producing fork-tender meat, a myriad of tastes, and a rich gravy. (You will need a very large roasting pan to accommodate the ingredients.)

Brisket tsimmes is similar to the short rib tsimmes of the previous recipe, but it is meatier yet, not quite as sweet, and even easier to cook. As in any tsimmes, once the ingredients are gathered, most of the work is complete. Enjoy brisket tsimmes during Passover or any time of year. A fine Sabbath meal during cold weather.

INGREDIENTS:

> 1 double recipe Knaidlach (page 91), uncooked
>
> 1 whole trimmed fresh brisket of beef (8 pounds trimmed weight)
>
> Salt (optional), freshly ground black pepper, paprika
>
> 2 tablespoons vegetable oil
>
> 1 pound carrots, peeled and cut into 1-inch rounds
>
> 1 pound yams or sweet potatoes, peeled and cut into chunks
>
> 1 pound white potatoes, peeled and cut into chunks

    1 package (12 ounces) mixed dried fruit, larger
        pieces cut in half or into thirds (substitute 2
        cups dried apricots or 1 cup each of dried
        apricots and prunes)
    3 tablespoons firmly packed dark brown sugar
    1 quart (4 cups) boiling water

DIRECTIONS:

1. Prepare the knaidlach mixture and refrigerate while browning the meat and assembling the other ingredients.

2. Adjust an oven rack to the middle of the oven. Preheat the oven to 250 degrees F.

3. Season the meat as desired. In a large stoveproof roasting pan, heat the oil over two adjacent burners until it is moderately hot. Brown the meat on both sides, fat side down first. Remove from the heat.

4. Scatter the carrots, yams, white potatoes, and mixed dried fruit around the meat. Shape the knaidlach mixture into 20 to 24 matzo balls, and place the dumplings in any empty spaces in the roasting pan. Sprinkle the brown sugar over the vegetables and knaidlach. Pour the boiling water into the roasting pan.

5. Cover the pan completely with aluminum foil, overlapping the foil as necessary. Crimp the edges securely.

6. Bake in the middle of the oven for a minimum of 6 hours. The tsimmes can be left in the oven at 250 degrees F. for as long as 10 hours. Serve the brisket tsimmes alone as a complete meal, or offer applesauce (page 236) on the side.

CHOLENT

Serves 6

Cholent—a masterpiece of ingenuity and resourcefulness—is the observant Jew's answer to the dilemma of the prohibition against doing any work (including kindling a fire) on the Sabbath vis-à-vis the tradition of enjoying a hot midday meal following the morning service on Saturday. A superb combination of meat, potatoes, beans, and barley, cholent (pronounced with a "tch" sound, and sometimes pronounced *tchulent*) is something between a stew and a very thick soup, filling and satisfying. Each of the three starches has a different texture and taste, making one want to eat slowly to savor the individual flavors that make up the whole dish.

As with many Eastern European preparations that have remained popular in Jewish cuisine, cholent was also a way for poor people to enjoy the taste of meat on the Sabbath by using a small piece of beef. Although the quantity of meat in this recipe is greater than the amount affordable many years ago, a fatty meat such as flanken, short ribs, or the top piece of a fresh brisket is still recommended to keep the cholent from drying out.

As a Sabbath meal, the food must be cooked before the Sabbath begins at sundown Friday. In some communities, the ingredients must be at least half-cooked; in others, the cholent must be fully cooked before the Sabbath. The preparation is then left overnight on a very low burner that has been covered with a *blech,* a Yiddish word for a sheet of metal that keeps the low heat evenly distributed. (Tin, aluminum, or asbestos coverings are used.) Or, the cholent can be left overnight in a slow oven.

Although all the work on the cholent is finished as soon as the temperature is reduced for the overnight warming, one must think about the preparation in advance: remember to soak the beans the evening before the Sabbath, and begin the cooking at least three hours before sundown.

Cholent can be served at any time, most fittingly on the Sabbath, a taste of the world to come. It is perfect.

INGREDIENTS:

> 3 pounds flanken or short ribs, or a 2-pound piece
> of brisket with fat
> Salt, freshly ground black pepper, paprika
> 2 tablespoons schmaltz (page 40) or vegetable oil
> 2 cups coarsely chopped onion
> 2 teaspoons minced garlic
> Water for cooking
> 1 cup dried baby lima beans, soaked overnight in
> 3 cups water, then drained
> 1 cup barley
> 1 pound potatoes, peeled and cut into halves or
> quarters

DIRECTIONS:

1. Season the meat generously with the salt, pepper, and paprika.

2. In a 6-quart pot, heat the chicken fat or oil. Brown the onion over moderate heat, stirring from time to time. Push the onion to the sides of the pot and brown the meat very well all over.

3. Sprinkle the garlic over the meat, add 2 cups of water, and bring to the boil over high heat. Reduce to a gentle boil, cover the pot, and cook for 1 hour.

4. Turn the meat over. Add the soaked, drained lima beans, the barley, potatoes, and another cup of water. Bring back to the boil, reduce to a gentle boil, cover the pot, and cook for another hour. Turn the meat over again. Taste and correct the seasoning.

5. Cook for an additional 30 minutes to 1 hour, until everything is very tender. The casserole will be moist, but most of the liquid will be absorbed. The cholent can be eaten at this point or prepared for the midday meal on Saturday.

6. To prepare the cholent for Sabbath lunch, prior to sundown on Friday night add enough boiling water to cover the ingredients by an inch. Cover tightly, then reduce the heat to the lowest possible setting. On a low enough burner, the liquid will be absorbed but the cholent will not have dried out when served the following day. A *blech* will help distribute the heat evenly. Or, place the cholent in an ovenproof casserole with a tight-fitting lid, add enough boiling water to cover by an inch, cover tightly (use aluminum foil if necessary for a tight seal), and place in a preheated 200-degree F. oven overnight.

Cholent is rich and substantial. A dish of applesauce (page 236) will complement it nicely, along with any challah left over from the evening meal. Or, serve a fruit compote (page 329) and sponge cake (page 336) for dessert.

Note: If you should forget to soak the beans overnight, there is an alternate method of rehydrating them. Place the dried lima beans in a 2-quart pot. Cover the beans with water by 2 inches. Bring to the boil over high heat, boil for 2 minutes, remove the pot from the burner, cover, and let stand for 1 hour. Drain the beans, rinse them with cold water, and use them in Step 4 of the recipe.

HAMIN

Serves 6

Among Sephardim, the Sabbath preparation that is prepared before sundown on Friday and left to stay warm all night is known as *hamin* (*dafina* in Morocco). Ladino (Spanish-Hebrew) for oven, *hamin* also derives from the Hebrew word for hot. Chickpeas or other legumes and meat or poultry are central to the preparation, which also features eggs that are cooked in their shells to become light brown inside. Some recipes include cracked wheat; others are spiced with the sweetness of cinnamon or the tempting aroma of cloves.

Although hamin is prepared most simply by placing all the ingredients in a large, deep ovenproof casserole then baking everything, you will find the casserole tastier if you brown the meat and onions first. Remember to soak the legumes the evening before you begin the actual cooking.

INGREDIENTS:

2 pounds boneless shoulder of lamb or beef,
    well trimmed and cut into 1½-inch cubes,
    or a 3-pound chicken, cut up
Salt and freshly ground black pepper
1 tablespoon olive oil
2 cups chopped onion
1½ to 2 cups dried chickpeas, soaked for a minimum
    of 12 hours in cold water to cover by 2 inches,
    then drained
¼ teaspoon turmeric
1 teaspoon cumin

**Pinch to 1 teaspoon allspice, cinnamon, and/or
cloves (optional)
6 eggs (graded large or extra large) in their shells
12 small potatoes, peeled
1 cup rice or cracked wheat (optional)
2 teaspoons minced garlic
1½ quarts (6 cups) water or broth**

DIRECTIONS:

1. Preheat the oven to 350 degrees F.

2. Season the meat generously with salt and pepper.

3. In a 12-inch skillet, heat the oil with the onion over moderate heat. Cook, stirring occasionally, until the onion browns lightly. Transfer the onion to a 5-quart ovenproof casserole (the insert of a 5-quart crock pot is ideal).

4. Now brown the lamb, beef, or chicken all over in the 12-inch skillet, adding a little more oil if necessary to keep the meat from sticking.

5. Mix the drained chickpeas and onion in the casserole. Sprinkle with the turmeric, cumin, any optional spices, and additional salt and pepper.

6. Carefully arrange the eggs and the potatoes on top of the chickpea mixture, then add the meat. Sprinkle the garlic over the meat. Add the water or broth, which should cover all the ingredients.

7. If you are using the rice or cracked wheat, place loosely in cheesecloth, tie with string, then place the filled cheesecloth in the liquid.

8. Cover the top of the casserole with a tight-fitting lid, or cover tightly with foil. No steam should escape. Bake at 350 degrees F. for 1½ hours.

9. Reduce the heat to 200 degrees F. Leave the hamin in the warm oven overnight, until serving time at the midday meal.

LAMB SHANKS WITH FRESH TOMATOES

Makes 4 servings

Lamb is significant in Judaism not merely as a culinary delight, but as a religious symbol. On Rosh Hashanah, the horn of the ram is used as the *shofar* because according to tradition the intended sacrifice of Isaac by Abraham occurred on Rosh Hashanah. At the last moment, Abraham found a ram caught in a thicket and used it as a substitute sacrifice.

On Passover, a lamb shank (*zero'a* in Hebrew) is one of the symbolic foods placed on the Seder tray, a reminder of "the mighty arm of God" which encouraged Pharaoh to release the Children of Israel from bondage. The lamb shank is also a reminder of the paschal lamb offered as the Passover sacrifice and eaten on the eve of Passover by all Jewish families in the days of the Temple. Many Jews now consider it inappropriate to serve lamb during the Seder meal because the Temple in Jerusalem and the sacrificial system no longer exist.

As a food, lamb was important to Jews in biblical days as the most widely available meat. Lamb remains the principal meat in many Mediterranean and Middle Eastern countries, where Sephardic Jews, as well as the general population, enjoy lamb kebobs and other ground mixtures, lamb roasts, and stews.

Leg of lamb is cut from the hindquarter and is not generally available from kosher butchers (see page 127), but Jews eat shoulder roasts and chops and foreshanks. Foreshanks can be rubbed with garlic and roasted uncovered in the same manner as leg of lamb. Or, they can be braised as they are here and cooked using ingredients commonly found in Sephardic kitchens of the Mediterranean. The meat is browned in olive oil, then smothered in onions and fresh tomatoes. The tasty sauce is punctuated with pieces of soft tomato and onion and the more firm chickpeas. Artichoke hearts are also partnered with lamb in Sephardic preparations, and they can be used in place of the chickpeas.

INGREDIENTS:

4 lamb foreshanks (1 pound each)

1 clove garlic for rubbing

Salt (optional), freshly ground pepper, paprika

2 tablespoons olive oil

2 cups chopped onion

4 teaspoons minced garlic, divided

2 pounds fresh tomatoes, chopped

½ cup chopped fresh parsley

2 cups cooked chickpeas or artichoke hearts

1 to 2 tablespoons freshly squeezed lemon juice

Extra chopped parsley for garnish

DIRECTIONS:

1. Rub the lamb shanks all over with the clove of garlic. Sprinkle the lamb with the optional salt, the pepper, and the paprika.

2. In a 10-inch skillet, heat the olive oil over moderately low heat. Place the lamb shanks in the oil, raise the heat to moderate, and brown the lamb well all over. Scatter the onion on and around the lamb. Cook for about 5 minutes, until the onion pieces wilt and some of them brown lightly. Now sprinkle the lamb with 2 teaspoons of the minced garlic. Scatter the tomatoes and then the ½ cup of parsley on top of the lamb.

3. Cover the skillet and reduce the heat to moderately low. Cook the lamb for 45 minutes, turning the shanks two or three times during the cooking. Adjust the heat so the lamb simmers in the sauce made by the tomatoes.

4. Sprinkle the remaining garlic over the lamb, and add the chickpeas or the artichoke hearts to the sauce. Cook for an additional 15 minutes or until the lamb is tender. Add lemon juice to taste and cook for a minute or two longer. Garnish lavishly with chopped parsley. Serve with rice.

STUFFED BREAST OF VEAL

Serves 4

Stuffed veal breast, a classic in Jewish cookery, gained popularity in a bygone era as an affordable way to provide a sizable portion of meat on the Sabbath and holidays. Although breast of veal is exceptionally bony, clever cooks extended each serving by cutting a "pocket" horizontally between the meat and the ribs, then filling the veal with an appetizing stuffing. The long period of braising required to tenderize the veal contributes to a delicious blend of tastes as the meat and stuffing flavor each other. The lengthy cooking also makes the bones tender enough to eat if one is so inclined.

Today, when breast of veal remains one of the most economical cuts of meat, even in affluent Jewish households one thinks of this succulent veal dish for an occasional Sabbath or holiday meal. During Passover, the pocket is stuffed with a sweet fruit-and-knaidlach filling (see the next recipe).

Ask the butcher to cut the pocket for you, or insert a sharp knife in one long side where the veal rests on the bone, and cut an even slit within half an inch of the other three sides. Allow at least a pound of veal breast per person. To serve, carefully slice between each rib, then turn the rib on its side so the filling shows. Serve with spätzle (page 262) or boiled potatoes on the side to absorb the rich gravy.

INGREDIENTS:

1 breast of veal (4 to 5 pounds), with pocket for
    stuffing
Salt (optional), freshly ground black pepper, paprika
2 tablespoons schmaltz (page 40) or vegetable oil

> 1 cup each diced onion and celery
> 6 cups cubed challah (page 300) or pareve white
>   bread (1/4-inch cubes)
> 1/2 cup each diced onion and celery
> 1 cup hot water, veal broth, or chicken broth
> Optional thickener: 1 tablespoon schmaltz (or oil)
>   and 1 tablespoon unbleached white flour

DIRECTIONS:

1. Preheat the oven to 325 degrees F.

2. Rub the veal with the optional salt, the pepper, and the paprika.

3. In a 10-inch skillet, heat the chicken fat or oil over moderately low heat. Sauté the cup each of onion and celery until wilted, about 5 minutes. Stir in the bread cubes. Season to taste with additional salt and pepper, and mix well. Remove the skillet from the heat.

4. Pack the veal pocket with the stuffing. It is not necessary to seal up the pocket because the veal is not turned once it is placed in the roasting pan. The filling will "set" during cooking and will not leak out. Place in a roasting pan just big enough to accommodate the veal comfortably.

5. Scatter the 1/2 cup each of uncooked onion and celery around the veal. Add the water or broth to the pan. Cover tightly with foil.

6. Bake at 325 degrees F. for 2 1/2 hours. Carefully remove the foil, raise the temperature to 375 degrees F., and bake for another 1/2 hour.

7. If desired, thicken the gravy as follows. First transfer the veal to a serving platter. Heat the tablespoon of chicken fat or oil in a 1-quart pot over moderate heat. Stir in the flour, cooking until the mixture is bubbly but not brown. Gradually add the gravy to the pot, stirring until smooth. Boil for a minute after all the gravy has been added.

FRUIT-STUFFED BREAST OF VEAL

Serves 4

You never have to worry about having too many matzo balls during Passover. True, you might run out of chicken soup and end up with extra knaidlach, but they can be sliced and fried for a side dish or combined with fruit in a moist, sweet stuffing for veal breast or chicken.

INGREDIENTS:

$\frac{1}{2}$ **cup each pitted prunes and dried apricots**
3 cups boiling water
1 cup coarsely chopped peeled apple
1 recipe Knaidlach (page 91), cooked
1 breast of veal (4 to 5 pounds), with pocket for stuffing
Salt (optional), freshly ground black pepper, paprika
1 cup hot water, veal broth, or chicken broth

DIRECTIONS:

1. In a medium-size heatproof bowl, place the prunes and apricots. Pour the boiling water over the fruit. Let stand for 15 minutes, then drain well. Cut the fruit into $\frac{1}{2}$-inch pieces, then mix the prunes and apricots with the chopped apple. Cut the cooked knaidlach into 1-inch chunks and mix with the fruit.

2. To stuff and cook the veal, follow the directions in the preceding recipe, but do not thicken the gravy. Serve with mashed potatoes (page 264), steamed carrots, and a green vegetable.

VEAL CHOPS

Allow 1 or 2 chops per person

When you grow up in an apartment in New York City, as you walk up the stairs, each level brings a characteristic aroma, and you can identify your neighbors with your eyes closed. "Oooh, brisket. The whole lobby smells good from the Silvermans in 1A." "Ah! Cabbage. Mrs. Cohen in 2C must be making a big pot of her stuffed cabbage today." "Hmmm. Nothing coming from 3B. I hope that means Mom is making veal chops tonight."

And when my mother _was_ making veal chops, she never minded when I stood right on top of her, waiting, savoring, anticipating. Picture a hungry youngster watching a very patient mother prepare breaded veal chops. Mom takes two bowls from the cabinet, beats an egg in one, and seasons breadcrumbs in another. She dips a rib veal chop into the egg, then coats it well with the breadcrumbs, then she carefully places it on the stove with the others in a pan of heated oil to cook slowly, slowly, oh, so slowly. She cooks the chops over low heat so they become golden without burning while cooking through. Actually, the whole process doesn't take much more than half an hour, but when you are young and you love breaded veal chops, the wait seems interminable.

Although it might have been faster to cook boneless veal cutlets, fixing meals quickly wasn't important in those days. We preferred chops to cutlets, because the bones on the rib chops gave the veal added flavor, and we enjoyed chewing on the bones afterwards to polish off every last scrap of meat.

In our home, the favorite accompaniments for breaded veal chops were plain white rice moistened with stewed tomatoes. Or, serve cabbage and noodles (page 245) along with a colorful tossed salad.

INGREDIENTS:

1 cup fresh breadcrumbs (substitute matzo meal
    during Passover)
¼ teaspoon each salt (optional), freshly ground
    black pepper, and paprika
1 egg (graded large or extra large)
6 rib veal chops (½-inch thick)
Oil for shallow frying

DIRECTIONS:

1. In a shallow bowl just big enough to accommodate one veal chop lying flat, mix the breadcrumbs or matzo meal with the optional salt, the pepper, and the paprika.

2. Beat the egg in a second bowl the same size.

3. Dip each chop into the beaten egg, then into the seasoned breadcrumbs. Cover the chops completely.

4. Pour ⅛ inch of oil into a 10-inch skillet. Heat the oil over moderately low heat.

5. Place the breaded veal chops in the oil. Cook for 10 to 12 minutes on one side, then cook the other side for 10 to 12 minutes. Regulate the heat so the chops do not brown too quickly. Pat dry on paper towels before serving. Serve with rice or potatoes, stewed tomatoes if you like, and a tossed salad.

CHICKEN FRICASSEE

Serves 6

A luscious yellow-brown gravy distinguishes chicken fricassee from other chicken stews. The gravy is marvelous over traditional Jewish dumplings and grains, for example spätzle (page 262) and kasha (page 268), or even plain rice, contributing to the popularity of chicken fricassee in Jewish cuisine. Some of the richness of the gravy comes from browning the chicken in schmaltz; the chicken fat is later used to thicken the gravy. (For those who do not care to use chicken fat, vegetable oil will brown the chicken nicely.)

Meaty pieces of tender stewing chicken are exceptionally tasty when bathed in fricassee gravy. As a bonus, leftover gravy can be used to make a second day's meal, a tasty soup.

INGREDIENTS:

1 stewing hen (6 pounds)

1 ½ cups unbleached white flour, approximately

½ teaspoon salt (optional)

½ teaspoon each freshly ground black pepper and
   paprika

¼ cup schmaltz (page 40) or vegetable oil

1 ½ quarts (6 cups) water

2 tablespoons additional unbleached white flour for
   thickening (optional)

DIRECTIONS:

1. Cut the chicken into wings, legs, thighs, and breasts. Cut the breasts in half or thirds, and the thighs in half.

2. Place the flour, optional salt, the pepper, and paprika in a small paper bag (lunch-bag size). Coat the chicken pieces with the mixture by placing a few pieces at a time in the bag and shaking the bag.

3. In a 5-quart pot, heat the chicken fat or oil over moderate heat. Brown the chicken slowly on both sides in two or three batches. Allow about 10 minutes for each batch. Remove the chicken to a bowl as browned.

4. Return all the chicken to the pot. Add the water. Bring to the boil over high heat. Reduce to a gentle boil, cover the pot, and cook until tender, about 2½ hours.

5. If the gravy needs thickening, skim off 2 tablespoons of the fat and transfer it to a 1-quart pot. (Substitute 2 tablespoons of oil if desired.) Place the pot over moderate heat, then add the 2 tablespoons of flour. Cook and stir until the mixture is bubbly but not brown. Gradually stir in a cup of liquid from the fricassee. Boil for 1 minute, then add this thickened liquid to the pot of fricassee, stirring all the while. Taste and correct the seasoning.

6. Serve with plenty of hot rice, spätzle (page 262), kasha (page 268), kasha varnishkes (page 270), or noodles.

   The leftover gravy is very rich. If you'd like, you can make a delicious soup by diluting it with water and adding cooked vegetables (carrot rounds, chopped celery, mushroom slices). Any leftover chicken can be pulled off the bones and served in the soup.

   Note: To use a 3-pound broiler or frying chicken, use 4 cups of water instead of 6. Cook the chicken for only about 45 minutes after browning.

CHICKEN IN THE POT WITH DUMPLINGS

Serves 4

A bowl brimming with hot chicken soup crowded with dumplings, carrots, and pieces of chicken—a splendid meal for an impoverished Eastern European family—remains enticing in a modern Jewish household. Chicken in the pot was an economical way to provide a meaty, filling, and nutritious meal for a large family.

Nowadays, it is perhaps the traditional dumplings that we savor more than the meat, whether they are knaidlach, as in this recipe, or spätzle (page 262) or kreplach (page 88). In place of dumplings, half a pound of noodles can be cooked in the soup just before it is served.

Small portions of chicken in the pot can be served as a first course (use a single recipe of knaidlach), or substantial portions as a main dish, along with plenty of bread. Since butter is not served with a meat meal in kosher cuisine, it is customary among some Jews to dip hunks of the bread into the soup to flavor the bread.

When chicken in the pot is the main dish, begin the meal with chopped liver (page 42) on a bed of lettuce, and serve a pareve cake (sponge cake, page 336, for example) with fruit for dessert.

INGREDIENTS:

1 whole chicken (3 pounds), cut into pieces
1 clove garlic, cut in half
Salt (optional), white pepper, and paprika
2 quarts (8 cups) water
1 cup chopped celery

1 cup peeled carrot rounds
1 teaspoon minced garlic
1 double recipe Knaidlach made with parsley
   (page 91), uncooked
Salt and white pepper
Additional chopped fresh parsley for garnish

DIRECTIONS:

1. Rub the chicken with garlic, optional salt, and the pepper and paprika.

2. In a 6-quart pot, bring the chicken and water to the boil over high heat. For clear broth, periodically skim off any scum that rises to the top. Reduce the heat to a gentle boil, then cover and cook for 30 minutes.

3. Add the celery, carrot, and minced garlic. Cook, covered, 30 minutes longer.

4. Shape the knaidlach into 16 to 20 balls. Drop into the soup. Cook, partially covered, for 40 minutes, until the matzo balls are fluffy and tender. Add salt and pepper to taste.

5. To serve immediately, remove and discard the skin. Pull the larger chunks of meat off the bones, discarding the bones. Serve in soup bowls, with knives, forks, and spoons. Sprinkle each portion of soup with fresh parsley.

6. To serve the next day, refrigerate before removing the skin and bones, but skin and bone the chicken before reheating.

ROAST CHICKEN

Serves 4

In the past, when ovens were by no means universal, potted chicken was more common than roast chicken. A potted chicken cooked with vegetables and a fine rich gravy served over a large portion of grain or potato could be made to go further than roasted meat. In the present day, the appeal of roast chicken with crispy skin covering tender meat and a well-filled cavity bursting with a savory filling makes roasting one of the most popular ways to cook chicken.

In many Jewish families, roast chicken is the traditional main course for the Friday evening Sabbath meal. While the chicken can be cooked unstuffed, more often it is filled with a marvelous stuffing, today aimed more at pleasing the palate than feeding a hungry family economically. Kasha (see the variation), rice, matzo balls (page 163), and bread stuffings made with vegetables or fruit and sometimes nuts are enjoyed as much as the meat.

Roasting chickens range from four to seven pounds. If you love the taste of chicken (but not turkey) and want a larger bird, try capon.

INGREDIENTS:

> 1 whole roasting chicken (4 pounds)
> 1 clove garlic, cut in half
> Salt (optional), freshly ground black pepper, and
>   paprika
> 2 tablespoons schmaltz (page 40) or vegetable oil
> 1/3 to 1/2 cup each chopped celery and onion
> 3 cups soft pareve bread cubes (1/4- to 3/8-inch cubes)
> Salt, freshly ground black pepper, and paprika

DIRECTIONS:

1. Preheat the oven to 350 degrees F.

2. Rub the chicken with the cut side of the garlic, then with the optional salt, and the pepper and paprika. Set aside.

3. In a 2-quart pot, heat the chicken fat or oil over medium heat. Cook the celery and onion until the onion is translucent, then stir in the bread cubes. Season to taste. Toss lightly until mixed, heated through, and the bread is just barely beginning to brown.

4. Stuff the chicken with the mixture. Transfer to a roasting pan. Roast for 1½ hours, until the skin is golden and crisp, and the meat tender. From time to time, baste with the pan juices.

   If the chicken is carved at the table, the stuffing can be left inside the cavity and spooned out with each serving of meat. If the chicken is cut up in the kitchen, arrange the legs, wings, and slices of meat on a platter and serve the stuffing in a separate bowl. Whether the chicken is brought to the table whole or already carved, it can be garnished with sliced stuffed *helzel* or *derma* (see next recipe). Note that a small chicken (3 pounds) can be roasted for 1¼ hours, then served in quarters.

   Leftover roast chicken is delicious served cold with a dish of homemade applesauce (page 236) on the side.

VARIATION:

Roast Chicken with Kasha Stuffing

Prepare the mushroom kasha variation (page 269) using chicken broth for the liquid. Stuff the mixture into the chicken, packing lightly. Bake any remaining kasha in a separate dish, covered, for 20 to 30 minutes.

STUFFED HELZEL
(*Poultry Neck Skins*)

Makes 3 neck skins

Here, chicken, duck, or goose neck skins are filled with a well-seasoned flour mixture then roasted until the skin is deliciously crisp and the flour-based filling is transformed into a moist stuffing rich with chicken fat and onions. Like so many vintage Jewish preparations, stuffed *helzel* originated as an inexpensive and filling but tasty way to make use of every edible part of the chicken.

In the old days chickens were purchased whole, and the neck and its skin were still attached to the chicken, often making it easier than now to obtain an untorn neck skin. Any tears in the skin can be sewn up with a strong needle and heavy thread. Even when the skin is not torn, you will need to sew up one end before filling the neck skin. The other end can be sewn shut or tucked under. Be sure to remove the thread before serving.

Stuffed helzel is usually cooked in the roasting pan along with a roast chicken. When cut into thin slices, it makes an unusual garnish for the chicken. It can also be roasted separately and served as a side dish with broiled or grilled chicken, or with stuffed breast of veal (page 161).

Stuffed helzel is related to stuffed *derma* (see the variation), also known by its Russian name, *kishke*. There is a certain romanticism associated with stuffed derma that can best be explained by the power of tradition. The word *derma* refers to beef casing—intestine—that is stuffed with a mixture similar to the one used in stuffed helzel. While one might not expect such a modest preparation to appear on the table with roast ribs of beef or chicken Wellington, stuffed derma is very likely to be served at the fanciest wedding and Bar and Bat Mitzvah receptions. As a home preparation, kishke is often roasted with poultry or veal, other times cooked in cholent and served on the Sabbath.

INGREDIENTS:

⅓ cup schmaltz (page 40) or vegetable oil

1¼ cups chopped onion

¼ teaspoon salt

½ teaspoon paprika

¼ teaspoon freshly ground black pepper

1 cup unbleached white flour (stir the flour, spoon
gently into a dry-measure cup, then level with
the edge of a spatula)

3 chicken neck skins, washed and patted dry

DIRECTIONS:

1. In an 8-inch skillet over medium heat, melt the chicken fat and sauté the onion until it is translucent. Stir in the seasonings, then the flour. Remove from the heat.

2. Stuff the neck skins with the filling, tucking under the ends. Place them in the roasting pan along with the chicken. Roast at 350 degrees F. for 1½ hours. Turn the neck skins over once or twice during roasting for even browning. The skins should be crisp and brown at the end of the roasting time. If they are not quite crisp, leave them in the oven while carving the chicken. Cut the helzel into half-inch slices to serve.

VARIATION:

Stuffed Derma (Kishke)

Decrease the onion to ¾ cup. Prepare the filling. Stitch together one end of each of two 8-inch lengths of well-cleaned beef casing. Pack half the mixture into each piece of casing, then stitch the other end. Bake with roast chicken, or bake separately at 350 degrees F. for 1½ hours, basting occasionally.

ROAST DUCKLING WITH FRUIT STUFFING

Serves 2 to 4

Perhaps the most elegant bird one can bring to the table is a whole roast duckling, its inviting golden-brown skin cooked to a crisp, dry perfection, its underlying dark meat juicy and appetizing. Duck specialties are known throughout the world, from the Peking (or Beijing) duck prized by the Chinese to the duck in pomegranate sauce (*fesenjan*) of Iran and the fruit-sauced ducklings of France. Most duck recipes can be used in kosher homes without adaptation, and roast and stewed duck preparations are enjoyed by Ashkenazic and Sephardic Jews everywhere.

Because duck contains more fat than many other fowl, a bread or matzo meal stuffing absorbs too much fat during roasting and is not recommended. A fruit stuffing does not absorb fat and complements the rich taste of the meat and skin. The stuffing is delicious when spooned over plain rice. Or serve roast duckling with a kugel or a pilaf (see Index for recipe listings) on the side, and a green vegetable or a tossed green salad. If the duck is roasted unstuffed, applesauce (page 236) is an excellent accompaniment.

Half a duck is a generous portion for one serving, but people who savor roast duck will appreciate the luxury. For a grand, festive meal where many other courses and dishes are served, one-quarter duck per person is sufficient. Note that the amount of stuffing will fill two ducks. If one duck is cooked to serve two people, you can cut the stuffing ingredients in half. If one duck is cooked for four people, use the full recipe but bake half of the stuffing separately (see the directions).

INGREDIENTS:

½ cup dried apricots

½ cup prunes

2 cups boiling water

4 cooking apples, peeled, cored and sliced thin

1 tablespoon freshly squeezed lemon juice

1 duckling (5 pounds)

Salt (optional), freshly ground black pepper, paprika

1 cup toasted almonds or cashew nuts

DIRECTIONS:

1. Place the apricots and prunes in a heatproof bowl. Pour the boiling water over them. Allow the fruit to stand for 15 minutes, then drain well.

2. Meanwhile, sprinkle the apples with the lemon juice.

3. Adjust an oven rack to the bottom third of the oven. Preheat the oven to 350 degrees F.

4. Remove and discard any visible fat from the duckling. Rub the duck with the optional salt, the pepper, and the paprika. Using a large kitchen fork, prick the skin all over.

5. Mix together the drained plumped fruit, the apples, and the toasted nuts. Stuff the cavity of the bird with half the mixture. Cook the remaining stuffing in a lightly greased casserole, tightly covered, for 1½ hours at 350 degrees F.

6. Lightly oil or grease the rack of the roasting pan. The roasting pan must be at least an inch deep to accommodate any fat that drips down. Place the stuffed duckling on the rack. Stretch out the neck skin so it will brown evenly. You will now roast the duck for 2½ hours, pricking the skin all over every 30 minutes. After 1 hour, carefully loosen the bottom of the duck so the skin doesn't tear, then turn over the duck. Continue to roast the duck,

turning as necessary to brown the skin all over. Roast duckling is ready when it is a gorgeous brown all over and a leg moves easily when prodded. Continue cooking for as long as an additional half hour if necessary.

7. To serve, use poultry shears to cut the duck in half or into quarters. Or use a very sharp knife to cut the duck in half through the breastbone, then cut in half through the backbone, then into quarters if desired. The stuffing can either be left in the duck cavity and served directly with the duck, or it can be removed before the duck is cut up and passed separately.

VARIATION:

Glazed Roast Duckling

Omit the stuffing. Cut the duck into quarters, then season and prick the skin as in Step 4. Place the quarters on a rack, making sure that extra skin that goes beyond the meat is stretched out so that it will brown thoroughly. The pieces should not touch each other. Roast at 350 degrees F. for 1½ hours, pricking every 20 minutes. It is not necessary to turn the duck pieces. Toward the end of the 1½ hours, heat 2 tablespoons of apricot or cherry jam in a pan of simmering water. Brush the duck pieces every 10 minutes with the jam. (Or use a bottled sweet and pungent sauce, unheated.) Roast the duckling for a total of 2 hours, until beautifully glazed.

ROAST GOOSE

Serves 6

"Take one-quarter pound of goose-oil..." begins the recipe for a Passover dessert pudding from a cookbook written in the early 1900s. While in *A Christmas Carol* Charles Dickens popularized the Christian tradition of dining on roast goose, there is a longstanding Jewish tradition of serving goose on Chanukah and setting aside some of its rendered fat for use on Passover.

Today, when most people no longer value the fat of fowl for food energy, rendered goose fat ("goose oil") has lost its desirability. In addition, the goose does not have nearly the amount of meat found on a capon or turkey of similar weight. Both the bone- and the skin-to-meat ratio are considerably higher in goose than in other poultry. But for those who look forward with pleasure to the crunch of a piece of crisp golden-brown skin from a roasted bird that has only succulent dark meat, goose is a treat. Consider roast goose for Chanukah, the Sabbath, or any holiday meal.

During the cooking process, the fat liquefies and would be absorbed by any breadlike stuffing, making a bread or matzo meal stuffing more fatty than most people would find satisfactory. The same stuffing used in the previous recipe for duck can be used. Or, if you are a nature lover and you live in an area subject to cold weather, during a snowy winter the birds will appreciate fat-soaked bread that has cooked in the cavity of a goose. Goose fat can be used in place of chicken fat in recipes for schmaltz, but it will impart a stronger taste.

Serve roast goose with roast potatoes or any kind of kugel (see Index for recipe listings), applesauce (page 236), and one or two fresh vegetables. A light dessert such as a sponge cake (page 336), along with fruit, makes a nice finale to the meal.

INGREDIENTS:

**Fruit stuffing from roast duckling (see previous
recipe), optional**
One goose (12 pounds)
Salt (optional), freshly ground black pepper, paprika

DIRECTIONS:

1. If you are stuffing the goose, follow Steps 1 and 2 on page 175.

2. Adjust an oven rack to the bottom third of the oven. Preheat the oven to 350 degrees F.

3. Remove and discard any visible fat from the goose. Rub the goose with the optional salt, the pepper and paprika. Using a large kitchen fork, prick the skin all over.

4. If you are stuffing the goose, mix together the drained plumped fruit, the apples, and the toasted nuts. Stuff the cavity of the bird with the mixture.

5. Lightly oil or grease the rack of a large roasting pan. The roasting pan must be well over an inch deep to safely accommodate any fat that accumulates. Place the goose breast side up on the rack. Roast the goose for a total of about 3¾ hours (3 hours if the goose is not stuffed), pricking the skin well every 20 to 30 minutes to allow fat to drip out. After the first hour, very carefully remove the roasting pan from the oven to avoid spilling fat. Spoon off accumulated fat and turn over the goose. Repeat after the second hour, turning the goose breast side up. The goose is cooked when the skin is a delicious-looking golden brown all over and the leg moves easily when grasped and pushed lightly with your fingers.

6. Very carefully remove the roasting pan from the oven. Transfer the stuffing to an ovenproof casserole, cover, and keep warm in a low oven. Carve the goose as you would a turkey.

Fish Specialties

Pickled, Fried, Baked, and Stuffed

Fish Specialties

The tradition of serving fish on Fridays goes back to the days when fish was a luxury that only the wealthy could afford. According to the Talmud (in Jewish literature, the most important written interpretation of the Bible), fish should be enjoyed by every family—including the poor—on the Sabbath. Eating fish is a reminder of Creation because, the Sages tell us, fish was created on the fifth day and man on the sixth, both to glorify the seventh day, the Sabbath. Fish was also linked by mystical teachings to the Messianic Age and immortality.

Fish fits into every kosher meal, meat or dairy, because it is considered pareve (neutral). In talmudic times it was thought to be unhealthy to eat fish and meat together, and some Jews still adhere to this tradition by not mixing fish and meat in the same preparation and by not serving the two on the same plate. In some homes, a bowl of soup separates the fish course from the meat to separate the flavors.

Because any fish with fins and scales is considered kosher, a large variety of tasty fish is available in Jewish cooking. All crustaceans are nonkosher, and in modern Jewish cooking there are attempts to make nonkosher fish look and presumably taste like kosher fish (for example, imitation crabmeat made of pollock; flounder or sole for the Chinese delicacy shrimp toast). But the traditional Jewish preparations are not attempts to imitate, and the range of flavors in preparing fish traditionally knows no bounds, from delicate to vinegary, subtle to spicy. Among the most popular fish in Jewish cuisine are whitefish, carp, salmon, herring, and mackerel. All methods are used for cooking fish, which may be pickled, stuffed, baked, broiled, boiled, fried, poached, or steamed.

This chapter begins with pickled herring, one of the most well known of traditional Jewish fish preparations.

PICKLED HERRING

Makes 2 cups; serves 6 to 8 as an appetizer

In days when most fish was unaffordable, the Jews of Eastern Europe ate herring, one of the most prolific and least expensive fish available. The fish were preserved by salting, pickling, or smoking. Pickled herring became especially popular to enliven an otherwise bland diet of black bread, cereal, and vegetables.

Pickled herring or a herring salad (see the chopped herring recipe on page 52) is served with challah and simple cakes at the light third meal of the Sabbath (*Seuda Shelishit*). It is also traditional to serve herring and other salty fish as part of the break-the-fast meal following Yom Kippur. This is in order to make one thirsty enough to replenish fluids lost during the day-long fast. In a more recent tradition, pickled herring is enjoyed by American Jews at Sunday brunch along with bagels and lox (smoked salmon).

Unlike fish that is cooked by heat and becomes flaky, pickled herring retains its solid consistency and, while tender, is chewy. When prepared and served with vinegar, the herring and sauce have a bit of a zing. Among Jews of Russian and Polish ancestry, pickled herring is often served in a sour cream sauce that takes out some of the bite (see the variation).

Today pickled herring is available in jars or sold in bulk, but as you will see, it is easy to prepare at home. For this recipe, as for chopped herring, use *schmaltz* herring, which is caught just before spawning, when it has much fat.

INGREDIENTS:

4 schmaltz herring (without heads, ½ pound each)
2 cups distilled white vinegar

½ cup granulated white sugar
½ cup water
1 cup sliced onion rings (¼-inch rounds)

DIRECTIONS:

1. Wash the herring, then soak them overnight in water to cover (minimum of 8 hours).

2. In a 1-quart pot, combine the vinegar, sugar, and water. Bring to a rolling boil, then boil for half a minute. Cool to room temperature.

3. Drain and rinse the soaked herring.

4. Open the herring out flat, then use your fingers to reach under the flesh and pull out the spine and the small bones that are attached. Use a sharp knife to separate the flesh from the skin. Or, remove the outer layer of the skin only (it will peel away easily with a sharp knife). Cut the fish into 1-inch pieces.

5. Place the fish slices and onion rings in a 1½-quart ceramic container. Pour the cool vinegar mixture over the herring and onions. Marinate in the refrigerator for 3 days, stirring occasionally. Drain before serving. Spear with toothpicks or serve with challah, crackers, or matzo. Or, serve small portions as a first course on a lettuce leaf garnished with tomatoes.

VARIATION:

Pickled Herring with Cream Sauce

Thin ½ cup of sour cream with 1 to 2 tablespoons of milk or light cream. Gently mix with the drained marinated herring from Step 5.

PICKLED SALMON

Serves 4

In this Ashkenazic preparation, fresh salmon cooks in a vinegary pickling spice mixture, then marinates in the cooking liquid. The tangy marinade preserves the fish, and the spices flavor the preparation, but the distinctive taste of the salmon is not lost. Pickled salmon can be prepared several days in advance, making it a good selection for a break-the-fast dish after Yom Kippur. Serve pickled salmon at a buffet brunch, doubling or tripling the recipe for a crowd.

INGREDIENTS:

1 cup thin-sliced onion rounds (do not separate into rings)
1½ pounds salmon fillets or salmon steaks
1 quart (4 cups) water
1½ cups distilled white vinegar
½ teaspoon dill seeds or 1 dill head
1 bay leaf, crushed
5 whole cloves
2 teaspoons granulated white sugar

DIRECTIONS:

1. Line the bottom of a 10-inch skillet with the onion rounds. Place the salmon on top of the onion rounds. Add the water. Bring to the boil over high heat, then immediately reduce the heat to a gentle boil, cover the skillet, and cook gently for 10 minutes.

2. Use a slotted spoon or a pancake turner to transfer the fish to a casserole or bowl just big enough to hold the fish and liquid (a 1½-quart square Corning Ware casserole is ideal).

3. Stir the remaining ingredients into the liquid in the skillet. Raise the heat to high. Bring to the boil over high heat. Boil for 1 minute.

4. Pour the liquid with all the seasonings over the fish. Cool to room temperature. Cover and refrigerate for a minimum of 12 hours before eating. Remove any bones before serving. Serve sliced or in big pieces, with the onions as garnish if desired.

VARIATION:

Salmon with Mixed Pickling Spices

Substitute a teaspoon of mixed pickling spices for the dill seeds or dill head, bay leaf, and cloves.

CHILLED SCHARFE FISH

Serves 6

Scharfe—that is, spicy—fish is cooked with mixed pickling spices, then either chilled and served in a jellied broth or served hot with a sauce made from the fish broth. When served cold, this dish is related to the pickled salmon of the previous recipe. Here, however, slices of fish are cut crosswise from a whole fish with the skin and bones intact. The fish is served with some of the pleasantly spicy jellied broth spooned over each serving.

The traditional fish used for scharfe fish is carp, one of the most popular fish in Jewish cuisine. The breeding of carp was spread through Europe through the trade routes of Jewish traders. Carp is enjoyed in spicy or sweet-and-sour dishes, and it is one of the primary fish used in preparing gefilte fish (see page 190).

Because chilled scharfe fish is refrigerated for two days before being served, it is an excellent choice for any occasion when advance preparation is required. Scharfe fish is an alternative to gefilte fish as the first course of the Friday night Sabbath meal, and it makes a fine buffet dish.

To serve scharfe fish hot, see the next recipe.

INGREDIENTS:

> 3 pounds sliced carp, trout, pike, or whitefish
> ($^3/_4$-inch slices)
> Salt
> 2 medium-size onions, peeled and cut into rounds
> $^1/_2$ cup celery, cut into $^1/_2$-inch slices
> 2 carrots, peeled and cut into $^1/_2$-inch rounds

1 teaspoon mixed pickling spices (suggested
    mixture: allspice, bay leaf, cardamom pods,
    cinnamon, cloves, coriander seeds, dill seeds,
    mustard seeds, black peppercorns)
1 quart (4 cups) water
1/3 cup distilled white vinegar
1 teaspoon granulated white sugar
Lemon wedges and parsley sprigs, for garnish

DIRECTIONS:

1. Sprinkle the fish all over with salt. Refrigerate for 1 to 3 hours.

2. In a skillet large enough to accommodate the fish in a single layer, bring the onions, celery, carrots, pickling spices, water, vinegar, and sugar to the boil over high heat. Reduce the heat so the water boils gently, partially cover the skillet, and cook for 15 minutes.

3. Rinse the fish under cold water, then place the fish in the skillet. Adjust the heat to a simmer. Cover the skillet. Simmer the fish (just below the boiling point) for 20 to 30 minutes, until it is cooked through but retains its shape.

4. Using a slotted spoon, carefully transfer the fish to a ceramic or glass dish that will accommodate the fish in one layer plus the liquid. Pour the liquid with the vegetables over the fish. (If you wish, first strain the stock to remove the spices. This will make the jellied sauce easier to eat but will reduce the spiciness of the dish.)

5. Cover the dish and refrigerate the scharfe fish for 2 days. Serve the fish with the skin intact. Remove the bones prior to serving if desired. Garnish with lemon wedges and sprigs of fresh parsley.

FISH WITH LEMON SAUCE

Serves 6

Here, the fish from the previous recipe is prepared with a zesty lemon sauce and eaten hot. Egg-lemon sauce is well known in Greek cookery as *avgolemono* sauce. Fish sauces thickened with egg and flavored with lemon juice may have come to the kitchens of Central and Eastern Europe by way of Sephardim. The same sauce can be used for any poached fish and is excellent with salmon or cod steaks. Serve as a main course with rice, noodles, kasha (page 268), or a wheat pilaf (page 272).

INGREDIENTS:

Scharfe fish from previous recipe (prepared
   through Step 3)
2 tablespoons unsalted butter or vegetable oil
2 tablespoons unbleached white flour
1 teaspoon grated lemon rind
2 cups strained fish broth
2 tablespoons freshly squeezed lemon juice
2 egg yolks
Lemon wedges and chopped fresh parsley,
   for garnish

DIRECTIONS:

1. Transfer the cooked fish to a heatproof serving platter. Keep the fish warm in a very low oven.

2. In a 1-quart pot, heat the butter or oil over moderate heat until warm. Stir in the flour and the lemon rind. Cook, stirring constantly, for 1 minute. Add the strained broth. Continue cooking until the mixture comes to the boil. Cook for an additional 30 seconds, then add the lemon juice and cook 30 seconds longer. Reduce the heat to low.

3. With a fork or a whisk, beat the egg yolks slightly in a heatproof mixing bowl. Gradually pour the hot sauce into the egg yolks, stirring rapidly and constantly. Now blend the mixture back into the 1 quart pot, return the pot to the stove, and cook for another 30 seconds, just long enough to heat the mixture without curdling the egg yolks.

4. Pour the sauce over the fish. Garnish with lemon wedges and chopped fresh parsley.

Gefilte Fish

Makes twelve 2-inch ovals; serves 6 to 8 as an appetizer

My grandmother used to call gefilte fish "filled fish," which I always mistook for a mispronunciation of *gefilte*. However, I later came to learn that Grandma Jennie's choice of words was correct.

The word *gefilte* (Yiddish for filled) refers to the fact that in earlier days a small amount of chopped fish was mixed with breadcrumbs or matzo meal, onion and seasonings, then stuffed back into the fish skin before being cooked. The family was presented with a fish that was filled with enough of the tasty mixture for everyone to enjoy.

From its humble beginnings as a poor man's fish preparation, gefilte fish has become the aristocrat of fish dishes in Jewish cuisine. Most people no longer use the least expensive fish available. Modern-day gefilte fish combines fresh whitefish, pike, and carp, which are at a premium in today's market. And although one can—in the traditional manner—cook the fish mixture in the skin and serve what looks like a whole fish, gefilte fish is more often shaped into ovals or balls. We no longer need to take a small amount of fish and make it look like a big stuffed fish.

Gefilte fish is the fish preparation that is traditionally eaten by Ashkenazim as part of the Sabbath meal on Friday night. Many Jews also serve gefilte fish at Rosh Hashanah and as part of the Passover Seder meal. Therefore, the three kinds of fish used in its preparation are featured in fish markets before these holidays. On Rosh Hashanah, when fish heads are served by some Jews to signify the hope that one will be a leader—not a follower—in the New Year, it is appropriate to prepare "filled fish" and bring the whole fish to the table.

Filleting and chopping the fish is something of a production, and chopped fish mixtures are available in many kosher fish markets. Even when using prepared mixtures, add plenty of fish skins to the cooking liquid for flavor, and fish bones and heads to make the liquid gel naturally. In some homes, onion skins are added to the cooking liquid to darken the outside of the fish ovals.

INGREDIENTS:

2 cups (1 pound filleted weight) chopped fish,
    preferably a mixture of whitefish, pike, and carp
3 tablespoons minced onion
3 tablespoons matzo meal
2 eggs (graded large)
1 tablespoon granulated white sugar (optional)
1 teaspoon salt
½ teaspoon freshly ground black pepper
3 pounds fish skins, heads, and bones
3 large carrots, peeled and cut into thick rounds
2 stalks celery
1 large onion, cut into quarters (leave the skin on if
    you want to darken the fish on the outside; peel
    the onions for whiter fish)
Water for cooking

DIRECTIONS:

1. In an old-fashioned wooden bowl, use a curved knife to chop the fish very fine. Chop in the onion, then the matzo meal, eggs, sugar, salt, and pepper. (Or use a meat grinder or a food processor, adding the ingredients in the order listed. Be careful not to purée the mixture to a paste in a food processor. A few seconds at a time on the pulse setting is all that is necessary.) Refrigerate for 1 hour (or until ready to use) to make forming the ovals easier. Fresh fish will keep up to 24 hours under very good refrigeration.

2. In an 8-quart pot, place the fish skins, heads and bones, the carrots, celery, and onion. Add enough water to cover the ingredients by 3 inches. Bring to the boil over high heat, then immediately reduce the heat to a gentle boil.

3. Wet your hands and shape the fish mixture into 12 ovals. Gently drop the ovals into the boiling liquid. Cover the pot and cook gently for 1 hour. The lengthy cooking improves the flavor and consistency of the fish. The fish absorbs a lot of water, so check the pot from time to time and add boiling water as necessary to keep the fish covered.

4. Transfer the fish to a container for refrigeration. Strain the broth, reserving the carrot rounds for garnish. Pour the strained broth over the fish. Refrigerate until serving time. The flavor of the gefilte fish will improve the longer the fish remains in the broth. When covered with broth, gefilte fish will keep for at least 3 days under modern refrigeration. Serve the fish ovals with carrot slices, and spoon some of the jellied broth over and around the fish. Horseradish (page 72) is the traditional accompaniment.

VARIATION:

Whole Gefilte Fish

If you would like to prepare old-fashioned "filled fish," have a 1½-pound whitefish filleted, leaving the skin and head intact. Prepare the fish mixture according to the basic recipe. Stuff the mixture evenly inside the fish. Using a heavy needle and thread, sew the fish together at the bottom. Lay the fish carefully in the boiling water, and proceed with the recipe. To serve, when the fish has chilled, use a very sharp knife to cut the cold fish into crosswise slices. The fish is served with the skin.

FRIED GEFILTE FISH

Makes about 2 dozen fish balls

A variation on gefilte fish, here the traditional fish mixture of whitefish, pike, and carp is shaped into balls, deep-fried, and served as an appetizer. The fish will be brown and crisp on the outside, soft inside. Or, shape into patties, dip into egg and matzo meal to form a thin crust, and fry (see the variation).

INGREDIENTS:

1 cup (½ pound) fish fillets, chopped fine
2 tablespoons minced onion
2 tablespoons matzo meal
1 egg (graded large)
1 teaspoon granulated white sugar
¼ teaspoon salt
⅛ teaspoon freshly ground black pepper
Oil for deep-frying

DIRECTIONS:

1. In an old-fashioned wooden bowl, use a curved knife to chop the fish very fine. Chop in the remaining ingredients except for the oil. Or, use a food processor on the pulse setting, taking care not to purée the mixture to a paste. Chill for at least an hour, up to 24 hours.

2. Just before serving, place 1½ inches of oil in a 4-quart pot. Heat until the oil is hot but not yet smoking, 375 degrees F.

3. With your hands, shape the fish into 1-inch balls. Carefully drop into the hot oil. Cook until golden all over. Regulate the heat so that the fish browns evenly while cooking thoroughly on the inside. Drain the cooked fish balls well on paper towels. Serve hot, with lemon wedges on the side.

VARIATION:

Fish Patties

Double the recipe for the fish mixture. Divide into 8 portions. Shape into patties with your hands. Dip into beaten egg, then into seasoned matzo meal. Fry in hot oil until golden on both sides. Drain well on paper towels. Serve as a main dish.

FRIED SMELTS, FLOUNDER, OR SOLE

Serves 4

Smelts were an important fish in Jewish cuisine when they were plentiful and comparatively affordable in years past, because even though they were very small, a few fish on each person's plate gave the appearance of a reasonable portion. The fish were traditionally rolled in flour and fried in oil, or dipped in egg then coated with flour, breadcrumbs, or matzo meal, making a thicker crust that made the fish look a little larger. Although smelts are still enjoyed in Jewish homes, people today are more likely to be able to afford the more expensive fillets of flounder or sole, which can be prepared in the same manner as fried smelts.

Here, the fish is fried in vegetable oil and served hot. An alternative manner of preparing fish was introduced to both non-Jewish Europeans and Ashkenazic Jews by Sephardim, who fried the fish in oil and served it cold. The olive oil imparted a good flavor without masking the taste of the fish. Cold fried trout, mackerel (see page 201), and other fish were enjoyed on the Sabbath. If you would like to fry fish in olive oil to be served either hot or cold, note that olive oil burns at a relatively low temperature and must be heated slowly to prevent burning.

INGREDIENTS:

> 1 egg (graded large or extra large)
> 2 tablespoons water
> 1 cup (approximately) matzo meal or unbleached
>   white flour
> 1 teaspoon salt

¼ teaspoon freshly ground black pepper

1½ pounds smelts (dressed weight), fillets of
    flounder, or fillets of sole

Vegetable oil for frying

½ cup toasted alomnds or pine nuts for garnish
    (optional)

Chopped fresh parsley and lemon wedges

DIRECTIONS:

1. In a shallow bowl large enough to accommodate the largest piece of fish, beat the egg with the 2 tablespoons of water.

2. In another bowl of comparable size, mix the matzo meal or flour with the salt and pepper.

3. Dip each piece of fish into the egg, coating completely, then into the matzo meal or flour mixture.

4. In a 10-inch skillet, heat ¼ inch of vegetable oil until it is hot but not yet smoking. Carefully add the fish, making sure the pieces do not touch each other. Cook until the fish is golden brown on one side, then turn and cook the other side. The total cooking time is about 10 minutes.

5. To serve, sprinkle the fish with toasted chopped nuts if desired. Garnish with chopped fresh parsley and serve lemon wedges on the side. Serve fried fish with rice or noodles as a starch, and a green vegetable or honeyed carrots (page 238) and a salad.

SWEET-AND-SOUR FISH

Serves 4 to 6

If you did not grow up in a household where gingersnaps were added to sweet-and-sour sauce, you may wonder why the gingersnaps. I, too, wondered as a child, and my mother knew exactly why. "Oh, you have to have gingersnaps. They make it taste better."

Some foods are passed down from one generation to the next because they are connected to religious holidays in special ways. Other preparations become traditional because they simplify a cooking procedure and make the food taste better as well. Here, gingersnaps take the place of the *einbren* (flour mixed with butter, oil, or schmaltz) also used traditionally in Jewish cooking to thicken sauces. The cookies bring out the sweetness while adding a hint of spice, making them especially suitable for sweet-and-sour sauces (see the recipe for tongue on page 148).

In fish preparations, the sauce is sweet and lemony, with a taste of the fish that has cooked in the sauce. Because the cooking time is relatively short, the onion textures the sauce with slightly firm pieces. When served hot, the sauce is marvelous over rice or noodles. When chilled, it thickens almost to a gel and is spooned over each portion of fish, to be enjoyed with each mouthful.

Fish fillets, steaks, even whole fish can be used in this recipe. Allow about ten minutes cooking time for fillets that are half an inch thick, fifteen minutes for one-inch fish steaks, about twenty minutes for a whole two-pound fish. For a larger fish, use one and one-half to two times the amount of each ingredient.

INGREDIENTS:

> 2 pounds salmon, cod, or other fish fillets
>   (approximately ¾-inch thick)
> 1 cup chopped onion
> 2 medium-size lemons, seeds removed, sliced into
>   ¼-inch rounds
> ½ cup firmly packed dark brown sugar
> 2 cups water
> 8 gingersnaps

DIRECTIONS:

1. Place the fish in a 10-inch skillet. Scatter the onion, lemon slices, and brown sugar on and around the fish. Add the water, then turn on the heat and bring to the boil over high heat. Immediately reduce the heat so that the water boils gently, cover the skillet, and cook for 12 to 15 minutes, until the fish is no longer translucent and flakes easily when poked with a fork.

2. Transfer the fish to a serving platter or bowl. Regulate the heat to keep the sauce simmering.

3. With a rolling pin, crush the gingersnaps between two sheets of wax paper, or use your fingers to crush the cookies into small pieces. Add them to the sauce, bring back to the boil, and cook while stirring until the gingersnaps are dissolved.

4. Pour the sauce over the fish, removing the lemon slices if desired. Serve hot as a main dish with rice, noodles, or kasha (page 268) to absorb the gravy. Or, chill the fish in the sauce and serve it cold as a first course, a buffet dish, or as the main course on a hot summer's day.

BAKED FISH
WITH FRESH TOMATO SAUCE

Serves 4 generously

Whole fish covered with a *sofrito* (Spanish sauce base) before being baked are enjoyed throughout the Mediterranean. Mackerel, one of many fishes that has fins and scales and is therefore kosher, is popular among Sephardim. It is a tasty fish and contrasts well with the mild sofrito. Trout, sweeter and less strong, perhaps more elegant, is a delicious alternative.

Olive oil, traditionally used in Sephardic cooking, is important to the characteristic taste of the baked fish in this recipe. There is a range of olive oils in taste and color, from green and fruity (cold-pressed from the first pressing) to almost white and mild-tasting (second or third pressing from heated olives). Cold-pressed is considered to be the best olive oil among connoisseurs, and while it is recommended for use with the mackerel, it will impart a strong taste to the preparation. A more mild-tasting olive oil is suggested for the trout.

One large whole fish or two pounds of fish fillets can be substituted for the four individual servings, but you will need to adjust the cooking time (more for a whole fish, less for fillets). The fish is done when it loses its translucent look and can be flaked easily with a fork.

INGREDIENTS:

$\frac{1}{4}$ **cup olive oil**

4 cups chopped onions

4 teaspoons minced garlic

2 pounds fresh tomatoes, chopped

1 cup packed chopped fresh parsley

$\frac{1}{4}$ **cup freshly squeezed lemon juice**

Salt and freshly ground black pepper
4 whole mackerel or trout (¾ pound each
    dressed weight), boned if desired
Olive oil
Boiling water if necessary
Optional garnishes: additional chopped fresh parsley
    and/or pine nuts sautéed in a little olive oil

DIRECTIONS:

1. Preheat the oven to 350 degrees F.

2. In a 10- or 12-inch skillet, heat the ¼ cup of olive oil over moderately low heat. Add the onion and garlic, raise the heat to moderate, and sauté until the onion is soft but not brown. Mix in the tomatoes. Cook until the tomatoes are warmed through but still hold their shape, then stir in the parsley and lemon juice. Season the sofrito to taste with salt and pepper.

3. Wash the fish and pat dry. Rub inside and out with salt and pepper, then with a little olive oil. Place the fish side by side in a baking pan, then spoon the tomato mixture over the fish.

4. Bake at 350 degrees F. for 20 minutes, then check the fish. If the vegetables appear to be drying out, add ½ to 1 cup boiling water to the pan, just enough to barely cover the bottom of the pan.

5. Raise the heat to 400 degrees F. Continue to bake the fish for another 10 minutes or until it becomes opaque and flakes easily with a fork. The tomatoes and onions may brown lightly, but if they are browning too much or are drying out, cover the baking pan with foil.

6. Serve one whole fish per person, with ¼ of the sofrito spooned over each serving. If you like, sprinkle with additional chopped fresh parsley and/or sautéed pine nuts. Serve with rice and a tossed green salad.

SPICE-AND-NUT STUFFED MACKEREL

Serves 4

The combination of fragrant spices, fruit, and nuts popular in Sephardic cooking makes a marvelous crunchy stuffing in this Turkish preparation. Stuffed mackerel is reminiscent of the Ashkenazic gefilte fish, and an excellent fish course for the Sabbath meal. During Passover, matzo meal is used in place of the breadcrumbs and flour. On Rosh Hashanah, when fish are presented with the heads intact, the mackerel are left whole; on Sukkot, when fruits, vegetables, and stuffed items are enjoyed, the recipe needs no changes.

Plan to serve the fried mackerel immediately after they are cooked, with hot rice or a wheat pilaf (page 272) and a green salad. The baked version makes an outstanding appetizer when sliced and served cold.

INGREDIENTS:

4 mackerel, heads and tails removed (each
   $1/2$ pound dressed weight)
2 tablespoons olive oil
1 cup chopped onion
$1/4$ cup pine nuts
$1/2$ cup chopped walnuts
$1/4$ cup dark raisins
$1/4$ teaspoon each ground allspice, nutmeg, and
   cinnamon
Pinch of ground cloves
$1/2$ cup chopped fresh parsley
$1/2$ cup soft breadcrumbs or matzo meal

1 egg (graded large), beaten (for fried version)
Flour or matzo meal for coating the fish (for fried
    version)
Vegetable oil for frying

DIRECTIONS:

1. Using a sharp boning knife, remove and discard all the bones from the fish. Carefully scrape the meat from the skin, leaving the skin intact. Wash the skin under cold water, pat dry, and set aside. Chop the fish coarsely. Set aside.

2. In a 10-inch skillet, heat the olive oil over moderately low heat. Before the oil begins to smoke, add the onion. Raise the heat to moderate and sauté until the onion is softened and golden but not brown. Stir in the pine nuts, walnuts, and raisins. Continue cooking for 2 minutes to lightly toast the nuts. Stir in the ground spices, the parsley, the breadcrumbs or matzo meal, and finally the chopped fish. Cook for 5 minutes longer, stirring often.

3. Divide the stuffing into 4 equal portions. Stuff each fish skin with a portion of the mixture. Secure the edges with toothpicks.

4. **To fry,** roll each fish in the beaten egg, then coat the fish completely with the flour or matzo meal. The fish can be refrigerated at this point. When ready to cook, in a skillet 12 inches or larger and at least 3 inches deep, heat an inch of oil to 375 degrees F. The oil should be hot but not yet smoking. Carefully add the fish to the oil, making sure that they do not touch each other. Fry the fish for a few minutes on one side, until golden, then carefully turn and fry the other side. Drain well on paper towels.

   To bake, preheat the oven to 400 degrees F. Omit the egg and flour coating. Line a baking sheet with foil and oil the foil. Place the fish on the foil. Bake in the middle of the oven for 15 to 20 minutes, until the stuffing is sizzling. Serve hot as a main dish, or chill the fish, slice crosswise into 1-inch pieces, and serve cold as an appetizer.

SALMON CROQUETTES

Makes 8 croquettes

In traditional Jewish cuisine, it is unusual to find a recipe that begins with "Take a can of...." Fresh meat, fish, vegetables, and fruit were eaten in the past, and one way of preserving the Jewish heritage is to continue to use fresh ingredients. Canned salmon and tuna fish are exceptions.

Jewish cookbooks that date back to the early 1900s contain recipes based on canned salmon, and even if Grandma ate smoked salmon and made pickled salmon (page 184) from fresh-caught fish, she used canned salmon for croquettes, patties, loaves, and salads. She could start with a canned product, then use seasonings and a cooking method to effect a homemade preparation.

Salmon croquettes feature the crunch of a crisp crust contrasting with a soft interior. Serve them as an appetizer with Sour Cream-and-Dill Sauce (recipe follows) or as a main dish with a noodle or rice kugel and a green vegetable and/or a tossed salad. For variety, substitute a large (12.5 ounces) can of solid white tuna fish for the salmon.

INGREDIENTS:

>   1 can (14.75 ounces) pink salmon, drained
>   2 tablespoons minced onion
>   2 eggs (graded large)
>   2 tablespoons minced fresh parsley
>   ¼ teaspoon freshly ground black pepper
>   ½ teaspoon salt (optional)
>   ⅔ cup breadcrumbs or matzo meal
>   ¼ cup vegetable oil for frying

DIRECTIONS:

1. Pick out the bones from the salmon. In a medium-size bowl, mash the salmon with a fork. Add the onion, eggs, parsley, pepper, the optional salt, and 2 tablespoons of the breadcrumbs or matzo meal.

2. Divide the mixture into 8 equal portions, then shape with your hands into croquettes (triangles with a round base). Roll the croquettes in the remaining breadcrumbs or matzo meal, covering completely. The croquettes can be transferred to a plate (sides not touching), lightly covered with plastic wrap or wax paper, and refrigerated for a few hours at this point.

3. In a 10-inch skillet, heat the oil over moderate heat until it is hot but not smoking. Carefully place the croquettes on their sides in the oil. Fry for 2 minutes on each side, then stand them upright and fry the bottoms. The croquettes will be crisp and golden brown all over. Drain well on paper towels. Serve hot, with lemon wedges on the side and Sour Cream-and-Dill Sauce.

SOUR CREAM-AND-DILL SAUCE:

> 1 cup (8 ounces) sour cream
> 2 tablespoons freshly squeezed lemon juice
> 1 teaspoon minced garlic
> 2 to 4 tablespoons minced fresh parsley
> 2 to 4 tablespoons minced fresh dill leaves
> Salt and freshly ground black pepper

In a small bowl, mix together all the ingredients, beginning with the smaller quantities of herbs. Taste and correct the seasonings. Cover and refrigerate until serving. The sauce will keep well in the refrigerator for several days.

5

Light Meals
Mostly Dairy

Light Meals

In a cuisine characterized by the complete separation of meat and milk products, dairy preparations are the basis of many meals. Fresh, uncured cheeses such as cottage, pot, and cream cheese are especially popular. Marvelous main dish casseroles (*kugels*) of noodles, cheese, and sometimes fruit; delicate *blintz* pancakes and strudels; simple cottage cheese-and-noodle mixtures—these are the traditional dishes savored in Jewish homes for dairy meals.

Eggs may be mixed with either meat or milk and are often hidden in Jewish dishes—when they moisten *kreplach* filling or naturally color and flavor noodle dough, for example. Eggs are also featured in light meals when scrambled with lox or mixed with matzo to make *matzo brei*. Eggs are symbolic of the unending cycle of life, and it is therefore customary to serve them to mourners at the Meal of Condolence that follows a funeral. Hard-cooked eggs dipped in salt water are served as an appetizer at the Passover Seder, a reminder of the holiday sacrifice brought in the days when the Temple stood in Jerusalem.

We begin this "mostly dairy" chapter with three traditional egg preparations that are enjoyed for breakfast or brunch. The chapter closes with a non-dairy sandwich that is included here because it is eaten as a light meal or snack. And while My Father's Favorite Sandwich may have little nutritive value, it will bring back memories to those who are over fifty.

EGGS WITH LOX AND ONIONS

Serves 4

Because it is forbidden to light a fire on the Sabbath, observant Jews do not cook on Saturday mornings. A simple, light, uncooked meal is eaten before morning worship services. Sunday is the day when a leisurely brunch featuring hot foods is enjoyed. Here is one of the traditional preparations eaten for Sunday brunch, along with bagels or a hearty bread (see Chapter Seven).

Even the most artful carvers of lox (salty) or nova (not salty) end up with pieces that can't be sold at the same price that hand-sliced smoked salmon commands. You can dice up slices or use the less expensive bits for this recipe.

INGREDIENTS:

2 tablespoons unsalted butter or vegetable oil
½ cup diced onion
8 eggs (graded large or extra large), beaten well
½ cup (¼ pound) diced lox or nova
Salt and freshly ground black pepper

DIRECTIONS:

1. In a 10- or 12-inch skillet, heat the butter or oil over moderate heat. Do not allow the butter to brown. Add the onion and cook until wilted.

2. Pour in the eggs, scramble until barely set, then scatter the lox or nova over the top. Continue scrambling until the eggs are cooked the way you like them, adding salt and pepper as desired while mixing. Serve immediately.

MATZO BREI

Serves 1 or 2

Matzo brei—fried matzo—is a Passover specialty that is also enjoyed year-round for breakfast or brunch. Matzo that has been softened in water is mixed with egg, then fried in butter. The mixture can be scrambled the way scrambled eggs are prepared, or allowed to set to make one big pancake.

If you follow the directions below, you will end up with a matzo brei that is crisp outside, soft inside, and never falls apart when flipped. You may wonder at the precision of the directions. While some cookbook authors follow their mothers around the kitchen to work out recipes, when it comes to matzo brei I watch my husband, and the recipe below describes his technique exactly.

Serve matzo brei plain, with preserves or a fruit sauce, with cinnamon and sugar, or with pancake syrup.

INGREDIENTS:

> 2 square matzos (7-inch square)
> Cold water
> 2 eggs (graded large or extra large)
> Salt and freshly ground black pepper (optional)
> 1½ teaspoons unsalted butter

DIRECTIONS:

1. Preheat a 7-inch cast-iron skillet over moderate heat (5 on a scale of 1 to 10). For a skillet that is not cast-iron, preheat on very low heat, 1 or 2, then raise the heat to 5 to melt the butter (Step 6 in this recipe).

2. Using your hands, in a medium-size mixing bowl break up the matzo into small (¼- to ½-inch) pieces. Add just enough cold water to cover. Set aside.

3. In another bowl, beat the eggs well. Add salt and pepper to the eggs if you wish.

4. Drain the matzo.

5. Add the beaten eggs to the drained matzo. Mix well with a fork.

6. Slice the butter into thirds and add all at once to the hot skillet, grasp the handle of the pan, and with a rapid motion of your wrist swish the butter in the pan so it melts without browning.

7. Immediately turn the matzo-egg mixture into the skillet all at once. Level with a fork. Cook for exactly 3 minutes in a cast-iron skillet, 3½ to 4 minutes if not cast-iron. Midway during the cooking, grasp the handle of the skillet and give the skillet a firm twist to break loose the pancake.

8. Flip the matzo brei onto a plate, then slide back into the skillet. Cook for 3 minutes on the second side (again, 3½ to 4 minutes if the skillet is not cast-iron). Serve hot.

Note: For a slightly softer crust, reduce the heat from 5 to 4 on a scale of 1 to 10.

CHALLAH FRENCH TOAST

Allow 2 or 3 pieces per serving

If you serve two *challot* (plural of challah) for Sabbath dinner and you are lucky enough to have a substantial part of one left over, consider challah French toast for Sunday breakfast. The recipe for challah is on page 300.

INGREDIENTS:

> 2 tablespoons unsalted butter, approximately
> 2 eggs (graded large or extra large)
> 1/4 teaspoon salt (optional)
> 8 or 9 slices challah (1/2-inch thick, roughly 2 x 5 inches)

DIRECTIONS:

1. In a 10-inch skillet, melt 1 tablespoon of the butter over moderate heat.

2. In a bowl large enough to accommodate at least one slice of challah, beat the eggs well. Add salt if desired. Dip a slice of challah into the eggs, turn to coat the other side, and place in the hot melted butter. Repeat until the skillet is full.

3. Cook until golden on one side, turn and brown the other side. Add more butter as necessary. Remove from the skillet. Serve immediately, or keep warm while cooking the remaining slices.

4. Serve hot with syrup, cinnamon and sugar, or jam.

VEGETABLES WITH COTTAGE CHEESE AND SOUR CREAM

Allow ½ to 1 cup cottage cheese per person

Early spring vegetables were a refreshing change from the winter vegetables (mainly beets and cabbage) eaten by Eastern Europeans. Radishes and scallions, among the first signs of spring, signaled an end to the harsh winter. The vegetables were crisp, sharp, and special because they were eaten fresh from the ground instead of from storage.

When mixed with creamed cottage cheese or the drier pot cheese, the vegetables became a light meal. Later on during the summer, cucumbers ripened and were added to the dish. The tomatoes are a modern addition.

A refreshing dairy lunch during the hot summer months, this dish is also enjoyed as the simple "Third Meal" of the Sabbath, *Seuda Shelishit*.

INGREDIENTS:

Cottage cheese
Sliced radishes, diced cucumber, sliced scallions
Red ripe tomatoes cut into chunks, seeds removed
Salt and freshly ground black pepper
Sour cream

DIRECTIONS:

1. Set out individual bowls of cottage cheese, and bowls of vegetables and sour cream to pass around.

2. Take what you want, season to taste, mix, eat.

BLINTZES

Cheese *blintzes* are the traditional blintzes of Jewish cuisine. Two cheese blintzes are traditionally eaten on Shavuot, the springtime holiday that celebrates the giving of the Torah on Mount Sinai, to represent the two tablets of the Ten Commandments received by Moses. It is customary to eat cheese products on the day the Torah was given on Mount Sinai because the words in the Song of Songs (4:11), "honey and milk under thy lips," imply that just as honey and milk products energize our bodies, the words of the Torah vitalize our spirits.

The blintz wrappers are related to the *crêpes* of France, the *mu shu* pancakes of China, the *palacsinta* of Hungary, and the *manicotti* of Italy. The Yiddish word *blintz* comes from the Russian *blini,* which are yeast pancakes that are usually topped with caviar and sour cream. Here, the thin pancakes are wrapped around a creamy cottage cheese filling, then fried in butter to a golden deliciousness and topped with sour cream.

In days gone by, a high fat content in cottage cheese was considered desirable as a way of adding calories to the diet. Nowadays, many people prefer to use a low-fat cottage cheese. Cheese blintzes can be made with whatever cottage cheese you usually use, or with the more old-fashioned pot cheese, which is made without the addition of cream. Traditional accompaniments for cheese blintzes are sour cream, applesauce, and a sprinkling of cinnamon and sugar. They are also excellent served topped with sliced strawberries or the berry sauce that appears at the end of this recipe.

Blintzes can be filled with a variety of tempting fillings other than cheese, including luscious fruits, cabbage, mushrooms, chopped liver, cooked brisket, or ground meat. Vegetable blintzes are fried in butter, oil, or chicken fat, depending on whether they are to be served with dairy or meat meals; meat blintzes are fried in oil or schmaltz. Blintzes are among the most versatile of traditional Jewish foods. They are eaten for breakfast, lunch, brunch, as the first course of a larger meal, as a buffet dish, as a light meal, or even as a dessert.

In addition to the cheese and fruit fillings presented here, one can use 2 cups of a meat kreplach filling (page 88), kasha (page 268), cabbage (page 250), or mushroom filling (page 252). Sour cream can be served with any blintzes that are not made with meat products.

There are four steps to making blintzes. First, the blintz pancakes are prepared and stacked. Next, the filling is made. (These steps can be reversed if desired.) The pancakes are then filled, and finally they are fried. If a berry sauce is desired, cook the sauce before frying the filled blintzes.

PREPARING THE BLINTZ PANCAKES

It may take a little practice to make thin, crisp blintz pancakes that do not tear. If the first few do not come out perfectly, enjoy them plain. There is enough batter for sixteen blintzes plus a few extras for practice. Stack the blintz pancakes as you go along, then fill them one by one when all the pancakes have been made.

2 eggs (graded large)
1¼ cups milk
1 cup unbleached white flour, sifted after measuring
Unsalted butter for coating the skillet
Unsalted butter for frying the blintzes (page 217)

1. In a medium-size mixing bowl, beat the eggs with a fork until well combined and beginning to thicken. Beat in the milk, then beat in the flour ¼ cup at a time. Press out any lumps with the back of a spoon, or strain to remove lumps. (Or, use a blender to mix the batter.)

2. Coat a 7-inch skillet (preferably cast-iron) with a thin layer of butter. Heat over medium heat. Pour the thinnest possible layer of batter into the skillet,

just enough to coat it evenly (about 3 tablespoons). Quickly tilt the pan as you pour in the batter so that the batter covers the skillet evenly. When the bottom of the pancake is light brown and the top surface is almost dried out (about 1½ minutes), loosen the edges with a thin metal spatula. Turn the skillet over onto a clean, hard (dentproof) surface and hit the skillet lightly. The pancake should pop out. If it does not come out and it seems a little wet, cook for a few more seconds. If it still does not pop out, use a metal spatula or a pancake turner.

PREPARING THE FILLING

Select one or more of the fillings below. If desired, the filling(s) can be readied in advance and refrigerated overnight.

COTTAGE CHEESE FILLING:

> **2 cups (1 pound) small-curd cottage cheese**
> **2 eggs (graded large)**
> **Cinnamon and sugar (optional)**
> **1 teaspoon grated orange rind (optional)**
> **2 tablespoons dark or golden raisins (optional)**

In a small mixing bowl, use a fork or spoon to beat together the cottage cheese and the eggs. If desired, sprinkle with a little cinnamon and sugar and/or grated orange rind, then add the raisins. Stir until the ingredients are distributed evenly. Set aside.

COOKED APPLE FILLING:

> **5 cups chopped peeled McIntosh, Golden**
> **Delicious, or other cooking apples**
> **¼ cup dark raisins (optional)**
> **¼ cup granulated white sugar**

½ teaspoon ground cinnamon
1 tablespoon freshly squeezed lemon juice
   (optional)

In a 2-quart pot, mix together the apples, the optional raisins, the sugar, and cinnamon. Cook over moderate heat for 4 to 5 minutes, stirring often, until the apples soften but retain their shape. The apples will cook down to less than half their original volume. Stir in the optional lemon juice. Set aside to cool to room temperature.

UNCOOKED APPLE FILLING:

2½ cups finely chopped peeled apples
2 tablespoons granulated white sugar
2 teaspoons freshly squeezed lemon juice
¼ teaspoon ground cinnamon

Mix together all the ingredients. Refrigerate if you will not be using within an hour. The apples soften somewhat when the blintzes are cooked, but not nearly so much as the cooked apple filling.

BERRY FILLING:

3 cups sliced hulled fresh strawberries or
   fresh blueberries
2 tablespoons granulated white sugar
2 teaspoons freshly squeezed lemon juice (optional)

Mix together the berries, sugar, and the optional lemon juice. The berries will become a little syrupy while the blintzes are being prepared and are best used shortly after they have been mixed with the sugar.

ASSEMBLING THE BLINTZES

Spread 2 level tablespoons of filling along the center of the cooked side of the pancake. Fold the sides over the filling to make a log, then tuck in the remaining sides so the filling doesn't leak out. Store in a single layer on wax paper. Repeat until all the batter and filling are used up. You will have approximately 16 filled blintzes. When all the blintzes have been filled, they can be refrigerated in a single layer or fried immediately.

FRYING THE BLINTZES

For final cooking, in a 10-inch skillet heat 2 tablespoons of butter over moderate heat until sizzling but not brown. Fry the blintzes flap side down until golden, then turn and fry the other side. Add additional butter for each batch as necessary. Serve hot with sour cream, applesauce (page 236), and cinnamon and sugar, fresh berries, or the berry sauce below.

BERRY SAUCE:

> **2 cups sliced hulled fresh strawberries or fresh blueberries**
> **¼ cup granulated white sugar**
> **1 teaspoon cornstarch**
> **2 tablespoons freshly squeezed lemon juice**

In a 1-quart pot, combine all the ingredients. Cook over moderately low heat, stirring constantly, until the fruit softens and the liquid that forms comes to the boil. Cook for 30 seconds longer, stirring all the while. Serve warm or at room temperature. Refrigerate leftovers.

CHEESE LATKES
(Pancakes)

Makes sixteen 3-inch latkes

Cheese *latkes,* which are traditionally eaten on Chanukah as well as on Shavuot (see pages 26 and 34), use the same basic ingredients as cheese blintzes, minus the milk in the batter, but they are considerably easier to prepare. The origin of the association of cheese with Chanukah has been traced to the Book of Judith in the Apocrypha. According to legend, Judith, a daughter of one of the Hasmoneans, fed cheese to the general of Nebuchadnezzar's army just before the general would have destroyed the Jewish people. The cheese made the general thirsty, he drank large amounts of wine, and when he became drunk, Judith beheaded him, ensuring a Jewish victory.

Like potato latkes (page 288), cheese latkes are golden and crisp on the outside with a soft interior. They have a pleasant cheese flavor which is complemented but not masked by traditional accompaniments of cinnamon and sugar, applesauce, and sour cream. They are also delicious when topped with sliced strawberries or the berry sauce of the previous recipe. Serve them for Sunday brunch or for a light supper with a salad and a hearty vegetarian soup to begin the meal.

INGREDIENTS:

> 1 cup (8 ounces) creamed cottage cheese
> 1 cup unbleached white flour (stir the flour, spoon
>   gently into a dry-measure cup, then level with
>   the edge of a spatula)
> 2 tablespoons sugar (optional)
> ¼ teaspoon cinnamon

4 eggs (graded large)

¼ cup (½ stick) unsalted butter for frying, approximately

Optional accompaniments: cinnamon and sugar, applesauce (page 236), sour cream, sliced strawberries, berry sauce (page 217)

DIRECTIONS:

1. In a medium-size mixing bowl, use a large spoon to beat together the cottage cheese, flour, sugar and cinnamon, and the eggs.

2. In a 10-inch skillet, melt half of the butter over moderate heat until the butter is sizzling but not brown.

3. Using 2 tablespoons of batter per latke, spoon the batter into the hot butter. Fry until set and brown on one side, then turn and brown the other side.

4. Add more butter to the skillet, and cook the remaining latkes.

5. Serve hot with any of the optional accompaniments above.

CHEESE STRUDEL

Makes two 14-inch rolls

Paper-thin layers of pastry filled with sweet, savory, or delicate combinations of fruit and nuts, vegetables or cheeses—*strudels* of all kinds are the pride of Hungary, Austria, and Germany, and of the Jews of those nations. Strudels came to the Austro-Hungarian Empire by way of Turkey, and are closely related to the phyllo pastries of Turkey and Greece.

In Jewish cuisine, a piece of strudel may be part of any course of a meal: small slices of vegetable or cheese strudels are eaten as appetizers or on the side with soups; larger slices make light main dishes; vegetable, cheese, or sweet strudels are eaten as tempting between-meal snacks just "to hold one over"; and the sweet fruit-and-nut pastries make delectable desserts.

Here, the pastry is easier to prepare than old-fashioned stretched strudel, and the results are excellent. The strudel recipe features a delicately flavored, custardy inside and a crisp golden brown crust. The cheese flavor is subtle, and the strudel goes especially well with a hearty pareve split pea (page 110) or lentil soup (page 112). It is light enough to be a marvelous nosh for people who are waiting for dinner. Large pieces (three to four inches) are served as a main dish, with a soup to start and a salad on the side. Cheese delicacies such as the strudel in this recipe are traditionally eaten on Shavuot and Chanukah, but they can be enjoyed any time of year.

INGREDIENTS:

> 1¼ cups unbleached white flour (stir the flour, spoon
>   gently into a dry-measure cup, then level with
>   the edge of a spatula)
> ¼ teaspoon salt (optional)

$\frac{3}{8}$ cup warm water (not over 100 degrees F.)

2 tablespoons beaten egg

1 tablespoon vegetable oil

1 cup (8 ounces) small-curd cottage cheese

$\frac{1}{2}$ cup (4 ounces) farmer cheese

2 eggs (graded large)

2 tablespoons melted unsalted butter

$\frac{1}{4}$ cup breadcrumbs

Beaten egg for brushing the top

DIRECTIONS:

1. For the dough, in a medium-size mixing bowl place the flour and salt. In a small bowl or a cup, mix together the water, 2 tablespoons of egg, and 1 tablespoon of oil. Add all at once to the flour. Stir with a wooden spoon until the mixture holds together and forms a dough.

2. Turn out the dough onto a clean, smooth work surface. Knead for about 3 minutes, until the dough becomes smooth and elastic. If necessary, dust the dough and the work surface with flour. Cover with a slightly damp, clean kitchen towel while preparing the filling.

3. For the filling, use a spoon to beat together the cottage cheese, farmer cheese, and the 2 eggs. Set aside.

4. Preheat the oven to 425 degrees F.

5. Grease a large baking sheet with butter or vegetable shortening.

6. Lightly flour a large clean, smooth work surface. Divide the dough in half. Work with one piece of dough at a time, keeping the other piece covered with the damp but not wet kitchen towel.

7. Flatten the dough between your hands, and gently stretch to a 6-inch circle. Place the dough on the floured surface. Place your hands under the dough, palms down. Now, working from the center outward, stretch the dough gently over the backs of your hands. If you are not making progress, use a rolling pin from time to time to stretch and even out the dough. The goal is a rectangle about 12 x 14 inches.

8. When the dough is the correct size, trim off the thick edges. Brush the dough thoroughly with 1 tablespoon of the melted butter, then sprinkle with half of the breadcrumbs. Spread half of the filling over the surface of the dough to within half an inch of the edges.

9. Roll up the dough as tightly as possible, as you would a jelly roll. Pinch the long edge against the filled roll, then pinch the ends and tuck under. Carefully transfer to the greased baking sheet. Brush all exposed surfaces with well-beaten egg.

10. Repeat Steps 7, 8, and 9 with the second piece of dough and the remaining filling.

11. Bake in the middle of the oven for about 15 minutes, until golden brown. Carefully transfer to a wire rack to cool slightly before slicing. Slice into serving-size pieces just before serving. Serve warm.

VARIATIONS:

Orange-flavored Cottage Cheese Strudel

Add 1 tablespoon of grated orange rind and 1 tablespoon of freshly squeezed orange juice to the filling in Step 3.

Cinnamon-Raisin Cottage Cheese Strudel

Mix 1 teaspoon of ground cinnamon with the filling in Step 3. Scatter ½ cup raisins over each half of the filling in Step 8.

NOODLES AND CHEESE

Serves 4

This simple combination of hot cooked noodles (*lokshen* in Yiddish) and cottage or pot cheese is based on a Hungarian noodles and cheese dish that is prepared with bacon. The kosher version of noodles and cheese is an uncomplicated, homey preparation that can be served with plain steamed vegetables or sweet honeyed carrots (page 238). Enjoy noodles and cheese with a cold fruit soup (page 123) for lunch or a light supper.

INGREDIENTS:

> 1 pound medium egg noodles
> 1 pound small-curd cottage cheese or pot cheese
> ¼ cup sour cream (optional)
> Salt

DIRECTIONS:

1. Cook the noodles in boiling water (salted if desired) until tender.

2. Meanwhile, in a medium-size bowl beat the cottage or pot cheese with a fork. Beat in the optional sour cream.

3. Drain the cooked noodles, return to the pot, and quickly stir in the cottage cheese-sour cream mixture while the noodles are still hot. Some of the cheese will melt, but most of the curds will remain. Add salt to taste. If the mixture is not hot enough, place over low heat until warmed through.

CREAM CHEESE-AND-PINEAPPLE NOODLE KUGEL

Serves 6

Anoodle *kugel,* or pudding, is a sweet or savory casserole of noodles made special when combined with fruits and sometimes nuts, along with cheese for dairy meals or chicken fat for meat meals. The noodles are mixed with eggs to make the preparation set when baked. Noodle kugels made with cheese are reminiscent of the lasagne of Italy, which layers noodles and cheese (often with meat, sometimes vegetables) in a main dish casserole that is served in squares.

Noodle kugel finds a place in Jewish cuisine as a Sabbath preparation for the Friday night meal, where nondairy kugels are made as side dishes to go with brisket, chicken, veal, or lamb. As a preparation that will feed many people, is easy to prepare and serve, and is delicious as well, noodle kugel is enjoyed on festive occasions in synagogues (Bar and Bat Mitzvah luncheon receptions, sisterhood brunches and dinners) and at family gatherings.

This recipe is for a rich, buttery dairy kugel flavored with pineapple and sweetened with a touch of sugar. Serve it as the main dish for a dairy meal or as a side dish with a plain broiled fish. A simple steamed vegetable, such as broccoli or carrots, and a tossed green salad round out the meal. Or, serve the kugel for Sunday brunch along with bagels and lox.

INGREDIENTS:

8 ounces medium to wide egg noodles

8 ounces (1 large package) cream cheese, at room temperature

6 tablespoons ($^3/_4$ stick) unsalted butter, at room temperature

2 tablespoons granulated white sugar

3 eggs (graded large)

1 cup (8 ounces) sour cream

1 can (8 ounces) crushed pineapple, well drained

½ cup crushed cornflakes

1 tablespoon unsalted butter, at room temperature

DIRECTIONS:

1. Preheat the oven to 350 degrees F.

2. Lightly butter a 2-quart baking dish (7 x 12 inches approximately).

3. Cook the noodles according to package directions. Drain well.

4. Meanwhile, in a large mixing bowl use an electric mixer to cream together the cream cheese and butter. Beat in the sugar, eggs, and the sour cream. Scrape the bowl and beaters and mix again. Stir in the drained pineapple, then the drained cooked noodles. Turn into the buttered baking dish. Level the top.

5. Use your fingers to mix together the cornflake crumbs and the tablespoon of butter until crumbly. Sprinkle the mixture evenly over the casserole.

6. Bake for 1 hour. The top will be toasted, the kugel set. Let cool for 10 minutes before cutting into squares.

VARIATION:

Cream Cheese-and-Apple Noodle Kugel

Omit the crushed pineapple. Substitute 1 cup of grated Golden Delicious, McIntosh, or other cooking apple that has been mixed with 1 teaspoon ground cinnamon.

COTTAGE CHEESE NOODLE KUGEL

Serves 6

I used to serve a dairy noodle kugel that had almost no sugar in it, and we always had lots of leftovers. When we visited my sister, she served a sweet version that my children devoured. I learn quickly. Here is a sweet, tasty main dish dairy kugel that your nieces and nephews will also devour.

In cold weather, begin the meal with a thick vegetarian soup, and serve fruit compote (page 329) and cake for dessert. In warm weather, select a chilled soup to start. For a luncheon meal or light supper, serve the noodle kugel with a tossed salad.

Small squares of the kugel can be served as a side dish. A delicious accompaniment to a simple baked or grilled salmon.

INGREDIENTS:

8 ounces medium or wide egg noodles

1 pound cottage cheese

1 cup (8 ounces) sour cream

½ cup granulated white sugar

2 eggs (graded large)

1 cup dark raisins

1 cup soft breadcrumbs or cornflake crumbs

DIRECTIONS:

1. Preheat the oven to 350 degrees F.

2. Grease a 9 x 13-inch baking dish.

3. Cook the noodles according to package directions. Drain well.

4. Meanwhile, in a large mixing bowl use a large spoon to beat the cottage cheese until it is creamy. Beat in the sour cream, the sugar, and finally the eggs. Stir in the drained cooked noodles, then the raisins. Turn into the greased baking dish. Level the top.

5. Sprinkle the breadcrumbs or cornflake crumbs evenly over the casserole.

6. Bake for 40 to 45 minutes. The top should be lightly toasted, the kugel set. Let cool for 10 minutes before cutting into squares.

VARIATION:

Fruited Dairy Noodle Kugel

Plump ¼ cup dried apricots by bringing them to the boil in water to cover by an inch. Remove from the heat. Cover the pot. Let the apricots stand in the water for 1 hour. Drain well. Dice the apricots. Reduce the sugar to ¼ cup and add the apricots with the raisins.

VEGETABLE AND FRUIT TSIMMES

Serves 6

"**D**on't make such a big *tsimmes* of it" isn't a message to a cook but an admonishment to not make such a fuss. The cook's big tsimmes is a mélange of vegetables, fruit, and sometimes meat that gets cooked together in an unhurried fashion. The popular meaning of the Yiddish word—a mix-up or a long procedure—derives from the fact that a tsimmes is made of a variety of ingredients mixed and cooked together over a long period of time.

Although preparing a tsimmes might sound like a big production, once the mixture is in the oven, all the work is done. And tsimmes reheats well, tasting even better the second day than the first, making advance preparation not only possible but desirable. Thus, tsimmes is served at Sabbath and holiday meals, one dish that can be fixed ahead of time when there are many last-minute things to do.

There is no one tsimmes, for the ingredients and flavorings that go into this classic dish vary according to locality and according to the individual cook. The preparation might be based on carrots, it can be a meaty dish (pages 150 and 152), or perhaps a vegetarian combination substantial enough to be served as the main dish.

In this tsimmes recipe, the vegetables are complemented by the mixed dried fruit and enlivened further by the lemon and orange flavors. The natural sweetness of the sweet potatoes, squash, and fruit is enhanced by the addition of brown sugar. The farfel, or egg barley, presents a contrasting, slightly chewy texture and absorbs the taste of the citrus, making it especially delicious. This is a filling tsimmes that can be served as a main dish with a light soup to begin the meal or as a side dish with brisket or roast chicken.

INGREDIENTS:

1 cup dried farfel (page 86)

2 cups mixed dried fruit (pitted prunes, apricots, peaches, pears) or 1 cup each pitted prunes and dried apricots

1 pound sweet potatoes or yams, peeled and cut into 1/2-inch rounds

1 pound white potatoes, peeled and cut into 1/2-inch chunks

1 pound butternut squash, peeled and cut into 1/2-inch rounds

1/2 cup firmly packed dark brown sugar

1/2 teaspoon ground cinnamon

Grated rinds of 1 lemon and 1 orange

2 tablespoons freshly squeezed lemon juice

1/4 cup freshly squeezed orange juice

2 cups boiling water

DIRECTIONS:

1. Preheat the oven to 325 degrees F.

2. Place the farfel on the bottom of a 9 x 13-inch baking dish.

3. Cut up the peaches and pears if they are larger than the other fruit. In a large bowl, mix together the dried fruit, sweet and white potatoes, and the squash. In a small bowl, mix together the brown sugar, cinnamon, lemon and orange rinds, and juices. Mix gently with the fruit and vegetables. Turn into the baking dish.

4. Carefully pour the boiling water over the casserole. Cover tightly with foil or a lid. Bake for 1 1/2 hours. Very carefully remove the foil or lid away from you so you don't get burned. Stir the tsimmes gently before serving. Serve hot. To reheat, add a little water as necessary.

MAMALIGA WITH CHEESE

Serves 6 to 8

As a child, a bowl of hot cooked yellow cornmeal was my favorite breakfast cereal, but quite frankly, I never associated it with Jewish cooking. I visited Jewish friends in the Bronx, Brooklyn, Manhattan (where I lived), Connecticut, and Long Island, but I never saw any of them eat a bowl of cornmeal. In fact, the only other person I ever knew to eat cornmeal mush was the father of a Puerto Rican friend, and it was one of his favorite breakfasts. To me, cornmeal mush was something only Puerto Ricans and my mother knew about.

I was surprised, then, to learn later in life of *mamaliga*, a Romanian preparation that was adopted by the Jews of that country along with the general population. Mamaliga is thick, so thick in fact that it can be shaped into a rectangle and cut into squares before being served (see the recipe for mamaliga in the chapter on breads, page 315). For dairy meals, the hot mamaliga might be mixed with cottage cheese, or it can baked with shredded cheese as it is in the recipe below.

INGREDIENTS:

2 cups yellow cornmeal

4 cups cold water

1 teaspoon salt

¼ cup (½ stick) unsalted butter

2 cups (8 ounces) shredded Cheddar cheese

DIRECTIONS:

1. Preheat the oven to 350 degrees F.

2. Grease a 1½-quart casserole.

3. In a 3- or 4-quart pot, mix together the cornmeal and the cold water. Stir in the salt. Bring to the boil over high heat, stirring constantly. As soon as the mixture comes to the boil, reduce the heat to low. Continue cooking for 5 minutes, stirring constantly to prevent lumps. The mixture will be smooth and very thick, becoming difficult to stir.

4. Stir in the butter, then 1 cup of the cheese. Spoon into the greased casserole, sprinkle on the remaining cup of cheese, and bake for 15 minutes or until the cheese topping has melted and is beginning to brown. Serve hot, with a salad on the side.

MY FATHER'S FAVORITE SANDWICH

Makes 2 open-faced sandwiches

My father loved to take a piece of fresh rye bread, smear it with a thick layer of schmaltz, salt the chicken fat, and cover it with thick slices of Bermuda onion. Mom claimed not to like this sandwich, but because of the onion, she ate it in self-defense. The cholesterol controversy changed all that, but if you want to get back to the heart and soul of the Jewish kitchen of yesteryear, try this sandwich.

INGREDIENTS:

> 2 slices seeded rye bread
> Schmaltz (page 40) to cover the bread
> Lots of salt
> 4 slices ($\frac{1}{4}$-inch thick) of a big Spanish onion,
> 　　3- to 4-inch diameter

DIRECTIONS:

1. Spread the rye bread with up to $\frac{1}{8}$ inch of chicken fat.

2. Sprinkle with salt (lavishly in the old days).

3. Cover with onion.

4. Munch.

6

Side Dishes

Vegetables and Grains,
Sweet and Savory

Side Dishes

Vegetables and grains of the peasantry—cabbage, potatoes, barley, kasha, for example—are transformed into noble preparations at the hands of Jewish cooks. Heaping bowls of deliciously robust red cabbage; crusty brown potato kugel; fruity noodle kugels; wholesome kasha mixed with homemade noodles; rice cooked with spices that flavor subtly while coloring delicately—a formidable array of traditional side dishes offers something for everyone.

Often, the most tempting Jewish side dishes make use of either leftovers or small quantities of ingredients on hand. *Piroshki, bourekas, kreplach, vareniki*—all are versions of a dough that is stuffed with vegetables, cheese, or meats to become dozens of mouthwatering pastries. Ordinary vegetables are prepared in combinations that add excitement to the meal. When cabbage is steamed and served as a colorless, unseasoned vegetable, it is not very interesting. But sauté the same cabbage with onions, and mix the vegetables with noodles, and now the table is adorned with an appealing mixture.

The attitude of the Jewish cook is not merely "I'll make do with what I have," but "How can I make this enticing?" A bowl of barley can be a nourishing cereal or a savory combination that includes mushrooms and broth baked into a tantalizing kugel. Plain baked potatoes are eaten, but it is the stuffed knishes and the crisp latkes that are remembered.

In Jewish cuisine, the side dishes do not simply round out the meal. They are appetizing, intriguing, memorable—conjuring up images of Grandma in the kitchen, using her hands and her eyes to measure everything from a cup of flour to a tablespoon of honey. Savor the sides: they are the heart and soul of Jewish cuisine.

APPLESAUCE

Makes 1½ quarts

"Why is the applesauce red?" If you have to ask the question, you have not yet enjoyed homemade applesauce, made red by being cooked with the skins left on the apples, rosier still by the addition of purple plums. And once you have made your own applesauce, it will be difficult for you to go back to the jars, which are more convenient but not comparable.

Applesauce is an accompaniment to many traditional Jewish preparations, including cheese blintzes and potato kugel. It is also a wonderful side dish with poultry, veal, and brisket, and makes a fine, light dessert. Peaches and pears can be added to make a fruit sauce, but note that the flavor of the pears will tend to dominate the preparation.

Food mills are among the kitchen gadgets that have been replaced by blenders and processors, but they are still being sold in kitchen supply stores, and they turn out the best applesauce. Your applesauce will be smooth, free of skins and seeds, but will not be puréed to the consistency of baby food.

Incidentally, if you are used to sweetened applesauce, you will be pleasantly surprised to find that the natural sugars in the fruit provide enough sweetness.

INGREDIENTS:

3 pounds McIntosh or other red cooking apples
6 to 8 fresh prune plums, pits removed
Water
Pinch cinnamon per serving (optional)

DIRECTIONS:

1. Wash the fruit well. Cut the apples into quarters. Do not peel the apples. It is not necessary to core the apples if the cooked apples will be run through a food mill later on. Do not peel the prune plums.

2. Place the fruit in a 5- or 6-quart pot with half an inch of water. Bring to the boil over high heat, reduce to a gentle boil, cover, and cook for 15 to 20 minutes, until the apples are tender. Stir two or three times during cooking.

3. When the fruit is very soft, stir again, then run through a food mill or use the back of a spoon to push through a strainer. Serve warm or chilled. If desired, sprinkle cinnamon on top of each serving. Refrigerate leftovers, or freeze in a freezer container, leaving an inch of headspace.

VARIATION:

Chunky Golden Applesauce

Omit the plums. Peel and core Golden Delicious apples. Cook the fruit as above until soft, but do not pass the fruit through a food mill or strainer. If desired, stir in half a cup of golden raisins while the fruit is still warm.

HONEYED CARROTS

Serves 4

Carrots sliced into rounds and glazed with honey are traditionally prepared for Rosh Hashanah. The Yiddish word for carrots, *meirin*, means "to increase," and carrots are therefore considered symbolic of the hope that one's fortune will increase in the New Year. The carrots are cut into rounds instead of strips because the rounds suggest coins, a symbol of prosperity. And because it is traditional to serve honey on Rosh Hashanah to usher in a sweet New Year, the carrots are cooked in honey.

Honeyed carrots can be enjoyed throughout the year as a tasty side dish for brisket, roast chicken, stuffed veal breast, and noodle-cheese kugels.

INGREDIENTS:

1 pound carrots, peeled and cut into thin rounds
½ cup water or ¼ cup each water and orange juice
¼ cup honey
¼ teaspoon cinnamon, nutmeg, or ground ginger
   (optional)

DIRECTIONS:

1. In a 1-quart pot, bring all the ingredients to the boil over high heat. Reduce the heat to a gentle boil, cover, and cook for 20 minutes or until the carrots are tender.

2. If the liquid is thin, remove the cover, raise the heat, and let boil down until the liquid is thickened and the carrots are glazed.

SEPHARDIC EGGPLANT SALAD

Makes about 3 cups

Although eggplant is the basic vegetable of this luscious salad, it is the liberal use of garlic that gives this Sephardic preparation much of its appeal. Garlic has been used as a seasoning since biblical days, when it grew wild in the Middle East. It is mentioned in the Bible as one of the vegetables that the Israelites ate in Egypt. In the days of the Talmud, garlic was purported to have aphrodisiac powers, and Ezra the Scribe wrote that garlic should be eaten on Friday nights because "it promotes and arouses sexual desires."

The cold-pressed extra-virgin fruity green olive oil of the Mediterranean will impart a stronger flavor than the milder olive oils that are sold in large containers in the United States. Use the more expensive fruity oil to duplicate the taste of the Sephardic salad. In the manner of Middle Eastern cookery, the eggplant and pepper are cooked until charred on the outside, tender inside.

This salad can be served on crackers or matzo as an appetizer; on a bed of lettuce, garnished with fresh tomatoes, as a salad; as a relish to accompany meats; or as a chilled vegetable. Because eggplant, tomatoes, and peppers are all harvested at the same time and prodigious quantities are often available at the end of the summer, it is appropriate to prepare this dish for Sukkot, the Festival of Ingathering.

INGREDIENTS:

> 1 eggplant, about 1¼ pounds (dark, shiny, long, and thin)
> 1 large green pepper (½ pound)
> 1 large red ripe tomato (½ pound)

1 tablespoon minced garlic
¼ teaspoon salt
2 tablespoons red wine vinegar
3 tablespoons olive oil

DIRECTIONS:

1. Prick the eggplant all over.

2. Preheat the broiler element of an electric oven (it is not necessary to preheat gas). Place the eggplant and pepper on a sheet of heavy foil, and broil about an inch from the heat source, turning frequently. The vegetables will be charred outside and tender inside in about 20 minutes. Turn off the heat. Cool the vegetables in the oven until they can be handled. (Alternatively, grill the vegetables over an open flame, turning frequently.)

3. Peel the skin off the eggplant. Slice the eggplant in half. Remove and discard the seeds if the eggplant is very seedy.

4. Peel the skin off the pepper. Slice the pepper in half. Remove and discard the core and seeds.

5. Slice the tomato in half. Scoop out the seeds.

6. In a big wooden chopping bowl, using a curved knife, chop the eggplant, pepper, and tomato coarsely. Sprinkle on the garlic, continuing to chop fine. Mix in the salt, vinegar, and olive oil. Taste and correct the seasonings. Serve chilled.

BULGUR SALAD

Serves 4 to 6

This refreshing bulgur (cracked wheat) salad, known in the Middle East as _tabooli,_ is widely enjoyed in Israel, where fresh vegetables such as cucumbers and radishes are often included. In the United States, the popularity of the all-natural combination of wheat, fresh herbs, an unsaturated oil, and raw fresh vegetables gives this dish appeal as well.

When soaked in water, the bulgur absorbs the water and triples in volume, becoming soft enough to eat. It is then drained, mixed with a noteworthy quantity of scallions and parsley, and a simple dressing of olive oil and lemon juice. Select an olive oil that you like: a fruity olive oil will have a pronounced taste; a milder-tasting olive oil will not be as noticeable. Tomatoes are added just before the salad is eaten so that their juice does not water down the mixture. The addition of other fresh vegetables is optional.

INGREDIENTS:

1 cup bulgur (cracked wheat)

3 cups cold water for soaking

$\frac{1}{2}$ to $\frac{3}{4}$ cup chopped scallions

$\frac{1}{2}$ to $\frac{3}{4}$ cup chopped fresh parsley

4 tablespoons olive oil, approximately

2 tablespoons freshly squeezed lemon juice, approximately

2 or 3 red ripe tomatoes, chopped

1 cup chopped seeded cucumber (optional)

$\frac{1}{4}$ to $\frac{1}{2}$ cup sliced radishes (optional)

Romaine leaves

DIRECTIONS:

1. Place the bulgur in a 1½- to 2-quart mixing bowl. Add the 3 cups of cold water. Cover the bowl with plastic wrap. Allow the bulgur to stand at room temperature for a minimum of 3 hours, as long as overnight. When it is ready, it should be chewy but no longer hard, and it will have absorbed most of the water. Drain well, pressing out excess water.

2. Mix in the minimum amounts of scallions and parsley. Stir in the olive oil and lemon juice. Taste, adding more scallions, parsley, oil, and lemon juice as desired. The salad can be served immediately or covered and refrigerated for later use. It will keep in the refrigerator for several days but should not be frozen.

3. Serve as a first course with large romaine leaves (the bulgur salad and romaine are eaten together as a "sandwich") or as a side dish to accompany grilled poultry, meat, or fish. Tomatoes, along with the optional cucumbers and radishes, can be mixed in just prior to serving, or they can be passed separately.

SWEET-AND-SOUR RED CABBAGE

Serves 4 to 6

Red cabbage is a popular vegetable in German and Hungarian cuisines, where it is cooked with sugar and vinegar to accompany beef, pork, duck, goose, and game. The Jews of these countries also cooked red cabbage to serve alongside brisket, veal, and poultry, and today sweet-and sour-red cabbage remains popular among Ashkenazim.

Vegetable and fruit combinations are well known in European cooking, and apples are often cooked along with the cabbage. Cooked red cabbage has a savory tartness to it, and the choice of apples can bring out the pleasantly sour taste of the cabbage or contribute to the sweetness of the dish. Green cooking apples will make the taste more tart; Golden Delicious will make it sweeter.

When you fill an eight-quart pot three-quarters to the top with shredded red cabbage, you may well think, "My, this is going to feed the whole neighborhood." But the cabbage cooks down, and by the time you finish tasting—once to see if it's tender, a few times to see if it's sour enough, again to see if it's sweet enough—you have just enough to fill the serving bowl.

INGREDIENTS:

1 head (3 pounds) red cabbage, cored and shredded

2 cups water

1 pound apples, peeled, cored, and shredded
   (optional)

1/4 cup firmly packed dark brown sugar

1/3 cup distilled white vinegar

2 tablespoons unbleached white flour

DIRECTIONS:

1. In an 8-quart pot, bring the shredded cabbage and water to the boil over high heat. Reduce the heat to a gentle boil, cover, and cook for about 15 minutes. Mix in the optional apples. Continue cooking for about 15 minutes, until the cabbage and apples are very tender.

2. Sprinkle the sugar over the cooked cabbage.

3. In a small bowl or a measuring cup, stir together the vinegar and flour to make a paste. Stir the mixture into the cabbage. Mix well. Bring the liquid back to the boil, stirring until smooth and thickened.

4. Cook for another minute or two, mix again, then taste and correct the seasonings. Serve hot as an accompaniment for brisket, veal breast, chicken fricassee, or any roast meat or poultry.

CABBAGE AND NOODLES

Serves 4

Another Ashkenazic preparation that originated in the kitchens of Germany and Hungary, this dish of the peasantry makes use of green cabbage, a vegetable that survives early frost and stores well during cold winters. The combination of sautéed cabbage and noodles is filling and tasty, and can be served as a main dish. The German preparation is presented in the basic recipe, the Hungarian version as a variation.

In today's more prosperous times, cabbage and noodles are eaten more as a side dish than as a light meal. In Jewish cuisine, the preparation can be served at any meal, because the vegetables can be sautéed in chicken fat for meat meals, butter for dairy meals, or vegetable oil for either. The contrasting tastes and textures of the mixture make it especially suitable to serve with plain broiled or grilled chicken, fish, veal, or lamb chops.

INGREDIENTS:

2 tablespoons schmaltz (page 40), vegetable oil, or
   unsalted butter
½ cup chopped onion
3 cups shredded green cabbage
Salt and freshly ground black pepper
3 cups cooked medium or wide egg noodles

DIRECTIONS:

1. In a 10-inch skillet, heat the chicken fat, oil, or butter with the onion over moderately low heat. Cook, stirring occasionally, until the onion just begins to brown.

2. Mix in the cabbage. Continue cooking, uncovered, for about 15 minutes, until tender. Stir from time to time to keep the cabbage from sticking. If the cabbage begins to brown, reduce the heat.

3. Add salt and pepper to taste, then mix in the cooked noodles. Serve hot as a side dish with broiled meat, poultry, or fish. As a dairy main dish, cook the vegetables in either oil or butter, and serve with sour cream on the side.

VARIATION:

Hungarian-style Cabbage and Noodles

In Step 1, cook the onion until wilted but not brown. Before adding the cabbage to the skillet, sprinkle 1 teaspoon of paprika on the onion and stir in 1 teaspoon of caraway seeds that have been slightly crushed with the back of a spoon.

CABBAGE STRUDEL

Makes two 14-inch rolls

Crisp, delicate layers of pastry filled with a prosaic vegetable might seem incongruous to us today. But to the impoverished of Austria and Hungary, cabbage strudel was a welcome addition to the repertoire of cabbage preparations. The contrast between the fine pastry and the commonplace but robust-tasting vegetable is one of the reasons cabbage strudel remains popular to this day. A tribute to ingenuity.

INGREDIENTS:

1 tablespoon schmaltz (page 40), unsalted butter, or
   vegetable oil

1 cup chopped onion

3 cups shredded green cabbage

1 teaspoon minced garlic (optional)

Lots of salt, freshly ground black pepper, and
   paprika

1¼ cups unbleached white flour (stir the flour, spoon
   gently into a dry-measure cup, then level with
   the edge of a spatula)

¼ teaspoon salt (optional)

⅜ cup warm water (not over 100 degrees F.)

2 tablespoons beaten egg

1 tablespoon vegetable oil

> 2 tablespoons melted schmaltz (page 40), unsalted
> butter, or vegetable oil for brushing the pastry
> before rolling up (Step 8)
> Beaten egg for brushing the top

DIRECTIONS:

1. For the filling, in a 10-inch skillet heat the chicken fat, butter, or oil over moderate heat. Add the onion and cook, stirring occasionally, until the onion is wilted and just beginning to brown. Stir in the cabbage and the optional garlic. Cook, stirring occasionally, until the cabbage is soft but not brown. Season well with salt, pepper, and paprika. Remove the skillet from the heat. The cabbage will continue to cook a bit from its own heat.

2. For the dough, in a medium-size mixing bowl place the flour and the optional salt. In a small bowl or a cup, mix together the water, 2 tablespoons of egg, and the tablespoon of oil. Add to the flour all at once. Stir with a wooden spoon until the mixture holds together and forms a dough.

3. Turn out onto a clean, smooth work surface. Knead for about 3 minutes, until the dough becomes smooth and elastic. If necessary, dust the dough and the work surface with a little flour. Cover with a slightly damp, clean kitchen towel and let rest for about 15 minutes.

4. Preheat the oven to 425 degrees F.

5. Grease a large baking sheet.

6. Lightly flour a large clean, smooth work surface. Divide the dough in half. Work with one piece of dough at a time, keeping the other piece covered with the damp but not wet kitchen towel.

7. Flatten the dough between your hands, and gently stretch to a 6-inch circle. Place the dough on the floured surface. Place your hands under the dough, palms down. Now, working from the center outward, stretch the dough

gently over the backs of your hands. If you are not making progress, use a rolling pin from time to time to stretch and even out the dough. The goal is a rectangle about 12 x 14 inches, larger if you can manage it.

8. When the dough is the correct size, trim off the thick edges. Brush the dough thoroughly with 1 tablespoon of melted chicken fat, or melted butter, or oil. Spread half of the filling in a strip an inch in from the long edge of the strudel, ½ inch from the sides. The cabbage will cover about 3 inches of dough.

9. Roll the dough tightly around the filling as you would a jelly roll. Pinch the long edge against the filled roll, then pinch the ends and tuck under. Carefully transfer to the greased baking sheet. Brush all exposed surfaces with well-beaten egg.

10. Repeat Steps 7, 8, and 9 with the second piece of dough and the remaining filling.

11. Bake in the middle of the oven for about 15 minutes, until golden brown. Slice into serving-size pieces and serve hot or warm as an appetizer, soup accompaniment, side dish, or a snack with tea. For a dairy meal, serve sour cream on the side.

PIROSHKI

Makes 20 to 22 piroshki

The small pastries called *piroshki* (a Russian and a Yiddish word) are popular in both Russian and Polish cuisines and are also favored by Ashkenazic Jews. Piroshki are related to the strudels of the Austro-Hungarian Empire (see the previous recipe) and the *bourekas* (page 253) of the Ottoman Empire. Large versions of piroshki are known as *pirogen* (plural of *pirog,* or pie).

Just as kreplach and knishes have an impressive variety of stuffings, piroshki come with numerous tasty fillings. The cabbage filling here, and mushrooms and potatoes (see the variations), are favorite vegetable fillings, and meat or cheese piroshki are enjoyed as well.

Enjoy piroshki as a soup accompaniment, an hors d'oeuvre, or as a tasty little snack.

INGREDIENTS:

1½ teaspoons vegetable oil
¼ cup finely chopped onion
1 cup finely chopped green cabbage
Salt and freshly ground black pepper
1 cup unbleached white flour (stir the flour, spoon
    gently into a dry-measure cup, then level with
    the edge of a spatula)
Pinch of salt
⅓ cup solid white vegetable shortening
2 tablespoons water, approximately
1 egg yolk beaten with 2 teaspoons water, for brushing

DIRECTIONS:

1. Grease a large baking sheet.

2. For the filling, in a small skillet heat the oil with the onion over moderate heat until the onion is wilted. Stir in the cabbage. Cook for about 5 minutes, stirring occasionally, until the cabbage is softened. Season well with salt and pepper. Leave the cooked cabbage in the skillet on the turned-off burner.

3. For the dough, in a small mixing bowl stir together the flour and a pinch of salt. Using a fork or your fingers, work in the shortening until the particles are small and evenly distributed, as for pie dough. Sprinkle in the water a tablespoon at a time, stirring until the dough forms a ball.

4. Preheat the oven to 400 degrees F.

5. Flatten the dough with your palms, then place between two sheets of wax paper. With a rolling pin, roll out the dough to a 12-inch circle. With a cookie cutter, cut as many $2\frac{5}{8}$-inch rounds as you can. Reroll the scraps and repeat until you've cut 20 to 22 rounds in all. Keep the cut rounds covered with a clean kitchen towel to prevent the dough from drying out.

6. Place a slightly heaping teaspoon of filling off-center on each round. Fold the dough in half over the filling. Press down to pinch the edges to seal. Place the filled pockets of dough on the greased baking sheet. Brush well with the beaten egg yolk.

7. Bake in the middle of the oven for 12 to 15 minutes, until golden. Transfer to a serving plate. Serve hot, with sour cream for dairy meals.

VARIATIONS:

Mushroom Piroshki

> Omit the cabbage. In Step 2, use a tablespoon of oil, increase the onion to half a cup, and substitute one and one-quarter cups of chopped mushrooms for the cabbage. Season the mushrooms with 2 tablespoons of chopped fresh parsley, two teaspoons of chopped fresh dill, and salt and pepper.

Potato Piroshki

> Prepare half of the filling for potato knishes on page 290.

Meat Piroshki

> Use the filling for kreplach on page 88.

Pirog

> For one large pirog, fill the whole twelve-inch circle of dough (Step 5) with the filling. Fold in half, pressing the edges to seal. Bake for about 30 minutes, until golden. Cut into wedges to serve.

CHEESE-AND-SPINACH BOUREKAS

Makes 36 bourekas

The holiday of Shavuot comes in late spring, when sheep and goats—the primary source of meat in Mediterranean and Middle Eastern countries since biblical days—are still feeding their young, and milk is especially plentiful. The tradition of consuming milk products and the availability of milk support and complement each other, therefore many special cheese preparations were eaten by the Jews of Greece and Turkey on Shavuot.

Among the most popular of the traditional dairy foods still eaten by Sephardim on Shavuot are exceptionally crisp, flaky pastries that use the paper-thin sheets of dough known as *phyllo,* including spinach-and-cheese pies *(spanakopita)* and triangular-shaped cheese-filled *tyropita.* A more general term for the pastries is *bourekas,* which can be large pies but more often refers to smaller pastries in the shape of logs or triangles. Bourekas are filled with cheese, vegetables (eggplant and spinach are especially popular), cheese-vegetable combinations, or meat.

The flaky pastry used in this recipe is prepared phyllo leaves, which are pliable when a fresh package is opened, but rapidly become dry and brittle. Always have all ingredients ready and at hand when working with phyllo. Work quickly, keeping the unused portions of dough completely covered with a clean kitchen towel until ready for use. It is helpful to practice the wrapping technique using a piece of wax paper.

INGREDIENTS:

> 1 cup cooked chopped spinach leaves, well drained
> then patted dry with paper towels
> ½ cup (4 ounces) feta cheese

½ cup (4 ounces) pot cheese or farmer cheese
¼ cup grated Parmesan cheese
Dash of nutmeg or cinnamon (optional)
1 egg (graded large), beaten
12 sheets phyllo dough (about ½ pound)
¼ cup (½ stick) unsalted butter, melted and mixed
    with ¼ cup olive oil

DIRECTIONS:

1. Butter or oil a 10 x 15-inch baking sheet, preferably one with raised sides. Set aside.

2. In a small mixing bowl, combine the spinach with the cheeses, the optional nutmeg or cinnamon, and the egg.

3. Spread the phyllo leaves open, and leaving them stacked, cut lengthwise into 3 strips. You now have 3 long stacks of dough, 12 strips in each. To prevent the phyllo from drying out, cover 2 stacks of dough completely with a slightly damp, but not wet, kitchen towel.

4. Preheat the oven to 400 degrees F.

5. Working on a clean, smooth surface with one stack of dough, carefully peel off one piece of phyllo. Cover the remaining stack of 11 strips. Using a pastry brush, brush the surface of the strip well with the melted butter and oil. Fold one long side of the strip toward the middle, then fold the other long side toward the middle (illustration 1). The two edges should meet in the middle, making one long, thin strip of dough. Now brush the newly exposed surface with the melted butter mixture. Place a heaping tea-spoonful of filling at one end of this long, narrow strip of dough (2). Fold the dough over the filling to make a triangle (3). Continue folding the dough to enclose the filling, keeping the triangle shape as you would to fold a flag (4). You will end up with many folds of pastry around the filling.

Place the filled triangle on the baking sheet. Repeat with the remaining dough and filling.

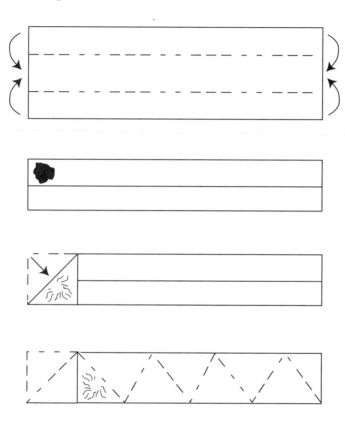

6. Brush the tops of the pastries with the butter and oil mixture. The pastries can be refrigerated at this point for up to 24 hours.

7. Bake in the middle of the oven for 10 to 15 minutes, until golden brown (allow a few minutes extra time for cold bourekas). Serve hot as an hors d'oeuvre or to accompany a vegetarian soup. Cheese bourekas are particularly good with the thick lentil soup on page 112.

CHEESE KREPLACH

There are many folktales that explain the custom of eating dairy dishes on Shavuot. One is that the Israelites abstained from eating meat dishes as a personal sacrifice before receiving the Torah. Another legend tells of the Israelites returning to their homes after receiving the Torah at Mount Sinai: there was little time to ritually slaughter and prepare a meat meal; therefore they put together a dairy meal that could be prepared more quickly. Others suggest simply that people drank milk after receiving the Torah because they were very hungry and milk was readily available. On a more spiritual level, some say that the Torah is as nourishing to the mind as milk is to the body, and therefore dairy products should be enjoyed on the holiday that celebrates the giving of the Torah to Moses and the Children of Israel.

Three-sided cheese kreplach are among the dairy treats enjoyed on Shavuot. The number three is significant in connection with the giving of the Torah because Moses was the third child of his parents, and the Torah was given in the third month of the Hebrew calendar, Sivan.

The traditional dough for kreplach, whether meat or cheese, is a basic noodle dough made of flour, eggs, and water (see page 89). The sour cream dough used in this recipe for dairy kreplach is a variation on the noodle dough. The sour cream makes a flaky, tender pastry that is easier to roll out than the traditional kreplach dough.

Whether cheese kreplach are boiled, fried, or baked, they are an excellent accompaniment to vegetable soups. Baked or fried kreplach can be passed around as hors d'oeuvres; the boiled version makes a tasty dessert with cinnamon and sugar or a fruit sauce (see page 217).

INGREDIENTS:

> 1½ cups unbleached white flour (stir the flour,
>   spoon gently into a dry-measure cup, then
>   level with the edge of a spatula)
> ½ teaspoon salt
> ½ teaspoon baking powder
> ½ cup (4 ounces) sour cream
> 1 egg (graded large), beaten
> ½ cup (4 ounces) pot cheese
> ¼ cup farmer cheese
> 2 tablespoons beaten egg
> Vegetable oil for fried kreplach
> Beaten egg yolk for glazing baked kreplach

DIRECTIONS:

1. For the dough, in a small mixing bowl use a fork to stir together the flour, salt, and baking powder. Stir in the sour cream and 1 beaten egg. Mix with a fork and your fingers until the dough comes together to form a ball. Cover with a clean kitchen towel while you mix the filling.

2. For the filling, in a small bowl stir together the pot cheese, farmer cheese, and the 2 tablespoons of beaten egg. Set aside.

3. Divide the dough in half. Work with one piece of dough at a time, keeping the other half covered. On a clean, lightly floured work surface, roll out the dough to a 12-inch square. Lightly flour the dough as necessary. If you find the dough difficult to roll out, allow it to rest for a few minutes, covered with a clean towel. (This will allow the gluten to relax.)

4. Cut the dough into sixteen 3-inch squares. Using half the filling, place 1 level teaspoon of filling slightly off-center on each square. Fold the dough over the filling to form a triangle. Press the edges together to seal well. Set the triangles aside on a floured plate or work surface, and cover with a clean kitchen towel.

5. Repeat the process with the reserved piece of dough, filling and shaping 16 more kreplach.

6. **To boil,** in a 6-quart pot bring 4 quarts of water to the boil. Quickly drop in the kreplach one by one. Partially cover the pot, reduce to a gentle boil, and cook for 3 to 5 minutes. Remove with a slotted spoon and serve immediately.

To fry, in a large skillet heat ¼ inch of vegetable oil until the oil is hot but not yet smoking, 375 degrees F. Add as many kreplach at a time as will fit comfortably. Fry until golden on both sides, which will take under a minute. Drain well on paper towels. Serve hot.

To bake, preheat the oven to 400 degrees F. Place the kreplach on a greased baking sheet. Brush with beaten egg. Bake for 12 to 15 minutes, until golden. Serve hot.

VARENIKI

Makes 24 vareniki

The Ukrainian version of filled dumplings is known as *vareniki*. In the general population of Ukraine, sauerkraut vareniki are especially popular; but as a Jewish preparation, cheese or fruit vareniki are more traditional. Other common fillings for the dumplings in both the broad population and among Jews of Ukrainian descent are seasoned potatoes, chopped liver, and mushrooms.

In vareniki, a homemade noodle dough is rolled thin, filled, then folded over to form a half-moon. Cheese vareniki are a tasty soup accompaniment, and like other dairy preparations, they are eaten on Shavuot. A big portion of cheese vareniki topped with sour cream can make a satisfying light meal. The fruit-filled version is a marvelous snack or dessert, especially with a cup of hot tea. Vareniki aficionados will argue that the twenty-four dumplings of this recipe are barely enough for one person, and you may want to double or even triple the recipe if such a devotee is coming to the table.

To prevent the noodle dough from drying out, first prepare one of the fillings, then the dough.

PREPARING THE FILLINGS

BLUEBERRY FILLING:

> **2 cups fresh blueberries**
> **3 tablespoons granulated white sugar**

In a 1-quart pot, cook the berries and sugar over very low heat, stirring occasionally, until the berries pop and the sugar dissolves. Set aside to cool.

CHERRY FILLING:

> 2 cups fresh sour cherries, halved and pitted
> 4 tablespoons granulated white sugar

In a 1-quart pot, cook the cherries and sugar over very low heat, stirring occasionally, until the cherries become soft and the sugar dissolves. Add a little more sugar if the cherries are too sour. Set aside to cool.

CHEESE FILLING:

> 1 cup (8 ounces) pot cheese
> 1 egg (graded large), beaten
> 2 tablespoons unbleached white flour
> 1 tablespoon granulated white sugar
> Optional additions: 1 teaspoon vanilla extract
> and/or 2 teaspoons grated orange rind

Mix together all the ingredients. Set aside.

PREPARING THE DOUGH

> ³/₄ cup unbleached white flour (stir the flour,
> spoon gently into a dry-measure cup, then
> level with the edge of a spatula)
> ¹/₄ teaspoon salt
> 1 egg (graded large)
> Water as necessary
> Additional flour for rolling

1. In a medium-size mixing bowl, stir together the flour and salt. Use your fingers to work in the egg. Add water a few drops at a time until the mixture clings together to form a ball of dough.

2. Turn out the dough onto a clean work surface and let rest, covered, for 10 minutes.

3. In a 4-quart pot, bring 3 quarts of water to the boil.

4. Divide the dough in half. Work with one piece of dough at a time, keeping the remainder covered. On a clean, floured surface use a rolling pin to roll out the dough to a 12-inch circle. Cut into 3-inch rounds. Reroll the scraps and cut more rounds, making 12 in all.

5. Place a teaspoon of filling off-center on each round. Do not overfill or the filling will leak out during cooking. Fold the dough over the filling to make a half-moon. Press the edges together to seal well.

6. Repeat with the second piece of dough and the remaining filling.

7. Drop the dumplings into the boiling water, cooking as many as will fit comfortably at once. Adjust the heat to a moderate boil. Cook the dumplings for 5 to 8 minutes. Remove with a slotted spoon. Serve immediately. If desired, drizzle melted butter on the vareniki. Serve sour cream and a cinnamon-sugar mixture on the side.

SPÄTZLE

Serves 4 to 6

The tender, irregularly shaped flour-and-egg dumplings known in Switzerland, Germany, and Austria as _spätzle_ use the ingredients of homemade rolled noodles in different proportions. They are produced when a thick batter is passed through the small holes of a colander or the larger holes of a spätzle-maker into boiling water. The small pieces that break off into the water are cooked within minutes, swelling to become light and fluffy.

Once you discover the fun of making your own spätzle, you may be motivated to buy a spätzle-maker from a kitchen specialty store. The spätzle-maker that looks like an open grater with $5/16$-inch holes and a hopper on top is easier to use than the version that looks like a food mill with large holes. If you use a colander, be sure that the bottom of the colander is at least an inch above the top of the water. Colander-produced spätzle will be daintier than those made from devices that have larger holes.

In Jewish cuisine, spätzle are particularly relished as a side dish with the rich gravies of brisket, fricassee, and veal. They are delicious when served with stews that have not been prepared with potatoes, or in place of pasta with any pasta sauce. Spätzle are also enjoyed as a main dish when mixed with butter or oil and topped with grated cheese.

INGREDIENTS:

> 3½ **cups unbleached white flour (stir the flour,**
> **spoon gently into a dry-measure cup, then**
> **level with the edge of a spatula)**
> 1 **teaspoon salt**

6 eggs (graded large or extra large)
$1/2$ to $3/4$ cup water

DIRECTIONS:

1. In a large mixing bowl, mix the flour and the salt. Make a well in the center, and add the eggs and $1/2$ cup of water. Beat with a large spoon or a heavy-duty electric mixer until the batter is smooth and begins to develop air bubbles on top. This will take 1 or 2 minutes with an electric mixer, 5 to 10 minutes by hand. Add a little more water if the batter is too stiff. It will be thicker than cake batter but must be fluid enough to easily go through the holes of the colander or spätzle-maker.

2. In an 8-quart pot, bring 4 quarts of water to the boil. If using a colander, hold the colander over the pot, pour the batter into the colander, and use the back of a large kitchen spoon to push the batter through. For a spätzle-maker, move the hopper back and forth or turn the handle to force the batter through. When all the batter is pushed through, stir the spätzle with a clean spoon, and cook for an additional 3 or 4 minutes, until tender and cooked through. Taste for tenderness.

3. Drain the cooked spätzle in a clean colander or a strainer. Return the spätzle to the pot and mix with a little oil to keep them from sticking to each other. (Use butter if they will be served with cheese.) Serve as soon as possible after the spätzle are cooked.

4. Although spätzle are most tender when served immediately after they are cooked, they can be prepared ahead of time. To prepare spätzle in advance, cook as above. Drain, then run cold water over the spätzle, cooling them thoroughly. Refrigerate or freeze. Reheat by steaming, or sauté the spätzle in oil or butter.

MASHED POTATOES

Serves 4

In kosher cooking, where meat and dairy products are not eaten together, mashed potatoes that are to be served with meat meals must be prepared with ingredients other than butter and milk to become creamy and tasty. Chicken fat and chicken broth, the traditional replacements, make rich-tasting potatoes. Oil and vegetable broth are used for flavorsome pareve potatoes. The broth can be omitted for drier potatoes.

Bits of potato are considered desirable in traditional Jewish mashed potatoes, and an old-fashioned potato masher is recommended for a coarse consistency. An electric mixer will yield smoother potatoes.

INGREDIENTS:

2 pounds white potatoes (about 6 medium)
2 tablespoons schmaltz (page 40), olive oil, or
    vegetable oil
¼ to ½ cup chicken broth or vegetable broth
    (optional)
Salt and freshly ground black pepper

DIRECTIONS:

1. Peel the potatoes, cut into quarters, and cook in boiling salted water until tender. Drain well.

2. With a potato masher, mash the potatoes. Add the chicken fat or oil, continue to mix, then mash in the broth to the consistency desired. Season to taste.

VARIATION:

Mashed Potatoes with Fried Onion

In an 8-inch skillet over moderate heat, cook 1 cup of chopped onion in 1 to 2 tablespoons of chicken fat, olive oil, or vegetable oil until the onion browns lightly around the edges. Add salt to taste. Mix the fried onion into the mashed potatoes.

VEGETABLE CUTLETS

Makes eight 3-inch cutlets; allow 2 or 3 per person

In the old days, no one ever heard the word "leftovers." Any food that was left over became something new. So it is with the vegetable cutlet, which consists of an assortment of vegetables bound together by a cup or so of mashed potatoes. And as with any other preparation that depends on what happens to be in the refrigerator, there were only two measurements: "Well, you know, add matzo meal until it looks right" and "A handful, that's how much."

In this updated recipe, more conventional measurements are used to produce an exceptionally tasty side dish. While you can start with fresh vegetables and cook them, no one will ever know if you use yesterday's peas and carrots. This recipe is for a pareve preparation. If leftover mashed potatoes that have been made with schmaltz are used, chicken fat can be substituted for the oil both for sautéing the onion and for frying the cutlets.

INGREDIENTS:

2 medium-size potatoes ($\frac{2}{3}$ pound), peeled and cut
   into halves or quarters
Salt and freshly ground black pepper
1 tablespoon vegetable oil
$\frac{3}{4}$ cup chopped onion
$\frac{1}{2}$ cup sliced fresh mushrooms
2 cups cooked mixed vegetables (peas, carrots,
   green beans)

1 egg (graded large), slightly beaten
¹/₂ cup matzo meal
2 tablespoons vegetable oil for frying

DIRECTIONS:

1. Cook the potatoes in boiling salted water until tender. Drain and mash with a fork or a potato masher. Season well with salt and pepper. Set aside. If you have leftover mashed potatoes, you will need 1¹/₃ cups of potatoes.

2. Meanwhile, in an 8-inch skillet heat the oil over moderately low heat. Add the onion and sauté until the onion is golden, then add the mushrooms. Cook, stirring occasionally, until the mushrooms are tender.

3. In a medium-size bowl, gently mix together the potatoes, onion, mushrooms, and the mixed vegetables. Taste and correct the seasoning. Stir in the egg, then mix in the matzo meal. Shape the mixture between wet hands into eight 3-inch patties.

4. **To fry,** in a 10-inch skillet heat 2 tablespoons of vegetable oil over moderate heat. Fry the cutlets until they are brown on one side. Add more oil if necessary, then turn and brown the other side. The cutlets should cook slowly enough so that they are heated through when browned.

   To bake, preheat the oven to 350 degrees F. Oil a baking sheet lightly. Place the cutlets on the baking sheet. Bake in the middle of the oven for 30 minutes or until they are golden.

KASHA

Makes about 4 cups

The hefty-tasting grain we call kasha, known in the United States as buckwheat groats, comes from Russia. In Russia, however, kasha is a term used both to refer to many different grains and to the preparation that results when grains are cooked to the consistency of porridge. The term can refer to buckwheat, oats, millet, or other grains, especially when cooked into a mush.

When kasha made its way across the ocean with Russian Jews in the early 1900s, the term was revised to become limited to one grain, buckwheat. Kasha is still eaten as a hot breakfast cereal, but in Jewish cuisine the grain is mixed with beaten egg and toasted before it is cooked in liquid, making each grain separate. The kasha is then served as a side dish at dinner (try kasha with brisket or chicken fricassee gravy), stuffed into a knish in place of potatoes, made into a kugel, or partnered with bowtie noodles in kasha varnishkes (see the following recipe).

Kasha has a hearty wheat taste that will be appreciated by those who enjoy strong but not spicy flavors. The robust flavor of the kasha is moderated when the grain is combined with vegetables (see variation) or with bowtie noodles.

INGREDIENTS:

> 1 cup kasha (buckwheat groats)
> 1 egg (graded large), beaten well
> 2 cups water (chicken or beef broth for a meat
>   meal)
> ¼ teaspoon salt (optional)

DIRECTIONS:

1. Preheat an electric burner to moderate. A gas burner does not need to be preheated.

2. In a 2-quart pot, use a fork to mix together the kasha and the beaten egg. Set the pot over moderate heat and cook, stirring constantly, until the grains separate and turn slightly dark, 3 to 4 minutes.

3. Meanwhile, bring the water or broth and the optional salt to the boil in another pot.

4. Pour the boiling water (or broth) over the toasted kasha, stirring with the fork. Turn the heat just low enough so the liquid boils gently, cover the pot, and cook for 15 minutes or until the kasha is tender and all the liquid is absorbed.

VARIATIONS:

Kasha with Onions

Sauté a cup of chopped onion in a tablespoon of chicken fat (for a meat meal), butter (for a dairy meal), or vegetable oil (meat or dairy meal). Mix with the cooked kasha.

Kasha with Onions and Mushrooms

Sauté a cup of chopped onion and 2 cups of sliced mushrooms in 2 tablespoons of chicken fat, butter, or vegetable oil. Mix with the cooked kasha.

KASHA VARNISHKES

Serves 4 to 6

For Eastern European Jews, the marriage of kasha and bowtie noodles, a preparation known as *kasha varnishkes,* was originally an association of economic necessity. Partnering the two starches in one dish made a nutritious and filling combination that was much more affordable than meat. While kasha varnishkes is now served as a side dish to accompany meat and poultry, in earlier times it might be eaten as the main dish, often along with some form of cooked cabbage to round out the meal.

The strong, wheaty taste of the grain is offset by the more delicate noodles. The addition of the sautéed onions gives the preparation a richer taste while somewhat muting the flavor of the kasha. This recipe uses one cup of cooked kasha to approximately two cups of cooked homemade bowtie noodles, but you can vary the proportions to taste.

I admit that giving ninety-six pieces of dough a quick twist to make bows becomes tedious, but it is very satisfying to bite into a homemade noodle, which will have more substance and more taste than a dried packaged noodle. (To substitute packaged noodles for fresh, cook half a pound of bowtie noodles as the package directs.) If using leftover cold kasha, steam to reheat.

INGREDIENTS:

1½ cups unbleached white flour (stir the flour,
    spoon gently into a dry-measure cup, then
    level with the edge of a spatula)

½ teaspoon salt

2 eggs (graded large)

2 tablespoons water, approximately

1½ **tablespoons schmaltz (page 40) or vegetable oil**
    (if onion is used)
1½ **cups chopped onion (optional)**
2 **cups hot cooked kasha (**½ **preceding recipe)**

DIRECTIONS:

1. In a medium-size mixing bowl, mix together the flour and salt. Using your fingers, a fork, or a spoon, work in the eggs. The dough will be slightly crumbly. Add water a little at a time until the dough holds together well. Turn out the dough onto a lightly floured work surface. Knead 20 times. Cover the dough with a bowl or a damp but not wet kitchen towel. Allow the dough to rest for 10 minutes.

2. If the optional onion will be used, in an 8-inch skillet heat the chicken fat or vegetable oil over moderate heat. Cook the onion until it is wilted and golden, just beginning to brown. Keep warm over very low heat.

3. Divide the dough in half. Roll each half into a 6 x 18-inch rectangle. Cut into 1½-inch squares. Repeat with the other half of the dough.

4. In a 4-quart pot, bring 3 quarts of water to the boil.

5. Meanwhile, shape each square into a bow by holding opposite sides and pulling gently while twisting your hands in opposite directions. When all the bows are twisted and the water is boiling, add salt to the water if you like, then drop in the bows as quickly as possible without squashing them when you pick them up. Cook for 3 minutes after the last bow has been added. Taste for tenderness, cooking a little longer if necessary. Drain in a colander.

6. Toss the drained hot noodles with the hot kasha and the optional onion. Serve as a side dish with brisket, chicken fricassee, or any meat dish that features a rich gravy.

WHEAT PILAF

Serves 6

Bulgur, a toasted cracked wheat product known in Israel and throughout the Middle East, is important in the diets of the inhabitants of the region. It can be prepared without further cooking by being soaked in water until it swells. The softened but coarse grains are then combined with herbs, olive oil, and lemon juice to become an intriguing salad (see page 241).

When bulgur is steamed in broth, it becomes the Turkish preparation known as wheat pilaf. The grains are more tender, the wheaty taste more subtle than in the uncooked wheat salad. Wheat pilaf is reminiscent of cooked kasha, but the taste of the grain is considerably more delicate. It can be prepared plain or laden with fruit and nuts. Enjoy wheat pilaf as a side dish with grilled chicken or other poultry, roast lamb, or broiled fish.

INGREDIENTS:

2 tablespoons olive oil
½ cup chopped onion
2 cups bulgur (cracked wheat)
4 cups chicken broth or other broth

DIRECTIONS:

1. In a 4-quart pot, heat the oil over moderately low heat. When it is warm, add the chopped onion. Raise the heat to moderate and cook the onion until it is wilted but not brown.

2. Stir in the bulgur, then add the broth. Raise the heat to bring the broth to the boil. Boil for 5 minutes without stirring, regulating the heat so the broth doesn't boil over. Reduce the heat to a simmer, cover the pot, and continue cooking for 20 minutes. Turn off the heat and allow the pilaf to finish cooking on the turned-off burner for another 20 minutes. Just before serving, fluff with a fork.

VARIATION:

Wheat Pilaf with Fruit and Nuts

While the pilaf is cooking, plump ½ cup dried apricots in 1 cup boiling water for 30 minutes. After the first 15 minutes, add ¼ cup raisins to the apricots. Drain well and cut the apricots into quarters. Meanwhile, toast ¼ to ½ cup pine nuts over moderate heat in a small cast-iron skillet. Shake the pan often, taking care not to burn the nuts. If you prefer, brown the pine nuts in a tablespoon of olive oil over low heat. Just before serving, mix the apricots, raisins, and pine nuts into the pilaf.

Yellow Rice Pilaf

Serves 6

Rice that steams in broth is known as *pilaf*. Originally a Turkish preparation, rice pilaf is popular throughout the Middle East and in the Mediterranean. Rice pilaf is often seasoned with aromatic spices, sometimes cooked with bits of lamb or chicken, and on festive occasions made special with slivered almonds and fruit. The seasonings and the additions of fruit, nuts, meat, or vegetables vary according to the country and the cook. In Jewish cuisine, the rice pilaf for meat meals is similar to the pilaf served by the general population; for nonmeat meals, vegetable broth is substituted for chicken broth.

The yellow color of the rice in this recipe comes from turmeric, which is used by many Sephardic cooks as an affordable alternative to the very expensive saffron of Spain. The rice is flavorful enough to stand on its own with lamb ke-bobs or other broiled meats, but subtle enough to mix with the gravies from stews or fricassees. For an even more delicate rice, omit the onion and cumin. For rice with a more pronounced flavor and aroma, see the variation.

INGREDIENTS:

2 tablespoons olive oil
1 cup chopped onion
½ teaspoon ground turmeric
½ teaspoon ground cumin
2 cups long-grain white rice
4 cups chicken broth or vegetable broth

DIRECTIONS:

1. In a 2- or 3-quart pot, heat the oil and onion over moderate heat for 3 to 5 minutes, stirring occasionally, until the onion is wilted but not brown. Stir in the turmeric and cumin, then the rice. Mix to coat the rice with the oil and spices.

2. Add the broth. Bring to the boil over high heat, then reduce the heat to a gentle boil. Cover and cook for 20 minutes. Reduce the heat as necessary to keep the water from boiling over. The rice can be served immediately or left on the turned-off burner, where it will remain hot for at least 20 minutes.

VARIATION:

Cinnamon-Clove Rice Pilaf

In place of the turmeric and cumin, substitute 1 teaspoon ground cinnamon and ½ teaspoon ground cloves.

RICE KUGEL

Serves 4

Although rice is more of a staple among Sephardim than among Ashkenazim, the grain is known throughout the world and is eaten by Jews everywhere. In Ashkenazic cuisine, rice is mixed with meat in stuffed cabbage (page 135), cooked with milk in dessert puddings, and enjoyed in kugels. When served as a side dish, rice kugel often finds itself on the table with a meat main dish. Accordingly, in the kosher home rice kugel is typically made without milk or butter.

The kugel bakes into a firm preparation that can be cut into squares. The top is crusty, the inside moist, compact, and slightly custardy. Two rice kugels are presented in this recipe: the first is made sweet with raisins and a little sugar; the unsweetened variation relies on chicken fat (or vegetable oil) and onion for its good flavor. Whether sweet or savory, rice kugel is a fine side dish to serve with roast meats, poultry, or fish.

INGREDIENTS:

> 3 eggs (graded large)
> 3 tablespoons granulated white sugar
> 3 cups cooked white rice (1 cup uncooked)
> ½ cup dark raisins

DIRECTIONS

1. Preheat the oven to 350 degrees F.

2. Grease a 1-quart casserole.

3. In a medium-size bowl, use a fork to beat the eggs with the sugar. Stir in the rice and the raisins. Turn into the greased casserole. Level the top.

4. Bake for 35 minutes.

VARIATIONS:

Savory Rice Kugel

Omit the sugar and raisins. Sauté ½ cup chopped onion in 2 tablespoons of melted chicken fat, vegetable oil, or olive oil until the onion is tender and golden. Season to taste with salt and pepper. Mix with the rice. Add the rice mixture to the beaten eggs, mixing thoroughly. Bake as above.

Rice Kugel for One

Following the basic recipe, use 1 egg, 1 tablespoon of sugar, 1 cup of cooked rice, and 2 to 3 tablespoons raisins. Bake at 350 degrees F. in a small casserole (1¼ to 1½ cups) for 25 minutes. If desired, dust with cinnamon and enjoy as a dessert.

SAVORY NOODLE KUGEL

Serves 4

The schmaltz in this recipe is both an ingredient and a sentiment, because if the lokshen (noodle) kugel is prepared with schmaltz and eaten by anyone who grew up enjoying chicken fat in traditional Jewish cooking, the dominant taste of the chicken fat is certain to evoke memories of what life was like in the old days. Crusty and chewy, tasting richly of onion, the kugel is an appropriate starch to serve with any meat meal. The cabbage variation changes the flavor of the kugel, with the taste of cabbage predominating—a solid version of the simpler cabbage and noodles on page 245. Those who prefer not to use schmaltz can prepare the kugel by using a vegetable oil or olive oil in place of the chicken fat.

INGREDIENTS:

8 ounces medium egg noodles

3 tablespoons schmaltz, page 40 (substitute part
or all vegetable oil or olive oil)

1 cup chopped onion

½ teaspoon salt

½ teaspoon paprika

¼ teaspoon freshly ground black pepper

3 eggs (graded large)

DIRECTIONS:

1. Preheat the oven to 350 degrees F.

2. Grease a 2-quart baking dish (7 x 12 inches, approximately) with a little chicken fat or vegetable shortening.

3. Cook the noodles according to package directions. Drain well.

4. Meanwhile, in an 8-inch skillet heat the chicken fat or oil over moderate heat. Cook the chopped onion until it is golden and just beginning to brown. Stir in the salt, paprika, and pepper.

5. Beat the eggs in a medium-size mixing bowl. Mix in the onion, then the noodles. Mix well. Turn into the greased baking dish. Level the top. Bake for 40 minutes. The top will be golden and crusty, the kugel will be set. Cool for 10 minutes before cutting into squares.

VARIATION:

Noodle Kugel with Cabbage

Cook the onion in a 10-inch skillet, using 4 tablespoons of chicken fat or oil. When the onion is golden, add 1 cup of shredded green cabbage to the skillet. Continue cooking, stirring occasionally, until the cabbage is tender, about 10 minutes. Season to taste with salt, paprika, and pepper. Proceed with the recipe above.

FRUIT-AND-NUT NOODLE KUGEL

Serves 6

Sweet noodle kugel is a favorite dish for people to bring to synagogue events. It can be prepared well in advance, it reheats well, serves many people, and it gives the cook a chance to be inspirational. By looking at the kugels you can tell who's at a sisterhood dinner without ever seeing the people. Bev's is made with pineapple, Marilyn brings four when you ask for one, Eleanor likes hers full of fruit and nuts.

Apples, raisins, and walnuts (sounds like a strudel filling, doesn't it?) are featured in the pareve kugel below. The basic recipe can be changed by varying the fresh fruit (pineapple, pears, plums, for example), adding mixed dried fruits that have been soaked in hot water for a few minutes, mixing the nuts with the noodles instead of sprinkling them on top, and such. To keep the apples from darkening, cook the noodles and have all the other ingredients measured before peeling the apples.

INGREDIENTS:

1 cup chopped walnuts

½ cup crushed cornflakes or soft fresh
   breadcrumbs

8 ounces medium egg noodles

4 eggs (graded large), beaten

½ cup golden or dark raisins

¼ to ½ cup granulated white sugar

1 teaspoon ground cinnamon

2 cups chopped or shredded apple (peeled and cored)

DIRECTIONS:

1. Preheat the oven to 350 degrees F.

2. Grease a 2-quart baking dish (7 x 12 inches approximately).

3. In a small bowl, stir together the walnuts and cornflakes or breadcrumbs. Set aside.

4. Cook the noodles according to package directions. Drain well.

5. In a large bowl, mix together the cooked noodles, eggs, raisins, sugar to taste, cinnamon, and the chopped or shredded apple. Turn into the greased baking dish. Level the top.

6. Sprinkle the nut mixture evenly over the casserole.

7. Bake for 40 to 45 minutes, until set and light brown on top. Let cool for 10 minutes before cutting into squares.

VARIATION:

Noodle-Applesauce Kugel

Omit the apples and raisins. In Step 5, mix together the cooked noodles, 3 eggs, ¼ cup of sugar, and 1 teaspoon cinnamon. Substitute 3 cups of home-made applesauce (page 236) for the chopped or shredded apple, but do not mix the applesauce in with the other ingredients. Instead, layer the noodles mixture with the applesauce in the casserole, beginning and ending with the noodles. Sprinkle with the nut mixture. Bake for 30 minutes. This kugel is traditionally served on the Sabbath as a side dish with brisket or roast chicken, but it can be the main course for brunch or a light lunch. While it is usually served hot, squares of cold kugel make a wonderful lunch box treat.

FARFEL KUGEL

Serves 4

As its alternate name—egg barley—suggests, *farfel* is similar to barley in size and texture, but the taste of egg is recognizable, just as it is in spätzle. This chewy moist kugel, richly flavored by broth, stands well on its own with any meat or poultry meal and is delicious when blanketed by a thick fricassee gravy. The savory pareve variation, which is flavored by aromatic vegetables and parsley, makes a tasty accompaniment for fish.

INGREDIENTS:

> 1 tablespoon schmaltz (page 40) or vegetable oil
> ½ cup finely chopped onion
> 1½ cups chopped fresh mushrooms
> 1½ cups dried farfel (page 86)
> 2 cups well-seasoned chicken or beef broth

DIRECTIONS:

1. Preheat the oven to 350 degrees F.

2. In a 2-quart pot, heat the chicken fat or oil over moderate heat. Add the onion and cook until light brown, stirring occasionally.

3. Stir in the mushrooms, then the farfel. Add the broth. Bring to the boil over high heat. Adjust the heat so that the broth boils gently with the cover off. Cook for 5 minutes.

4. Transfer to a 1½-quart ovenproof casserole. Cover with a lid or with foil and bake for 30 minutes. Remove the cover and bake the kugel for an additional 5 minutes to brown the top. Serve hot.

Note: A 1½-quart square Corning Ware casserole that is both stoveproof and ovenproof can be used for both the initial cooking and the baking.

VARIATION:

Farfel and Vegetable Kugel

Use vegetable oil and 1 cup of chopped onion, 1 cup of diced carrot, and ⅔ cup of diced celery in place of the onion in Step 2. Cook, stirring occasionally, for 10 minutes, until the vegetables are softened but not brown. In Step 3, add 1 cup of chopped fresh mushrooms, 1½ cups of farfel, ½ cup of chopped fresh parsley, 2 cups of water or vegetable broth, and salt and pepper to taste. Continue as directed.

BARLEY KUGEL

Serves 6

Barley, the sustaining grain of biblical days (see page 104), remains popular in traditional Jewish cuisine in soups, cholent (page 154), and in kugels. When barley is baked with vegetables and chicken broth, the grain absorbs the delicious flavor of the broth and has the consistency of a very thick soup. But when beaten eggs are added to the casserole, the "soup" thickens and sets, making barley kugel almost a solid version of a mushroom and barley soup. Serve the kugel as a side dish with meat or poultry. The pareve variation is recommended when fish is the main dish.

INGREDIENTS:

2 tablespoons schmaltz (page 40) or vegetable oil
1 cup chopped onion
2 cups sliced fresh mushrooms
1 cup barley
4 cups well-seasoned chicken broth
Salt and freshly ground black pepper
2 eggs (graded large)

DIRECTIONS:

1. Preheat the oven to 375 degrees F.

2. In a 2-quart pot, heat the chicken fat or oil over moderate heat. Add the onion and cook until light brown, stirring occasionally. Stir in the mush-

rooms, next the barley. Cook for a minute or more, until the mushrooms are wilted.

3. Pour in the chicken broth. Transfer to a deep 2-quart ovenproof casserole. Cover with a tight-fitting lid or foil. Bake for 45 minutes to an hour, until the barley is tender.

4. Remove the barley casserole from the oven. Taste for seasoning, adding salt and pepper as desired.

5. In a medium-size mixing bowl, beat the eggs. With a large spoon, mix the barley into the beaten eggs a spoonful at a time, stirring rapidly so that the eggs do not curdle. When all the barley has been mixed in with the eggs, return the mixture to the casserole. Bake, uncovered, 15 minutes longer. The barley should be set, the top brown. Serve hot.

Note: A 2-quart square Corning Ware casserole that is both stoveproof and ovenproof can be used for both the initial cooking and the baking.

VARIATION:

Barley Kugel, Pareve Version

Substitute vegetable oil for the chicken fat, and vegetable broth for the chicken broth.

POTATO KUGEL

Serves 6

Crisp, dense, moist, tender. It's no wonder that potato kugel, also called potato pudding, is on the menu for most Jewish holiday meals in Ashkenazic homes. A combination of grated potatoes and onions mixed with eggs and chicken fat, it was originally a Lithuanian Jewish preparation called *kugelis* by the people of the Baltic States. Potato kugel finds a place on the table at many Friday night Sabbath meals as an accompaniment to brisket or roast chicken.

Grated potatoes turn pinkish-gray shortly after coming in contact with the air, and the old-fashioned method was to grate the potatoes into a bowl of water, then drain well and mix with the other ingredients. However, if you work quickly and have the onion grated and the eggs beaten, you can grate the potatoes directly into the egg-onion mixture. Or, grate the potatoes and onions in a food processor, then mix them with the remaining ingredients.

Select a casserole that will make the potato mixture a bit less than an inch high and you will have just the right ratio of brown crust to soft interior.

INGREDIENTS:

¹/₂ cup grated onion

2 eggs (graded large), beaten

2 pounds potatoes (enough to make 4 cups grated)

¹/₃ cup unbleached white flour or ¹/₄ cup matzo meal

2 tablespoons melted schmaltz (page 40) or
    vegetable oil

1 teaspoon salt

¹/₂ teaspoon freshly ground black pepper

DIRECTIONS:

1. Preheat the oven to 350 degrees F.

2. Grease a 2-quart baking dish (7 x 12 inches, approximately).

3. Place the grated onion and beaten eggs in a large bowl.

4. Peel all the potatoes, then grate or shred them directly into the bowl, stirring after adding each potato.

5. Stir in the flour or matzo meal, the chicken fat or oil, and the salt and pepper. Turn into the greased baking dish. Level the top.

6. Bake at 350 degrees F. for 1¼ hours. The potatoes should be cooked, the top brown. Serve hot, with applesauce (page 236) on the side. Leftovers can be reheated in the oven or in a microwave. Cold potato kugel with applesauce has a following also.

Potato Latkes

Makes sixteen 3-inch latkes

Can you imagine having *happy* memories of grating potatoes on a hand grater until your fingers ached? So it is for my husband, one of many grandsons who took turns grating potatoes for their Grandma's *latkes* (pancakes). What might be considered a task today was a privilege, an honor. Sure, you can use a food processor or blender to make potato latkes, but if you want to pass along a unique memory, try a hand grater.

The potatoes can be coarsely shredded or grated to a mush. Coarsely grated potatoes will be very crisp when fried, tender but slightly chewy inside. Finely grated potatoes are more even-textured, crisp outside, very soft inside. Because the potatoes oxidize and turn color when they make contact with air, potato latkes are best when fried immediately after they are grated and mixed with the other ingredients. However, if you must make up the mixture in advance, cover the top with a thick layer of flour, then carefully remove as much of the flour as you can just before frying the latkes. Mix any excess flour into the batter.

Originally a German preparation, potato latkes are associated with the holiday of Chanukah among Jewish people everywhere. Latkes are fried in oil, thus a reminder of the miracle of a one-day supply of oil burning for eight days when the Temple was cleansed and rededicated in the days of the Maccabees. While latkes are always served during Chanukah, they can be enjoyed any time of year. Small potato pancakes are often served as hors d'oeuvres at Bar and Bat Mitzvah and wedding receptions.

Applesauce and sour cream (for dairy meals) are the traditional accompaniments for potato latkes.

INGREDIENTS:

1 medium-size onion (1/3 cup grated,
   approximately)
2 eggs (graded large), slightly beaten
2 pounds potatoes (approximately 6 medium)
2 tablespoons unbleached white flour or matzo meal
1 teaspoon salt
1/2 teaspoon freshly ground black pepper
Vegetable oil for shallow frying

DIRECTIONS:

1. Place the grated onion and beaten eggs in a large bowl.

2. Peel all the potatoes, then grate or shred them directly into the bowl, stirring after adding each potato.

3. Stir in the flour or matzo meal, salt, and pepper. Mix well with a large spoon.

4. In a large skillet, heat 1/8 inch of oil until it is hot but not yet smoking, 375 degrees F. For each potato pancake, spoon about 1/4 cup of potato mixture into the oil, flattening slightly with the back of the spoon to make a 3-inch pancake. Cook until crisp and brown on one side, then turn and brown the other side.

5. Drain well on paper towels. Serve hot, with sour cream and/or applesauce.

6. Although they taste best when eaten immediately, latkes can be prepared in advance and refrigerated or frozen. Reheat in a single layer on an ungreased baking sheet in a 350-degree F. oven until hot and crisp.

POTATO KNISHES

Makes eight 4-inch knishes

The potato knishes made famous on the boardwalk of Brooklyn's Coney Island—still sold from pushcarts in New York City and featured in Jewish delicatessens—are substantial stuffed pastries made of a thin dough wrapped around a well-seasoned filling of potato and onion. These large knishes are related to a meat-stuffed Russian pastry, *beliashi*, which is made of a yeast dough. Served as a snack or side dish, today's knishes are also filled with kasha or cabbage. Dairy knishes are filled with a cottage cheese or farmer cheese mixture.

Fried knishes are crisp; baked are more crusty. In California, knishes are sold using egg roll wrappers for the dough, and one can buy kosher egg roll wrappers to use with a homemade filling. Knishes are served hot, but if you should nosh on a piece of a cold knish, you will notice that the flavor of the filling changes when the knish reaches room temperature—the onion flavor comes out more in the potato knish, the kasha is more wheaty, the cabbage tastes stronger than in the hot knish.

INGREDIENTS:

FOR THE FILLING:

> 3 tablespoons schmaltz (page 40) or 3 tablespoons
>   vegetable or olive oil for pareve knishes
> 1⅓ cups minced onion
> 2 cups cooked mashed potatoes (page 264)
> Salt and freshly ground black pepper
> 1 egg (graded large or extra large)

FOR THE DOUGH:

> **1 cup unbleached white flour (stir the flour, spoon
>   gently into a dry-measure cup, then level with
>   the edge of a spatula)**
> **¼ teaspoon salt**
> **2 tablespoons solid white vegetable shortening**
> **1 egg (graded large or extra large)**
> **2 tablespoons water, approximately**
> **Vegetable oil for fried knishes**
> **Beaten egg for glazing baked knishes**

DIRECTIONS:

1. For the potato filling, in a small skillet heat the chicken fat or oil with the onion over moderate heat, stirring occasionally, until the onion is lightly browned.

2. Add the onion to the mashed potatoes, scraping in all the chicken fat or oil. Season to taste with salt and pepper. Use a large spoon to beat in the egg. The filling can be refrigerated at this point.

3. For the dough, in a small mixing bowl mix together the flour and ¼ teaspoon salt. Cut in the shortening with a fork until the pieces are small and evenly distributed, then stir in the egg. Stir in a tablespoon of water, then add water a few drops at a time as necessary to make a smooth dough that is soft enough to roll out but is not at all sticky.

4. Form the dough into a ball, knead 8 to 10 times, then divide into 8 equal pieces. Form each piece into a ball. Cover the balls of dough with a clean, slightly damp kitchen towel. On a clean, lightly floured work surface, flatten a ball of dough, roll out to a 3-inch circle, pick up the dough to make sure it is not sticking, put it down flat, then go on to the next ball of dough until you have rolled out all 8 pieces. Cover the circles of dough with the

damp towel and allow the dough to rest for 2 or 3 minutes. This will make it easier to roll thinner.

5. Now, working with one ball of dough at a time (keep the remainder covered), roll out each ball of dough to a thin circle that will eventually be about 6 inches in diameter. Roll from the center to the outside, pick up the dough and rotate ¼ turn, roll again from the center to the outside.

6. When the dough is at or near a 6-inch circle, place ¼ cup of filling in the center. Bring the dough around the filling from opposite sides to overlap slightly in the center, then bring the other 2 sides toward the center, covering the filling completely. Gently flatten the filled dough to a 4-inch square.

7. **To fry the knishes,** heat ½ inch of vegetable oil in a large skillet until hot but not yet smoking, 375 degrees F. Carefully place the knishes in the hot oil, flap side down. Fry until golden on one side, turn and fry the other side. Drain well on paper towels. Serve hot. Fried knishes can be reheated in a 350-degree F. oven until warmed through.

   To bake the knishes, preheat the oven to 400 degrees F. Place the knishes flap side down on a greased baking sheet. Brush the knishes with beaten egg. Bake for 15 to 20 minutes, until golden and heated through.

VARIATION:

Kasha or Cabbage Knishes

For kasha knishes, substitute 2 cups of cooked kasha (page 268) for the potatoes. For cabbage knishes, use the filling for cabbage strudel on page 247.

POTATO CHREMSLACH

Makes ten to twelve 2-inch chremslach

Potato chremslach are, in effect, a combination of mashed potatoes, potato knishes, and potato latkes. The deliciously crusted potato balls begin with mashed potatoes (leftovers or freshly prepared) that are seasoned well and mixed with sautéed onion and whole eggs, then fried crisp. If you like the taste of chicken fat, fry the chremslach in chicken fat or a combination of schmaltz and oil. While olive oil is not traditionally used in Ashkenazic dishes, it makes a tasty alternative to chicken fat. To fry in olive oil, see the note following the recipe.

Small chremslach can be passed around as appetizers; regular-size potato chremslach are eaten as a side dish. For a crowd, the recipe can be doubled or tripled.

INGREDIENTS:

> 1 pound potatoes (3 medium)
> 2 tablespoons schmaltz (page 40), vegetable oil,
>   or olive oil
> 1 cup minced onion
> Salt and freshly ground black pepper
> 3 eggs (graded large)
> Schmaltz or oil for frying, or a combination of the two

DIRECTIONS:

1. Peel the potatoes, cut them into quarters, and cook in boiling (salted if desired) water until they are tender. Drain well, then mash them with a potato masher until they are smooth. Or, use 2 cups of leftover mashed potatoes.

2. Meanwhile, in an 8-inch skillet heat 2 tablespoons of chicken fat or oil over moderate heat. Cook the onion until it is golden and just beginning to brown. Mix the onion with the mashed potatoes. Season the mixture liberally with salt and pepper.

3. When the potatoes are cool enough not to curdle the eggs, use a spoon to beat the eggs into the potato mixture. The potatoes will now be very creamy. The mixture can be refrigerated at this point.

4.   In a 4-quart pot, heat 2 inches of chicken fat and/or vegetable oil until it is hot but not yet smoking. Carefully drop well-rounded tablespoons of the potato mixture into the fat or oil. The chremslach will sink at first, then they will float to the top as they cook. If they do not turn over on their own, turn them once to brown them all over. Regulate the heat so the chremslach cook through while browning—they should not brown so quickly that the insides do not cook. Remove with a slotted spoon, drain well on paper towels, and serve immediately. Although they are best when eaten as soon as they are cooked, leftovers can be reheated until sizzling in a 325-degree F. oven.

Note: To deep-fry chremslach in olive oil, heat the oil slowly over low heat to prevent burning.

7

Breads Fresh from the Oven

Nine Ethnic Delights

Breads Fresh from the Oven

Hot bagels for Sunday brunch, crusty rye breads baked as free-standing loaves, golden challah warm from the oven in time for the Sabbath. The three most celebrated breads in Jewish cuisine are among the most widely known of Jewish foods. But while everyone eats bagels, in the Jewish home the bagel is covered with cream cheese and lox, the rye bread piled high with corned beef or pastrami.

More than just a convenience for eating meats or for spreads, bread is the most important food in Jewish tradition. Wheat (from which most bread is made) is mentioned before all other foods in the Book of Deuteronomy. When the blessing over bread (*Hamotzi* in Hebrew) is recited at the beginning of the meal, it covers all foods that will be eaten during the meal. The custom of breaking bread following the blessing and distributing it to those at the table has its roots in the Talmud.

In addition to its historical and religious significance, bread is important as a sustaining food; in talmudic times, the meals of rabbinical students sometimes consisted only of bread. Pocket breads of the Middle East have always been used as a vehicle for eating other foods, but are eaten for nourishment as well. Dark, chewy, hearty pumpernickel breads of Eastern European countries supplemented cabbage and other vegetable soups to make the main meal of the day. Other breads not quite so filling go with the meal but are not considered part of the main course. *Mamaliga* and the onion-topped *pletzel* and *bialys* add a pleasing touch at mealtimes.

A WORD ABOUT YEAST

Yeast is a fungus that grows when it "devours" carbohydrates in a warm, moist atmosphere, producing tiny leavening bubbles of carbon dioxide. Wheat flour contains gluten, a plant protein that stretches to form a meshlike framework that holds the gas bubbles developed by the yeast. In short, yeast makes the bread rise while gluten makes the bread hold its shape.

Originally, yeast was packaged in small compressed "cakes" for use in home baking. Although cake or compressed yeast is still sold and can be used if an old-fashioned method is desired, it sometimes becomes moldy even when refrigerated under good conditions. Cake yeast does not remain viable as long as dry yeast does.

Currently there are two kinds of active dry yeast on the market, regular and rapid-rise. Both are sold in small triple packages. Each individual sealed package contains two level teaspoons and weighs one-quarter ounce. Rapid-rise yeast has smaller granules than regular yeast, granules that mix well with flour, eliminating the need to dissolve them first. Rapid-rise yeast is more tolerant of hot water than is regular yeast, and one can begin with warmer water.

Regular active dry yeast is usually dissolved in water to become active. If one wants to "prove" that the yeast is viable before preparing the dough, the yeast is mixed with small amounts of sugar (flour can be added as well) and is dissolved in water. Within a few minutes, the yeast goes to work on the carbohydrates, and one can see the activity in the form of small bubbles. In traditional recipes, this is called "proofing" the yeast.

The recipes in this cookbook have been tested using regular active dry yeast, the most widely available of the three kinds of yeast. (Brewer's yeast, which is used in cooking as a nutritional supplement, will not make bread rise.)

The amount of time it takes for dough to rise is partly dependent on the quantity of yeast one has started with. Although one can speed up the rising time by using double the quantity of yeast, it is generally agreed that long, slow risings produce a better flavor than hasty risings. The temperature of the environment in which the dough is rising also affects the rising time. A dough will eventually rise in a 65-degree F. room, but the time required will be much greater than in an 80-degree F. area. Thus, if you like eating bread hot from the oven, you can control when you actually bake the bread: move the dough to a cool area (even the refrigerator) for a time to slow down the rising, or help it along in a warm environment. Salt, which retards the growth of yeast, affects the rising time. If you omit the salt from a recipe because of a special diet, the dough will rise more quickly.

When you have mastered the recipes and are comfortable with them, you may decide to experiment with different amounts of yeast. For example, for my own home baking I often start bread in the evening, using as little as a quarter-teaspoon of yeast (I use rapid-rise for this overnight method). In the morning, the dough has risen, and I can proceed at whatever pace the day permits.

A WORD ABOUT MEASURING FLOUR
FOR BREAD BAKING

The amount of white flour listed in a bread recipe is given as an approximate measure. In bread baking, the amount of flour needed may vary slightly with humidity and altitude. The correct amount of flour to use in a kneaded dough is determined by the "feel" of the dough: in most breads, sprinkles of flour are added toward the end of kneading until the dough loses its stickiness. Unless you live in a very damp area where the flour becomes lumpy when it is stored at room temperature, it is not necessary to sift the flour for bread doughs. For a further discussion about measuring flour, refer to page 328.

The use of unbleached white flour for recipes in this cookbook is in keeping with the general philosophy that natural foods go hand-in-hand with traditional Jewish cooking. Unless otherwise noted, white flour refers to all-purpose flour.

CHALLAH

Makes 2 loaves

You may have **eaten** *challah,* the braided egg-rich loaf that is served as the traditional Sabbath bread, but do you "**take** challah"? If you break off a small piece of dough before shaping the loaves and bake it until it has burned, you are "taking challah," a symbol of the portion of bread taken from the loaf and brought to the Priests in the days before the destruction of the Second Temple.

Among other customs that go back to biblical times are serving two *challot* (plural of challah), symbolic of the double portion of manna sent down before the Sabbath, and dipping challah in salt, a reminder of the days when salt was used with the sacrifices brought on the altar. The challot are covered with a decorative white cloth, because in Jewish tradition the Sabbath has been compared to a bride, who wears white and covers her face. Just as the veil of the bride is removed after the blessings under the canopy have been recited, so are the challot "unveiled" after the blessing over the bread is recited.

Modern-day cooks often use part whole wheat flour, but traditionalists prepare the Sabbath bread with all white flour. If you like raisins in your challah, scatter in half a cup during the last few minutes of kneading.

INGREDIENTS:

1 teaspoon granulated white sugar
1 tablespoon unbleached white flour
1 package ($1/4$ ounce) active dry yeast
$3/8$ cup warm water (6 tablespoons), approximately
     105 degrees F.
5 cups unbleached white flour, approximately
$1/4$ cup granulated white sugar

1 tablespoon salt
$^3/_4$ **cup hot water (120 degrees F.)**
$^1/_4$ **cup mild-tasting vegetable oil**
2 eggs (graded large or extra large)
Beaten egg for glazing
Poppy or sesame seeds (optional)

DIRECTIONS:

1. In a small bowl or a glass, mix together the teaspoon of sugar, the tablespoon of flour, and the yeast. Stir in the $^3/_8$ cup of warm water. The liquid will start bubbling and rising. (This step is called proofing the yeast. The bubbling and rising are proof that the yeast is active.) Set aside until about doubled, which will take 10 to 15 minutes.

2. Meanwhile, in the large bowl of a heavy-duty mixer with a dough hook, or in a large mixing bowl with a wooden spoon, combine 2 cups of the flour, the $^1/_4$ cup of sugar, and the salt. Stir in the $^3/_4$ cup hot water and the oil, then beat in the eggs. When the yeast mixture has doubled, stir it in. Beat on a low speed with the mixer for about 2 minutes, until the ingredients are combined, or by hand with the wooden spoon until smooth. Now blend in the remaining flour $^1/_2$ cup at a time. If the dough is sticky, add more flour.

3. **For machine kneading,** knead on a low speed for 6 minutes under the dough hook, sprinkling in additional flour if the dough becomes sticky. Turn out the dough onto a clean, lightly floured work surface and knead for an additional minute. The dough should feel light and springy, and an imprint should not remain when you lightly poke a finger into the dough.

    For hand kneading, turn out the dough onto a clean, lightly floured work surface. Knead for about 8 minutes, until the dough is smooth and springy. Sprinkle in a little flour if the dough becomes sticky. To test if the dough is kneaded enough, lightly poke a finger into the dough. The imprint should not remain.

4. Place the dough in a clean bowl large enough to accommodate it when it doubles in volume. (It is not necessary to grease the bowl.) Cover the bowl tightly with a clean kitchen towel or a piece of plastic wrap. Allow the dough to rise in a warm place until doubled in volume. The amount of time will depend on the temperature in the room. At 85 degrees F., the dough will take a few hours. In the refrigerator, it will take all night. To speed up the rising, place a pan of hot water in a cool oven, and place the bowl of dough on a rack above the pan of water. Or place the dough in an oven that has a pilot light.

5. When the dough has risen enough, if you poke a finger into the dough, the indentation will remain and the dough will not be sticky.

6. For the second rising, remove the towel or plastic wrap, punch down the dough, then work the outside edges of the dough toward the center until the top is smooth again. Recover the bowl tightly and allow the dough to rise again. The second rising will take less time than the first.

7. To shape, punch down the dough again, then knead on a clean, dry work surface for half a minute. While it should not be necessary to work in extra flour at this point, if the dough is very sticky, work in a few sprinklings of flour until the dough can be handled easily. Divide the dough into 6 equal pieces. Roll each piece into a rope about 8 inches long. Braid 3 ropes together for each challah. Place on a greased baking sheet. Cover with a clean kitchen towel or plastic wrap. Let rise again in a warm draft-free place for about 45 minutes (all day in the refrigerator).

8. Toward the end of the rising time, preheat the oven to 350 degrees F. Brush the loaves thoroughly with the well-beaten egg. If you like, mix the beaten egg with a teaspoon of sugar before brushing; this will darken the glaze. Sprinkle the challot with poppy or sesame seeds if desired. Gently brush again with the beaten egg. This will prevent the seeds from falling off during and after baking.

9. Bake for 30 to 35 minutes in the middle of the oven, until a lovely brown and baked through. A metal cake tester or a toothpick inserted in the center of the loaf should come out clean and dry. Carefully transfer to a wire rack to cool. Serve warm or at room temperature.

VARIATIONS:

Large Challah

For one large challah, divide the dough into 3 equal pieces. Roll each into a rope about 12 inches long. Braid. Let rise on a greased baking sheet. Brush as above (Step 8). Bake at 350 degrees F. for about 45 minutes.

Round Challah

For Rosh Hashanah, when it is traditional to serve round challot, roll the dough into two 18-inch ropes for two small challot, or one 36-inch rope for 1 large challah. Beginning from the center outward, form the rope of dough into a flat coil. Or, braid the dough as in Step 7. Gently elongate the braided dough, then shape the dough into a coil. Let rise and bake as above.

Ladder Decoration

For Shavuot, there is an old tradition in which the challah is decorated with a ladder to commemorate the ascent of Moses to Mount Sinai to receive the Torah. For a ladder decoration on the 2 small challot, for each loaf break off ¼ cup of dough, cover the small pieces of dough well with plastic wrap, and let them rest at room temperature. Braid each challah and let rise as above.

Just before baking, shape the ladders. For each challah, use one ¼-cup piece of dough to make a ladder with 6-inch sides and four 1-inch rungs. Brush the challah with the egg glaze, lightly press the ladder into the challah, and brush the ladder with egg.

For one large challah, use ½ cup of dough for a ladder that will be about 9 inches long with five 1½-inch-wide rungs.

RYE BREAD

Makes 2 loaves

Light-colored rye bread speckled with caraway seeds—the bread traditionally used for corned beef and pastrami sandwiches in Jewish American delicatessens—has its antecedents in the dark pumpernickel peasant breads of Eastern Europe. The medium rye flour used in this recipe produces a loaf with a finer texture and a milder flavor than the coarse black bread made from dark or pumpernickel rye flour (see the following recipe).

Rye flour has little capacity for developing the gluten structure that traps the fermented gases produced by activated yeast, so bread made with rye flour alone will be dense and heavy—it will never rise. Wheat flour, whether white or whole wheat, contains gluten, a plant protein that does form an elastic network when developed by kneading, allowing the loaf to expand. For most rye breads, rye flour is mixed with at least an equal amount of wheat flour, which can be white or whole wheat. In Jewish rye bread, a higher ratio of white-to-rye flour contributes to the light color of the bread. Even lighter colored rye breads are made in bakeries which use white rye flour, the lightest of all the ryes in color and texture.

Enjoy rye bread with your corned beef and pastrami sandwiches, cut thick slabs for My Father's Favorite Sandwich (page 232), or toast the bread for breakfast.

INGREDIENTS:

1 package ($^1\!/_4$ ounce) active dry yeast
2 cups warm water (105 degrees F.)
2 tablespoons granulated white sugar
2 tablespoons mild-tasting vegetable oil

2 cups medium rye flour

4 cups unbleached white flour, approximately

2 teaspoons salt

2 tablespoons caraway seeds

2 tablespoons beaten egg for glazing

DIRECTIONS:

1. In a medium-size mixing bowl, dissolve the yeast in the water. With a wooden spoon, stir in the sugar, oil, and 1 cup each of the rye and white flours. Beat for half a minute. Cover with a clean kitchen towel or plastic wrap and let rise in a warm place for 30 minutes.

2. Beat in the salt, caraway seeds, and the remaining cup of rye flour. Beat for about 50 strokes, then stir in a cup of white flour, then work in another.

3. Spread the fourth cup of white flour in an 8-inch circle on a clean work surface. Turn out the dough. Knead for 10 minutes, working in as much flour as the dough absorbs. Use additional flour if necessary.

4. Place the dough in a bowl large enough to accommodate it when it doubles in volume. Cover the bowl tightly with a clean kitchen towel or with plastic wrap. Allow the dough to rise in a warm place (80 to 85 degrees F.) until it has doubled. A warm room, a gas oven with a pilot light, or an oven with a pan of hot water on the bottom rack and the bowl of dough on the rack above will do. To test the dough to see if it has risen enough, press your finger into it. The indentation will remain and the dough will not be sticky. The rising time will take anywhere from 1½ hours to 4 hours, depending on the temperature where the dough is rising.

5. Grease a large baking sheet.

6. Punch down the dough, turn it out onto a clean work surface, and knead 4 or 5 times, until it is smooth again. Using a sharp knife, divide the dough

in half. Shape each half into a ball then elongate into an oval that will be 4 x 6 inches. Place on the greased baking sheet, allowing plenty of room between the breads for rising. Cover with a clean kitchen towel or wax paper and allow the loaves to rise in a warm draft-free place for 45 minutes.

7. Toward the end of the rising time, preheat the oven to 400 degrees F.

8. Brush the loaves all over with the beaten egg. Bake the loaves on the middle rack of the oven for 35 minutes. A metal cake tester or a toothpick inserted through the center of the loaf should come out clean. Pick up a loaf and thump the bottom with your fingers—the thump should be loud and clear, not muffled.

9. Serve warm as a bread to be buttered, at room temperature for sandwiches. Wrap well to store, or freeze when completely cool.

PUMPERNICKEL BREAD

Makes 2 loaves

Dark, coarse, heavy, and chewy, this peasant bread from Russia and Ukraine bears little resemblance to the packaged sliced loaves available on grocery shelves. Substantial and filling, it was a sustaining bread in Eastern Europe, the "meat" of a meal that might consist only of cabbage soup and bread. No longer a bread of the poor, homemade pumpernickel is now enjoyed as a treat. It is a nutritious bread with a hearty flavor, a refreshing change from purchased white breads.

Dark and pumpernickel rye flours are coarsely ground and have bran particles that will cut through the gluten structure during rising, producing a more compact loaf than the medium rye flour. The coffee powder and un-sweetened chocolate are both used more to make the bread dark than for flavor, but they do make a subtle difference in the taste.

INGREDIENTS:

4 cups medium, dark, or pumpernickel rye flour

4 cups unbleached white flour, approximately

1 cup wheat bran (not cereal)

2 packages ($1/4$ ounce each) active dry yeast

2 tablespoons caraway seeds

1 tablespoon instant coffee powder or instant espresso

1 tablespoon salt

1 tablespoon granulated white sugar

$2^{1}/_{2}$ cups tap water

$1/4$ cup distilled white vinegar

¼ **cup molasses**
¼ **cup solid white vegetable shortening**
1 ounce (1 square) unsweetened baking chocolate
Glaze: ½ cup cold water and 1 tablespoon cornstarch

DIRECTIONS:

1. In a large mixing bowl, combine 1 cup each of the flours, the bran, yeast, caraway seeds, instant coffee, salt, and sugar.

2. In a 2-quart pot, mix together the water, vinegar, molasses, shortening, and the unsweetened chocolate. Heat over moderately low heat, stirring from time to time. As soon as the shortening and chocolate melt but before the liquid becomes hot (130 degrees F.), remove the pot from the heat.

3. Blend the liquid into the dry ingredients, and beat for 2 minutes with a wooden spoon. Now add 1 cup each of the rye and white flours, beat for another minute, then add another cup of each flour and continue beating. Mix in the final cup of rye flour.

4. Spread the last cup of white flour on a clean, smooth work surface. Turn out the dough onto the flour, cover it with the mixing bowl, and allow it to rest for 15 minutes.

5. Knead the dough for 8 to 10 minutes, adding sprinklings of white flour if the dough becomes sticky. The dough is ready when it is springy and not at all sticky.

6. Place the dough in a clean, dry bowl large enough to accommodate it when it doubles in volume. Cover the bowl tightly with a clean kitchen towel or with plastic wrap. Allow the dough to rise in a warm place (80 to 85 degrees F.) until it has doubled. A warm room, a gas oven with a pilot light, or an oven with a pan of hot water on the bottom rack and the bowl of dough on the rack above will do. To test the dough to see if it has risen enough, press your

finger into it. The indentation will remain and the dough will not be sticky. The rising time will range anywhere from 1½ hours to 4 hours, depending on the temperature where the dough is rising.

7. Lightly grease a large baking sheet on opposite ends, where the loaves will be placed.

8. Punch down the dough, turn it out onto a clean work surface, and knead 4 or 5 times, until it is smooth again. Using a sharp knife, divide the dough in half. Shape each half into a ball, and place on the greased baking sheet. Cover with a clean kitchen towel or wax paper and allow the loaves to rise in a warm draft-free place for 45 minutes.

9. Toward the end of the rising time, preheat the oven to 350 degrees F. Bake the loaves on the middle rack of the oven for 1 hour. A metal cake tester or a toothpick inserted in the center of the loaf should come out clean. Pick up a loaf and thump the bottom with your fingers—the thump should be loud and clear, not muffled.

10. Just before the bread is done, in a 1-quart pot mix the cornstarch and cold water. Bring to the boil over medium heat, stirring often, then boil for 5 to 10 seconds, stirring constantly. Open the oven door, pull out the rack, and quickly brush the loaves with the cornstarch glaze. Return the loaves to the oven, close the door, and allow the bread to remain in the oven for 2 minutes. Transfer to a wire rack to cool. Serve warm or at room temperature. Wrap well to store, or freeze when completely cool.

PITA

Israeli flat bread, also known as *pita* and pocket bread, is the bread of the Middle East. It is a yeast bread that is flattened like a pancake then baked at a very high temperature. The initial impact of hot air creates a burst of steam inside the flat bread, making a crusty bread that inflates somewhat like a balloon. When cool, the bread is left with a "pocket" on the inside. The top of the small "loaf" is cut or torn off, and fillings are stuffed inside. Or, for hummus (page 48) and eggplant preparations (page 50), pieces of the bread are torn off and the food is scooped up.

INGREDIENTS:

1 package (¼ ounce) active dry yeast
1 cup warm water (105 degrees F.)
2 cups whole wheat flour
1 teaspoon salt
1 cup unbleached white flour, approximately

DIRECTIONS:

1. In a medium-size mixing bowl, sprinkle the yeast over the water. When the yeast has dissolved, use a wooden spoon to beat in the whole wheat flour and the salt. Beat for 1 minute. Stir in half a cup of the white flour.

2. On a clean, dry work surface, spread the remaining ½-cup flour in a 6-inch circle. Turn out the dough onto the flour. Knead for about 8 minutes,

working in all the flour. Sprinkle on additional flour as necessary to prevent the dough from becoming sticky. The dough should feel light and springy, and an imprint should not remain when you lightly poke a finger into the dough.

3. Place the dough in a clean bowl large enough to accommodate it when it doubles in volume. Cover the bowl with plastic wrap. Allow the dough to rise at about 80 degrees F. until it has doubled.

4. Punch down the dough. Turn out the dough onto a clean work surface and knead for 30 seconds. Divide the dough into 6 equal pieces. Form each piece into a smooth ball. Flatten each ball between your hands, then, with a rolling pin, roll each ball into a 5-inch round. Place the rounds of dough on a clean, smooth surface. Cover the dough with plastic wrap or clean kitchen towels. Allow the breads to stand at room temperature for 1 hour before baking.

5. Adjust an oven rack to the lowest position in the oven, and preheat the oven to 500 degrees F. (Be sure that the oven temperature reaches 500 degrees F.) Place the breads on an ungreased baking sheet, turning each round over so that what was the top surface is now touching the baking sheet. If all the pita do not fit on one baking sheet, bake the first batch before placing the remaining breads on a second baking sheet.

6. Bake the pita for 5 minutes, then immediately transfer to a wire rack. If you will be baking the breads in two batches, be sure the oven has reached 500 degrees F. again before putting in the second batch. The pita can be eaten warm or kept for later use. Store in foil at room temperature for one day, or wrap well and freeze.

CORN BREAD

Makes 2 loaves

Unlike American corn bread, a quick bread based on corn flour or cornmeal, Jewish corn bread is a rye bread that derives its name from the German word for grain, which is *Korn*. Round but irregularly shaped on top, with a thick crisp crust characteristic of European breads, an oatmeal-colored very moist interior, and a sourdough flavor, corn bread is heavy, chewy, dense, yet full of large air pockets. And if bagels (page 316) are not usually produced in the home kitchen, so much the moreso for Jewish corn bread.

If you talk with the head baker at a Jewish bakery, you will discover that corn bread is made with a sourdough starter using a light rye flour not usually available to the home baker, a water rising method, and steam baking. The medium rye flour used in the recipe below makes a darker bread with more of a rye taste than a bakery-made corn bread. It is moist, marvelously crusty, with a pleasantly sour flavor, and as close to the bakery bread as you are likely to ever be able to produce at home. While it is always a good idea to read through a recipe before you begin, it is mandatory for Jewish corn bread.

INGREDIENTS:

FOR THE SOURDOUGH STARTER:

1 package ($\frac{1}{4}$ ounce) active dry yeast
2 cups medium rye flour
$1\frac{1}{2}$ cups warm water (105 degrees F.)

FOR THE DOUGH:

> 1 package ($^1/_4$ ounce) active dry yeast
> 1 cup warm water (105 degrees F.)
> The Sourdough Starter
> $^1/_4$ cup mild-tasting vegetable oil
> 2 tablespoons granulated white sugar
> 1 tablespoon salt
> 2 tablespoons firmly packed brown sugar
> 1$^1/_2$ cups medium rye flour
> 5 cups unbleached white flour, approximately
> Optional glaze: $^1/_2$ cup cold water and 1 tablespoon
>   cornstarch

DIRECTIONS:

1. For the sourdough starter, in a large mixing bowl mix together the package of yeast and the 2 cups of rye flour. Stir in the 1$^1/_2$ cups of warm water. Use a large wooden spoon to beat for half a minute. Cover the bowl tightly with plastic wrap. Allow the mixture to stand at room temperature for a minimum of 24 hours, up to 3 days. The mixture will ferment and rise, then fall.

2. On the day of baking, mix the second package of yeast in a cup of warm water. Add the yeast and water to the sourdough starter, then add the oil, sugar, salt, brown sugar, and the 1$^1/_2$ cups of rye flour. Use a wooden spoon to blend the ingredients. Beat for 100 strokes, then beat in a cup of the white flour. Stir in a second cup, then a third. Mix in the fourth cup (this will be difficult). Spread the remaining cup of white flour in an 8-inch circle on a clean work surface. Turn out the dough onto the white flour.

3. Knead for about 5 minutes, until as much of the flour as possible is absorbed and the dough is smooth. Add a little more flour if necessary. The dough should not be at all sticky at this point.

4. Place the dough in a large clean bowl. Add cool tap water to cover the dough by 2 inches. Allow the dough to rise in the water, which will contribute to the moist, dense interior of the loaf. It will take 30 to 60 minutes for the dough to reach the top, depending on the temperature of the room.

5. Grease two baking sheets. Divide the dough in half. Shape each half into a large ball and place one on each of the baking sheets. Cover the dough with clean kitchen towels or a greased piece of wax paper. Allow the loaves to rise until doubled in size. The rising time will depend on the temperature of the area where the dough is rising. About 80 degrees F. is ideal. At that temperature, the dough will take 45 minutes to an hour to rise.

6. Toward the end of the rising time, prepare the oven(s). If you have only one oven, bake the breads one at a time. Place a pan with 2 cups of hot water on the bottom rack of the oven(s). This will create steam that will increase the crustiness of the bread. Preheat the oven(s) to 375 degrees F. Using a sharp knife, make an x in the top of the loaves, about $1/4$-inch deep. Brush the tops with cold water. Bake the breads on the middle rack for 40 to 45 minutes, until crusty and baked through. Pick up a loaf and tap the bottom crust. The sound should be hard and hollow, a distinct thump.

7. If a glaze is desired, just before the bread is done, in a 1-quart pot mix the cornstarch and cold water. Bring to the boil over medium heat, stirring often, then boil for 5 to 10 seconds, stirring constantly. Open the oven door, pull out the rack, and quickly brush the loaves with the cornstarch glaze. Return the loaves to the oven, close the door, and allow the bread to remain in the oven for 2 minutes. Transfer to a wire rack to cool. Serve warm or at room temperature. Wrap well to store, or freeze when completely cool.

    Note: For 4 smaller loaves, divide the dough into 4 equal pieces, shape into 4 small balls, and place 2 on each baking sheet. Let rise for 30 minutes. Bake for 30 to 35 minutes.

MAMALIGA

Serves 4

The national dish of Romania, *mamaliga* has always been enjoyed by the Jewish population. It is a versatile cornmeal preparation that is served as a porridge, sliced and fried, mixed with cheese (see page 230), or cut into squares as it is here and served as a breadlike side dish. In the traditional method of slicing mamaliga, a string is held taut between the fingers and pulled through a firm slab of the mixture to cut it into squares. Serve the cut squares with stews or other meats.

INGREDIENTS:

2 cups yellow cornmeal
4 cups cold water
1 teaspoon salt

DIRECTIONS:

1. In a 3- or 4-quart pot, mix together the cornmeal and the cold water. Stir in the salt. Bring to the boil over high heat, stirring constantly. As soon as the mixture comes to the boil, reduce the heat to low. Continue cooking for 5 minutes, stirring constantly to prevent lumps. The mixture will be smooth and very thick, becoming difficult to stir.

2. Turn out the mixture onto a clean, dry work surface. Use a spatula and your hands to shape the cornmeal into a 6 x 6-inch square that is 1 inch high. Hold a 15-inch length of string taut between the thumb and index fingers of your hands, slide the string under the slab of mamaliga, and quickly lift up both your hands, making a clean cut. Repeat to cut into small squares.

BAGELS

Makes 12 bagels

In the early 1600s in Eastern Europe, bagels were thought to have magical powers. They were given as gifts to midwives as it was believed that bagels could ward off evil demons that might be present during birth. Because they are circular with no beginning or end, bagels have also come to symbolize the continuous cycle of life. Therefore, it is traditional in Judaism to enjoy bagels not only in celebration of birth, but at the simple meal served at home following a funeral.

In the United States, bagels first became popular as a New York phenomenon. In the 1950s small shops devoted exclusively to selling fresh bagels sprung up in New York City and spread to Long Island. Even today, bagel stores in other parts of the country have signs in the window boasting "New York bagels." In the early 1960s the bagel industry was revolutionized by the Lender family in the New Haven area of Connecticut. The Lenders discovered the power of frozen foods and put bagels in supermarkets throughout the United States, broadening the popularity of bagels from a Jewish "roll" served on Sundays with lox and cream cheese to a toasted breakfast item or sandwich roll enjoyed daily by the population at large.

Bagels differ from other breads or rolls in their texture. They are boiled before being baked, giving them a characteristically chewy texture. The boiling time is the most critical stage for the home baker. If the bagels are boiled too long, they will rise and collapse; then, when baked, they will emerge from the oven heavy and hard but not chewy. If they are boiled for too short a period of time, they will not rise enough and they will seem to be already stale when they come out of the oven. While bagels are most often purchased and rarely prepared at home, they are fun to turn out of your own kitchen. They keep for several days at room temperature, or they can be frozen for later use.

INGREDIENTS:

> 1 package (½ ounce) active dry yeast
> ¼ cup warm water (105 degrees F.)
> 5 cups unbleached white flour, approximately
> 1½ teaspoons salt
> ¼ cup granulated white sugar
> 1¼ cups hot water (120 degrees F.)
> 3 tablespoons mild-tasting vegetable oil
> Beaten egg for glazing the bagels
> Optional toppings: sesame seeds, poppy seeds,
>   chopped onion, minced garlic

DIRECTIONS:

1. In a cup or a small bowl, dissolve the yeast in the ¼ cup of warm water.

2. In a large mixing bowl, stir together 2 cups of the flour, the salt, and sugar. Gradually add the water and the oil, stirring all the while. Using a heavy-duty electric mixer or a wooden spoon, beat for a minute. Beat in the dissolved yeast. Mix in 1 cup of the flour, then another cup, mixing just until the mixture is blended. Spread the remaining cup of flour in a small circle on a clean work surface. Turn out the dough onto the flour. Knead for about 5 minutes, until all the flour is absorbed and the dough is smooth. Add a little more flour if necessary. The dough should not be at all sticky at this point. (If you have a heavy-duty mixer with a dough hook, the kneading can be done by the mixer.)

3. Place the dough in a clean bowl just large enough to accommodate it when doubled in volume. Cover with plastic wrap. Allow the dough to rise in a warm place until doubled. Punch down. Turn onto a clean, dry work surface and knead for about 10 seconds.

4. Divide the dough into 12 equal pieces. Roll each piece into a 10-inch log. Shape into a circle. Overlap the ends slightly, twisting them together and pinching the edges securely to ensure that the ends will not break apart during boiling.

5. Set the circles of dough on a clean, lightly floured work surface. Cover with clean kitchen towels. Let rise for 45 minutes at room temperature.

6. Toward the end of the rising time, adjust an oven rack to the middle of the oven. Preheat the oven to 400 degrees F.

7. At the same time, in an 8-quart pot bring 4 quarts of water to the boil. Carefully drop in 4 bagels, sides not touching. Partially cover the pot. *Do not cover the pot completely or the bagels will absorb too much water.* Adjust the heat so that the water continues to boil rapidly but not violently. Cook the bagels for exactly 4 minutes. The bagels will puff up and more than double in size. Remove with a slotted spoon and transfer to a large greased baking sheet. Cook the remaining bagels 4 at a time, transferring them to the baking sheet.

8. Brush the bagels with the beaten egg. Sprinkle with any of the optional toppings, pressing in lightly. Bake for 18 minutes, until golden. Cool on a wire rack. Serve for brunch with cream cheese and slices of lox, or a cream cheese spread, along with sliced onion and tomatoes. Store leftover bagels in a paper bag for a day or two. (They will become uncharacteristically soft if stored in a plastic bag or container.) If they will not be eaten within two days, freeze the bagels. Freshen them in a warm oven before serving, or toast the bagels if desired.

BIALYS

Makes 8 bialys

If you look quickly at a *bialy* (named after Bialystok, Poland) from the side, you might mistake it for a bagel, but a top view will reveal a thin indented center covered with onions. So a bialy looks much like a bagel (preceding recipe) whose hole is filled in with *pletzel* (onion board, next recipe). The bialy is closer to a roll than to a bagel in taste and texture. While the bagel is chewy throughout, the bialy has a clearly defined crisp crust with a soft, breadlike interior.

Second only to bagels as a vehicle for cream cheese and lox, bialys are usually served at breakfast or brunch. They are delicious split and buttered, an excellent roll to accompany scrambled eggs with lox (page 208) or an omelet.

Experienced bakers may want to double the recipe, but the first-time bialy baker will do well to begin with the more manageable three cups of flour and eight bialys to shape and bake.

INGREDIENTS:

1 package ($\frac{1}{4}$ ounce) active dry yeast

$\frac{1}{4}$ cup warm water (105 degrees F.)

3 cups unbleached white flour, approximately

2 teaspoons granulated white sugar

$\frac{1}{2}$ teaspoon salt

$\frac{3}{4}$ cup hot water (120 degrees F.)

1 tablespoon vegetable oil

1$\frac{1}{4}$ cups chopped onion

Salt

1 egg (graded large), beaten

DIRECTIONS:

1. In a cup or a small bowl, dissolve the yeast in the ¼ cup of warm water.

2. In a large mixing bowl, mix 1½ cups of the flour with the sugar and the ½ teaspoon salt. Stir in the ¾ cup of hot water. Use a wooden spoon to beat for a minute until smooth. Stir in the dissolved yeast and ½ cup of the flour, then another ½ cup of flour. Spread the remaining ½ cup of flour in a small circle on a clean work surface. Turn out the dough onto the flour. (Or, mix the dough in a heavy-duty machine with a dough hook, adding the final half-cup of flour to the bowl.)

3. Knead for about 6 minutes, until the dough is smooth and springy and all the flour is absorbed. Poke a finger into the dough. The indentation should not remain.

4. For the rising, place the dough in a clean bowl just large enough to accommodate it when double in volume. Cover the bowl with a clean kitchen towel or plastic wrap. Let the dough rise at room temperature until it has doubled. This will take about an hour in a 72-degree F. room. Poke a finger into the dough. The indentation should remain, and the dough should not be sticky.

5. Punch down the dough. Turn out the dough onto a clean work surface and knead 3 or 4 times.

6. To shape the bialys, divide the dough into 8 equal pieces. Roll each piece into a ball. Flatten with the palms of your hands, then use a rolling pin or your fingers to enlarge each piece into an even circle about 5 inches in diameter. Transfer to a large greased baking sheet.

7. Cover lightly with a clean kitchen towel or plastic wrap and let the dough rise for about 45 minutes at room temperature (72 degrees F.).

8. In a small skillet, combine the oil and the onion. Cook over moderate heat for a few minutes until the onion is wilted but not yet beginning to brown. Sprinkle with salt to taste. Set aside.

9. Toward the end of the rising time, adjust an oven rack to the middle of the oven. Preheat the oven to 400 degrees F.

10. After the 45 minutes of rising, the dough should be slightly puffy, about double in height. Use your fingers to make a 3-inch indentation in the center of each piece of dough. Brush the surface of the bialys all over with the beaten egg. Fill the indented centers with the cooked onion. Spread evenly.

11. Bake immediately in the 400-degree F. oven for 20 minutes or until crusty and brown. Cool on a wire rack. Bialys can be served warm or at room temperature, and they freeze well.

ONION BOARD
(*Pletzel*)

P*letzel,* a Yiddish word that refers to something flat, is also the word for onion board. A crisp, flat dough smothered with onions and often dotted with poppy seeds, pletzel is related to a German onion tart that is made with bacon and sour cream. As a Jewish preparation, the bacon is omitted, and in its simplest form pletzel is made as a pareve bread without sour cream.

It is likely that onion board originated as a peasant preparation in Europe, much the same way as pizza—an extra piece of dough is stretched thin and covered with ingredients on hand (fresh tomatoes and herbs for pizza, chopped onions and poppy seeds for pletzel). In America, pletzel became a popular item in Jewish bakeries, a thin but chewy and crusty breakfast or brunch treat that could be cut into pieces to be enjoyed by everyone in the family.

The basic dough is easy for the home baker to work with, the topping simple but rich and appetizing. Serve onion board with breakfast or brunch, as a snack at any time, or as a dinner bread with a beef or lamb stew (page 139).

INGREDIENTS:

1 package (¼ ounce) active dry yeast

¼ cup warm water (105 degrees F.)

4½ cups unbleached white flour, approximately

1 teaspoon salt

1 tablespoon granulated white sugar

¾ cup hot water (120 degrees F.)

1 tablespoon vegetable oil

2 eggs (graded large)

3 cups chopped onion
2 tablespoons vegetable oil
Salt and freshly ground black pepper
4 teaspoons poppy seeds

DIRECTIONS:

1. In a cup or a small bowl, dissolve the yeast in the ¼ cup of warm water.

2. For the dough, in a large bowl mix 1 cup of the flour with the teaspoon of salt and the sugar. Mix the ¾ cup of hot water with a tablespoon of oil and, using a large kitchen spoon or a heavy-duty electric mixer with a dough hook, stir the liquid into the flour mixture. Beat in the eggs, then the dissolved yeast. Add 3 cups of the remaining flour 1 cup at a time, stirring until the flour is absorbed.

3. Spread the remaining half cup of flour on a clean, smooth work surface. Turn out the dough onto the flour. Knead for 8 to 10 minutes, working in as much flour as the dough absorbs. Sprinkle on additional flour as necessary. (Or, use the heavy-duty mixer with a dough hook to knead the dough, adding the final half-cup of flour to the bowl.) The dough has been kneaded enough when an indentation springs back when you poke the dough with a finger.

4. Place the dough in a clean, dry bowl just large enough to accommodate it when double in volume. Cover with plastic wrap. Let the dough rise in a warm place until doubled. The rising time will be 1 to 1½ hours, depending on the temperature where the dough is rising.

5. Meanwhile, in a 10-inch skillet sauté the onion in 2 tablespoons of oil over moderate heat until translucent. Sprinkle with salt and pepper to taste. Set aside.

6. When the dough has doubled, punch it down. Knead for 10 seconds to work out any bubbles, then form the dough into a ball.

7. Grease a large baking sheet. Place the dough on the center of the baking sheet, flatten with your hands, then use your fingers to push the dough from the center to the outside to make a rectangle approximately 14 x 16 inches. Pinch the edges up. (Or, shape the dough into two circles, each 12 inches in diameter.)

8. Preheat the oven to 375 degrees F.

9. Spread the cooked onion on the dough, then sprinkle on the poppy seeds.

10. Bake the pletzel on the bottom rack of the oven for 20 to 25 minutes, until the dough is crisp, baked through, and lightly browned. The top should be golden to light brown. Serve warm or at room temperature, cut into squares or rectangles.

8

Desserts and Sweets

Cakes, Pastries, Cookies, and Other Delicacies

Desserts and Sweets

Traditional Jewish cakes, pastries, and cookies are homey rather than gourmet. A thick slice of babka will be dunked into coffee, and a substantial portion of strudel or cheesecake is more likely to be served than a sliver.

In any culture, part of the appeal of food is how it looks. In traditional Jewish cooking, while presentation is a consideration, the emphasis is more on how the food tastes. Thus, a Jewish cook will be proud if the kuchen looks like it came out of a fancy bakery, but disappointment will reign if the kuchen is not eaten and enjoyed. It is the tastiness of the food savored in an atmosphere of warmth that is emphasized, from appetizers all the way through desserts.

Fruit has been important in Jewish cuisine since biblical days, when major holidays were agricultural festivals that celebrated fruit and vegetable harvests. In later years, fresh fruit represented health and wealth to the peasantry of Eastern Europe. Fresh or dried fruit has always been served at the conclusion of the meal among Sephardim. In any modern Jewish household, it remains appropriate to serve fresh, dried, stewed, or even canned fruit at the end of a meal. Typically, at least one kind of cake or pastry will accompany the fruit. Many traditional Jewish cakes contain fruit, with apples and raisins appearing most often. Almonds and pecans are widely used as well.

In Jewish cuisine, any mixing of meat and milk, whether in cooking or eating, violates the laws of *kashrut* (see page 15). Furthermore, depending on the community and the rabbinical authority, observant Jews wait anywhere from one to six hours between eating meat and dairy foods. For those who wait the full six hours, nondairy desserts must follow meat meals. Those following a less rigorous tradition have two options: they can sit and talk for hours while waiting for dairy desserts, or they can serve pareve desserts immediately following the meal (in which case they will still sit and talk for hours).

A modern approach to the culinary problem of wishing to follow a meat meal with a dairy dessert is to use nondairy substitutes. However, in keeping with tradition, only natural ingredients are used in this cookbook, desserts included. A broad range of desserts is covered, from sponge cake to rich coffee-cakes and luscious strudels. Many are pareve, others include milk, cheese, or butter. We begin with a fruit compote, and conclude with one of New York's most famous beverages.

A WORD ABOUT MEASURING FLOUR
FOR CAKES AND PASTRIES

The processing of flour has changed during the last twenty years, and the flour industry no longer considers it necessary to sift flour before measuring. However, flour packs down when it sits on a supermarket or a pantry shelf, and stirring the flour just before measuring is always recommended. In order to avoid packing down the flour when measuring, the flour is spooned gently into a dry-measure cup, then leveled off with the edge of a metal spatula.

Unless otherwise noted, in testing the recipes the flour was not sifted before being measured. If you notice that your flour becomes lumpy upon storage (typically under conditions of high humidity), or if you notice any tiny balls of undissolved flour in your baked products, sift the flour *after* measuring.

If exact measurements were absolutely necessary for successful baking, one would need to weigh the flour to ensure precision. Indeed, in most European cookbooks measurements are by weight. In the recipes in this cookbook, the baker does not need to measure flour by weight to produce excellent baked goods.

As noted previously, the use of unbleached white flour is in keeping with the general philosophy that natural foods go hand-in-hand with traditional Jewish cooking. Unless otherwise noted, white flour refers to all-purpose flour.

COMPOTE OF DRIED FRUIT

Makes 4 cups; serves 6 to 8

Fruit has always been both symbolically and nutritionally important in Jewish cuisine. A plentiful harvest of dates and figs in biblical days was a good omen for the coming year. In later years, Jews living in climates where harsh winters were normal depended on fresh, dried, or reconstituted fruit for vitamins and minerals and to enliven otherwise bleak meals.

A simple compote (stewed fruit) of tender, plump, slightly sweetened prunes and apricots makes a pleasant dessert after a heavy meal and is often featured following lavish holiday meals. It is an excellent way to begin breakfast, and compote makes a satisfying snack as well.

To use four cups of mixed dried fruit in place of the prunes and apricots, cut the dried peaches and pears so they are about the size of the other fruit. If you like the taste of citrus in your compote, note the variation.

INGREDIENTS:

2 cups pitted prunes

2 cups dried apricots

1 cup water

2 tablespoons granulated white sugar

4-inch stick cinnamon, broken into 3 or 4 pieces

Chopped pecans, walnuts, or almonds for garnish
   (optional)

Whipped cream for garnish (optional)

DIRECTIONS:

1. In a 2-quart pot, bring the prunes, apricots, water, sugar, and cinnamon stick to the boil over high heat. Stir gently. Reduce the heat to a gentle boil, cover the pot, and cook for 30 minutes. Make sure that the liquid doesn't boil away, leaving the fruit to burn. Add a little water as necessary.

2. Remove the pot from the heat. Cool the compote in the covered pot. Remove the cinnamon stick, then chill.

3. To serve, spoon into individual dessert dishes. Garnish with chopped nuts if desired. After a dairy meal, you might enjoy topping your compote with whipped cream.

VARIATION:

Compote of Dried Fruit with Lemon and Orange

In place of the cup of water, use ½ cup water, ½ cup orange juice, and 2 tablespoons of freshly squeezed lemon juice. Taste the mixture after the first 15 minutes of cooking. Add a little more sugar as necessary.

APPLE CAKE

Makes one 9-inch tube cake

It is not always easy to find a really good pareve cake to serve after a meat meal, and it was even more difficult in the days before pareve margarine became accessible and widely used. Apple cake made with oil in place of butter may be disappearing from modern cookbooks, but for those who do not use margarine, this moist, fruity cake is a treat as a snack any time or after any meal.

When mixing the apples into the cake batter, you might wonder if you've read the recipe correctly. There will hardly be any cake around the apples. But when the cake has baked, you will see that the proportions are just right. Golden Delicious apples are excellent for cakes because they bake through but do not become too soft. McIntosh lose their shape somewhat but are acceptable. For variety, substitute four cups of unpeeled fresh prune plums, halved and pitted, for the apples. Or use two cups each of apples and plums.

A tube pan with a removable bottom is recommended for this cake. When cooled as directed, the cake will come out of the pan without difficulty.

INGREDIENTS:

> 5 or 6 large apples (enough for 4 cups sliced)
> ¼ cup granulated white sugar mixed with
> > ½ teaspoon cinnamon
> 3 cups unbleached white flour (stir the flour,
> > spoon gently into a dry-measure cup,
> > then level with the edge of a spatula)
> 2 cups granulated white sugar

1 tablespoon baking powder

4 eggs (graded large)

1 cup mild-tasting vegetable oil

¼ cup orange juice

DIRECTIONS:

1. Adjust an oven rack to the bottom third of the oven. Move any other racks below so the tube pan will fit in. Preheat the oven to 350 degrees F.

2. Grease a 9-inch tube pan.

3. Peel, core, and slice enough apples to make 4 cups. Immediately mix the sliced apples with the sugar and cinnamon mixture to prevent darkening.

4. In a large mixing bowl, mix the flour, the 2 cups of sugar, and the baking powder. Add the eggs, oil, and orange juice all at once. Using an electric mixer or a large wooden spoon, beat well until the batter is smooth, about 2 minutes with the mixer, 3 minutes by hand. This is a heavy batter and will be a little difficult to mix.

5. Fold in the apples. Do not use the mixer at this point.

6. Spoon the batter into the tube pan, leveling with a spatula. Bake for 1¼ to 1½ hours, until a toothpick inserted in the center comes out clean and dry.

7. Remove the tube pan from the oven. Place the pan on a wire rack. Do not invert the pan. Allow the cake to cool completely in the pan. When the cake has cooled, use a thin metal spatula or a long, sharp knife to cut around the outside of the cake, then cut around the inner tube. Push up on the bottom of the pan and remove the sides of the pan. Now cut around the bottom of the cake to completely release it from the pan. (Always take care to cut close to the pan so that you do not cut into the cake.) Invert and remove the tube part of the pan, then gently transfer the cake to a serving platter.

MARBLE CAKE

Makes one 9 x 5 x 3-inch loaf

The pound cake, historically made from a pound each of flour, butter, sugar, and eggs, with smaller quantities of flavorings, became part of the Jewish American repertoire as marble cake. Areas of chocolate that taper into striations make marble cake somewhat fancier than the basic pound cake. It is moist and tasty but not overly sweet or rich, and goes well with ice cream, fresh fruit, or compote (page 329).

Part of the popularity of marble cake may be attributed to its availability as a pareve cake both at home and in bakeries, making it ideal for a guest to bring into a kosher home where one might not be sure whether meat or dairy is being served. For the home baker, whether preparing a dairy or pareve marble cake (see the variation made with orange juice), one can put special touches on the marble cake that make it one's own. The cake can be served unfrosted or with a chocolate frosting for the dairy cake, an orange glaze for the pareve. Note that this cake uses an electric mixer and a simplified method of mixing that turns out a moist, even-textured loaf.

For me, marble cake has special meaning. My grandfather enjoyed playing a game with marble cake. Grandma brought the loaf to the dinner table, and Grandpa sliced the cake with one hand, and rolled real marbles down with the other, making it look as though the marbles actually came out of the cake. Of course we all knew that it was just a trick of Grandpa's, but we went along with the act, delighting in seeing the marbles roll onto the table from the cake. So it goes when you love your grandfather.

INGREDIENTS:

> 1 ounce (1 square) unsweetened baking chocolate
> 2 cups unbleached white flour (stir the flour,
>   spoon gently into a dry-measure cup,
>   then level with the edge of a spatula)
> 1 cup granulated white sugar
> 1 tablespoon baking powder
> ¾ cup milk
> ½ cup (1 stick) unsalted butter, at room temperature
> 2 eggs (graded large)
> 2 teaspoons vanilla extract

DIRECTIONS:

1. Melt the chocolate in a small heatproof cup or dish placed in a pan of simmering water. Remove from the heat as soon as the chocolate has melted. Set aside.

2. Adjust an oven rack to the middle of the oven. Move any other racks below so the cake will have room to rise above the pan. Preheat the oven to 350 degrees F.

3. Grease a 9 x 5 x 3-inch loaf pan.

4. In a large mixing bowl, place all of the ingredients except for the melted chocolate. Using an electric mixer, beat on a low speed for 30 seconds to blend the ingredients. Scrape down the bowl. Beat on a moderate speed for 3 minutes, pausing to scrape the sides of the bowl as necessary.

5. Pour half a cup of the batter into a small bowl. Mix the cooled melted chocolate with the half-cup of batter.

6. Pour the remaining batter into the loaf pan. Spread evenly with a spatula. Now spoon the chocolate batter onto the top by tablespoons. To create the marble effect, use a knife to cut through the batter two or three times lengthwise and six or eight times crosswise, swirling the chocolate into the white batter.

7. Bake for 60 to 70 minutes. Check after an hour, then every few minutes as necessary. The top will be brown, no imprint will remain when the cake is touched lightly with the fingertips, the sides will just begin to pull away from the pan, and a cake tester inserted in the middle of the loaf will come out clean. Remove the loaf pan from the oven. Cool right side up on a wire rack for 10 minutes, then loosen the sides of the cake with a knife. Quickly turn the cake upside down. It will drop out of the loaf pan in one piece. Turn the cake right side up. Cool, then wrap well. The cake will keep at room temperature for several days, but it is at its best when eaten within a day or two of baking. It freezes very well.

VARIATION:

Orange-flavor Marble Cake

For a pareve cake, substitute orange juice for the milk and a mild-tasting vegetable oil for the butter. If desired, instead of the 2 teaspoons vanilla extract, use 1½ teaspoons vanilla extract and ½ teaspoon almond or lemon extract for flavoring.

LEMON-ORANGE SPONGE CAKE

Makes one 9-inch tube cake

Highly versatile, sponge cake batter can be baked in a tube pan and glazed, in a jelly-roll pan and filled with jam, as cupcakes, or in layers and filled and topped with whipped cream and fruit. Unlike the French *genoise,* which is made with butter, or the chiffon cake, which is made with oil, the sponge cake contains no shortening or oil. While sponge cake can be made with baking powder, the oldest traditional Jewish recipes rely on beaten eggs alone for leavening. The basic sponge cake is made without dairy products and is a fine finale for any meal. The subtle flavorings of lemon and orange in this recipe make this sponge cake especially suitable as a snack at tea time.

Sponge cake is light and airy in texture, and more precision is necessary in measuring the flour than for less delicate cakes. Therefore, the flour is sifted before being measured. If the sugar is lumpy, sifting is recommended as well. To bake as a tube cake, a tube pan with a removable bottom is necessary to ensure that the cake will come out in one piece without any tearing.

INGREDIENTS:

> 6 eggs (graded large), separated
>
> 1½ cups granulated white sugar
>
> ½ cup orange juice
>
> 1 teaspoon vanilla extract
>
> 1 teaspoon lemon extract
>
> 1½ cups sifted unbleached white flour (stir the
> flour, spoon gently into a dry-measure cup,
> then level with the edge of a spatula)

DIRECTIONS:

1. Adjust an oven rack to the lower third of the oven. Move any other racks below. Preheat the oven to 325 degrees F.

2. In a medium-size mixing bowl, use an electric mixer to beat the egg yolks and the sugar on high speed for 5 minutes. The egg yolks will become very thick and pale yellow.

3. Mix together the orange juice and the vanilla and lemon extracts. On a low speed, blend the liquid into the egg yolks.

4. Remove the beaters from the bowl. Resift the flour ½ cup at a time directly onto the egg-yolk mixture, then use a rubber spatula to fold the flour into the mixture. You can *gently* stir for even mixing at this point, but do not beat.

5. In a large clean, dry bowl, with clean, dry beaters, beat the egg whites until they hold stiff peaks but are still moist. Using a rubber spatula, gently fold (do not stir) half the egg whites into the yolk mixture, then fold the mixture back into the whites. The object is to combine the ingredients as quickly as possible without collapsing the beaten egg whites. To fold the whites into the yolk mixture, spoon about a cupful of egg whites at a time on top of the batter. Use a rubber spatula to cut through the center of the egg whites and the batter all the way down to the bottom of the bowl. Bring the spatula up against the side of the bowl, turn the bowl a quarter turn, cut through again. Repeat until half the whites have been mixed in, then reverse the procedure, gently folding the egg yolk mixture into the remaining whites.

6. Turn the batter into an ungreased 9-inch tube pan that has a removable bottom. Cut through the batter gently to make sure there are no large air pockets. Level the top. Bake for 1 hour or until the cake is brown, it springs back when lightly touched, and a cake tester comes out clean.

7. Invert the tube pan and cool the cake completely before removing. When the cake has cooled, use a long, sharp knife to cut around the outside of the

cake, then cut around the inner tube. Push up on the bottom of the pan and remove the sides of the pan. Now cut around the bottom of the cake to completely release it from the pan. (Always take care to cut close to the pan so that you do not cut into the cake.) Invert and remove the tube part of the pan, then gently transfer the cake to a serving platter.

Sponge cake freezes well either unfrosted or frosted with a confectioners' sugar glaze (below) or a buttercream or fudge icing.

ORANGE-FLAVORED CONFECTIONERS' SUGAR GLAZE:

Mix the grated rind of 1 orange with 2 cups of sifted confectioners' sugar. Resift the sugar into a medium-size bowl. Blend in freshly squeezed orange juice a tablespoon at a time until the mixture is just thin enough to spoon over the cooled cake. You will need about 1/4 cup of juice. Spoon the glaze over the top of the cake, allowing some to drizzle over the sides.

VARIATION:

Jam-filled Sponge Layer Cake

To bake in layers, line the bottoms of three 8-inch cake pans with wax paper. Preheat the oven to 350 degrees F. Follow the recipe above, dividing the batter among the cake pans. Bake on the middle rack (and upper if necessary) of the oven. The sides of the pans should not touch each other. Bake for 20 to 25 minutes or until done (see Step 6). Cool upside down on wire racks. Remove the layers from the pans when they are cool.

For the filling, mix together 1/2 cup each of seedless raspberry and apricot jam. Spread half the mixture on each of 2 layers, stacking the layers. To dust the top layer with confectioners' sugar, place about a tablespoon of confectioners' sugar at a time in a sifter. Sift directly onto the cake, moving the sifter as necessary to cover the layer completely.

PASSOVER CHOCOLATE ROLL

Makes one 10-inch chocolate roll

This cakelike dessert is based on a thin spongelike layer that contains neither the potato flour nor the matzo cake meal used in most Passover cakes. Nonetheless, it has enough substance from its beaten egg structure to make a fine jelly roll. Dark in color, light in texture, and deliciously chocolate, it is elegant when filled with whipped cream.

INGREDIENTS:

12 ounces semisweet chocolate pieces

4 tablespoons brewed coffee

7 eggs (graded large), separated

¾ cup granulated white sugar

DIRECTIONS:

1. Lightly grease a 10 x 15-inch jelly-roll pan with vegetable shortening. Line the pan with a piece of wax paper, and lightly grease the wax paper as well.

2. Preheat the oven to 350 degrees F.

3. Place the chocolate pieces and the coffee in a heatproof container set into a pan of simmering water. Melt the chocolate. Stir to combine the chocolate and coffee and remove the mixture from the heat.

4. In a medium-size mixing bowl, use an electric mixer to beat the egg yolks with ½ cup of the sugar on high speed for 5 minutes. The mixture will become

very thick and pale yellow. Stir the melted and somewhat cooled chocolate mixture into the beaten egg yolks.

5. In a large clean, dry mixing bowl with clean, dry beaters, beat the egg whites on high speed until they are frothy. Gradually add the remaining ¼ cup of sugar and continue beating until the egg whites hold stiff peaks.

6. Fold the egg whites into the chocolate mixture. To fold, turn out the beaten egg whites on top of the chocolate batter. Use a rubber spatula to cut through the center of the egg whites and the batter all the way down to the bottom of the bowl. Bring the spatula up against the side of the bowl, turn the bowl a quarter turn, cut through again. Repeat until the egg whites have been gently mixed in. The whole procedure should take under a minute.

7. Spread the batter evenly in the jelly-roll pan. Bake on the middle rack of the oven for 15 minutes or until the top springs back when lightly touched.

8. Meanwhile, cut a sheet of wax paper a little bigger than the size of the jelly-roll pan. Sprinkle the wax paper with granulated sugar. Remove the cake from the oven. Loosen the edges and immediately place the jelly-roll pan upside down on the sugared sheet of wax paper. If the layer does not come out, tap the bottom of the pan with a large metal spoon or spatula. Carefully peel off the wax paper. Beginning with the 10-inch edge, tightly roll up the cake, including the sheet of wax paper on which it was placed. The wax paper will be removed after the rolled cake has cooled. Cool the roll on a wire rack. Note that whatever filling is selected, the cake must first be rolled up unfilled, cooled, then filled and rerolled.

9. For a pareve dessert, spread the chocolate roll with a cup of apricot or seedless raspberry jam, or a mixture of the two, and roll tightly into a jelly roll. For a luscious dairy dessert, spread the chocolate roll with sweetened whipped cream, roll up carefully, and chill.

PASSOVER NUT TORTE

Makes one 9-inch torte

Here is an exceedingly rich pareve nut torte, deliciously spiced with cloves and cinnamon, topped with preserves for extra enjoyment. Small pieces of this luxurious torte are especially good with hot tea. A splendid dessert for Passover or any occasion.

INGREDIENTS:

4 eggs (graded large), separated
1½ cups granulated white sugar
1 cup coarsely ground walnuts
⅛ to ¼ teaspoon ground cloves
¼ teaspoon ground cinnamon
1 teaspoon lemon juice
¼ cup sweet Passover wine
¼ cup seedless raspberry preserves
¼ cup apricot preserves

DIRECTIONS:

1. Adjust an oven rack to the middle of the oven. Move other racks as necessary to allow room for the springform pan. Preheat the oven to 350 degrees F.

2. Grease the bottom and 1 inch up the sides of a 9-inch springform pan.

3. While the oven is heating, in a small mixing bowl use an electric mixer on high speed to beat the egg yolks with the granulated sugar for 5 minutes. The yolks will become very thick and pale yellow.

4. In a large mixing bowl, mix the ground nuts with the cloves to taste and the cinnamon. Sprinkle the lemon juice and wine over the nut mixture.

5. In a medium-size clean, dry mixing bowl, with clean, dry beaters, beat the egg whites until they hold stiff peaks but are still moist. Pour about a third of the egg yolk mixture at a time on top of the beaten egg whites and fold the yolks into the whites. To fold, use a rubber spatula to cut through the center of the egg yolks and whites all the way down to the bottom of the bowl. Bring the spatula up against the side of the bowl, turn the bowl a quarter turn, cut through again. Repeat until the yolks have been gently mixed in. Fold in another third of the yolk mixture, finally the remainder. The whole procedure should take under a minute.

6. Stir the nut mixture to mix in the lemon juice and wine. Now fold the egg mixture into the nuts. Turn out into the springform pan. Level the top.

7. Bake for 45 minutes. The top of the torte will be crusty, the filling will be set. A cake tester inserted in the torte will come out clean. Cool the torte in the springform pan on a wire rack. Do not remove the outer ring until the torte has cooled.

8. Before serving, run a knife around the outside of the torte. Release the ring of the springform. Mix together the raspberry and apricot preserves. Spread the jam mixture on top of the torte, leaving ¼ inch margin around the edges. Do not attempt to remove the torte from the bottom of the spring-form pan. The torte can be left to stand at room temperature for several hours, but eventually it needs to be refrigerated. To store, put the ring back on the springform. Cover the top of the springform with aluminum foil. This will prevent refrigerator odors from permeating the cake.

HONEY CAKE
(*Lekach*)

Makes two 8½ x 4½-inch loaves

The word *lekach,* Yiddish for honey cake, can be traced to the Book of Proverbs (4:2): "Because I give you good instruction [*lekach*], do not forsake my teaching." The instruction refers to the Torah portions that are studied. Based on this connection, it has become traditional among Ashkenazim to serve honey cake on Rosh Hashanah to express the hope that one will be blessed with "a good portion," which is taken to mean a healthy, good, sweet year.

Honey cake is sweet and moist, keeps well at room temperature for several days when wrapped tightly, and it freezes well.

INGREDIENTS:

3 cups unbleached white flour (stir the flour,
   spoon gently into a dry-measure cup,
   then level with the edge of a spatula)

1 teaspoon baking soda

1 teaspoon baking powder

1 teaspoon ground cinnamon

4 eggs (graded large)

1 cup granulated white sugar

1 cup honey

¼ cup mild-tasting vegetable oil

1 cup brewed coffee, at room temperature

DIRECTIONS:

1. Adjust an oven rack to the middle of the oven. Move other racks below to allow the loaves enough rising space. Preheat the oven to 350 degrees F.

2. Grease two 8½ x 4½-inch loaf pans.

3. In a medium-size mixing bowl, stir together the flour, baking soda, baking powder, and cinnamon. Set aside.

4. In a large mixing bowl, use a rotary beater or an electric mixer to beat the eggs with the sugar until very thick and light in color. Gradually beat in the honey, then the oil.

5. Add the flour mixture and the coffee alternately, beating just enough after each addition to make the batter smooth.

6. Pour into the prepared pans. Bake for 55 to 60 minutes, until brown on top and baked through. If the cakes brown too quickly, cover the tops loosely with foil. A toothpick or cake tester inserted in the middle of the loaves will come out clean when the loaves are done.

7. Place the pans right side up on a wire rack for 5 minutes. Loosen the sides of the honey cakes, turn over the pans, and remove the cakes from the loaf pans. Cool before slicing. Honey cake keeps well at room temperature if tightly wrapped in foil, and it freezes well.

VARIATIONS:

Honey Cake with Raisins and Nuts

Stir 1 cup of dark raisins and 1 cup of chopped walnuts into the batter.

Honey Cake with Orange Flavor

Scatter 1 tablespoon of grated orange rind over the dry ingredients, stirring with a fork to distribute the rind evenly. Substitute ¾ cup brewed coffee and ¼ cup freshly squeezed orange juice for the 1 cup of brewed coffee.

COTTAGE CHEESE CAKE

Makes one 9-inch cake

Old-fashioned Eastern European cheesecakes began with homemade cottage or pot cheese. Cottage cheese is an uncured cheese that was introduced to Eastern Europeans hundreds of years ago by marauding Mongols as a way of using surplus milk. Skimmed milk left in a warm area will naturally sour and separate into curds and whey. The curds, when drained and crumbled, become dry cottage cheese, which is salted and then mixed with cream and/or butter to restore some of the butterfat. Additional cream is added for creamed cottage cheese. For Jews observing the dietary laws, cottage cheese is especially appealing because no rennet (an animal product) is required for coagulation.

In Russia, the festive cheesecake specialty for the general population is the molded *paskha,* while the everyday cheesecake is *vatrushki,* a pot-cheese tart. Hungarian cheesecakes are covered with a top layer of dough, and German cheesecakes begin with a cookielike dough for a crust. The cheesecakes that evolved into traditional Jewish cheesecakes are usually made with a bottom crust of zwieback or graham cracker crumbs. If there is a topping, it is likely to be crushed pineapple, a sour cherry mixture, or another fruit topping.

For the filling, cottage cheese might simply be mixed with eggs, sugar, and a little lemon juice or vanilla extract for flavoring, or—as in this recipe—made rich and custardy with egg yolks and cream, light with separately beaten egg whites. Today's bakers enjoy using exotic flavorings such as amaretto or orange liqueur (see the variation).

In traditional Jewish homes, cheesecake is a favorite dessert for Shavuot, when cheese products are consumed.

INGREDIENTS:

1¼ **cups graham cracker crumbs**

¼ **cup (½ stick) unsalted butter, melted**

2 **cups (16 ounces) creamed cottage cheese**

4 **eggs (graded large), separated**

1 **cup granulated white sugar**

1 **cup light cream**

2 **teaspoons freshly squeezed lemon juice**

1 **teaspoon vanilla extract**

DIRECTIONS:

1. For the crust, in a medium-size bowl mix together the graham cracker crumbs and the melted butter with a fork. Turn out into a 9-inch spring-form pan. Using your fingers or the back of a spoon, press the crumbs even-ly on the bottom and ½ inch up the sides of the pan.

2. Adjust an oven rack to the lower third of the oven. Adjust any upper racks to leave room for the springform pan. Preheat the oven to 350 degrees F.

3. Purée the cottage cheese in 2 batches in a blender. If you do not have a blender, pass the cottage cheese through a food mill or a sieve. This step is essential for a smooth, custardy filling.

4. In a large mixing bowl, use an electric mixer on a medium speed to mix together the cottage cheese and the egg yolks. Beat in the sugar, the cream, and the flavorings. The batter will be thin.

5. In a small clean, dry mixing bowl, with a clean, dry whisk or beaters, beat the egg whites until they hold stiff peaks but are still moist. Gently fold the egg whites into the cheesecake mixture. To fold, spoon about a cupful of egg whites at a time on top of the batter. Use a rubber spatula to cut

through the center of the egg whites and the batter all the way down to the bottom of the bowl. Bring the spatula up against the side of the bowl, turn the bowl a quarter turn, cut through again. Repeat until the first cup of egg whites has been gently mixed in. Continue with the remaining beaten whites. The whole procedure should take under a minute so that the egg whites do not deflate.

6. Pour the mixture into the prepared springform pan. Immediately reduce the heat to 325 degrees F. Bake for 45 minutes. If you take a quick peek at the cheesecake at this point, you will note that the cake has risen and the top is lightly browned. The top will yield to the gentle pressing of the fingertips. Turn off the oven and leave the cheesecake in the oven with the door closed until it has cooled completely. The slow cooling away from drafts will help prevent fissures from forming as the cheesecake cools. When it has reached room temperature, cover and refrigerate the cheesecake.

7. Before serving, run a knife around the outside of the cake. Release the ring of the springform. Do not attempt to remove the entire cheesecake from the bottom of the springform. The cake will keep in the refrigerator for several days. It should be wrapped well to avoid picking up odors from other foods.

VARIATION:

Cottage Cheese Cake with Amaretto or Orange Liqueur

Omit the lemon juice and vanilla extract. Substitute a tablespoon of amaretto or an orange liqueur.

CREAM CHEESE CAKE

Makes one 9-inch cake

Traditional Jewish cheesecakes are made with cottage (or pot) cheese or cream cheese. This recipe, which uses cream cheese, produces a creamy but solid cake that is typical of New York-style cheesecakes. During baking, the cake will rise, and as it cools, it will fall. Sometimes, even if the cheesecake bakes at a moderate temperature and cools gradually, a crack develops in the top. This does not affect the taste, and a blanket of sliced fresh strawberries or a fresh fruit sauce (see variation) is a delicious way to cover the crack.

INGREDIENTS:

1¼ cups graham cracker crumbs

¼ cup (½ stick) unsalted butter, melted

2 packages (8 ounces each) cream cheese, at room
temperature

4 eggs (graded large)

1 cup granulated white sugar

2 cups (1 pint) sour cream

1 teaspoon vanilla extract

DIRECTIONS:

1. For the crust, in a medium-size bowl mix together the graham cracker crumbs and the melted butter with a fork. Turn out into a 9-inch spring-form pan. Using your fingers or the back of a spoon, press the crumbs evenly on the bottom and ½ inch up the sides of the pan.

2. Adjust an oven rack to the middle of the oven. Move other racks below. Preheat the oven to 325 degrees F.

3. For the cheesecake, in a large mixing bowl use an electric mixer to beat the cream cheese on a moderate speed until it is creamy. Scrape the cream cheese off the beaters. Beat in the eggs one at a time. Beat in the sugar, then the sour cream, and finally the vanilla. The mixture should be smooth.

4. Pour the mixture into the prepared springform pan. Bake at 325 degrees F. for 45 minutes. Turn off the oven and leave the cheesecake in the oven for 30 minutes, then open the oven door and allow the cheesecake to cool to room temperature. Cover the cheesecake and refrigerate.

5. Before serving, run a knife around the outside of the cake. Release the ring of the springform. Do not attempt to remove the entire cheesecake from the bottom of the springform. Cheesecake will keep in the refrigerator for several days. It should be wrapped well to avoid picking up odors from other foods. The plain cheesecake can be frozen whole or in slices if wrapped well.

VARIATION:

Cheesecake with Fresh Fruit Sauce Topping

You will need 2 cups (1 pint) of fresh strawberries or blueberries for the topping. In a 1-quart pot, mix 1 cup of hulled and mashed fresh strawberries or 1 cup of whole fresh blueberries with 2 tablespoons of granulated white sugar, 2 teaspoons of cornstarch, and a teaspoon of freshly squeezed lemon juice. Bring to the boil over moderate heat, reduce to a gentle boil and cook for 2 minutes, stirring frequently. Cool to room temperature. Arrange 1 cup of hulled whole fresh strawberries or blueberries on top of the cheesecake. Spoon the cooled sauce over the cake. Chill until serving.

Fresh Fruit Kuchen

Makes one 8-inch square cake

Rich and buttery coffeecakes of Germany were brought to America by the Ashkenazim. Although many traditional Jewish coffeecakes use yeast and therefore require advance planning, the exceptionally tasty biscuitlike dough in this recipe is ready in a matter of minutes. Fruit *kuchen* (the German word for cake) is a delectable coffeetime snack or dessert that is nutritious as well, taking advantage of fresh fruit in season. Serve warm from the oven. Leftovers will keep for a day or two at room temperature.

INGREDIENTS:

1 cup unbleached white flour (stir the flour,
   spoon gently into a dry-measure cup,
   then level with the edge of a spatula)

¼ cup granulated white sugar

1 teaspoon baking powder

¼ cup (½ stick) unsalted butter, at room
   temperature

1 egg (graded large or extra large), beaten

1 tablespoon water or milk if necessary

3 to 4 large apples, peaches, or nectarines (enough
   for 2 cups sliced), or 12 prune plums

¼ cup granulated white sugar mixed with
   ½ teaspoon ground cinnamon

DIRECTIONS:

1. Preheat the oven to 375 degrees F.

2. In a medium-size mixing bowl, use a fork to stir together the flour, sugar, and baking powder. Break up the butter with your fingers or a pastry blender and work it into the dry ingredients until the particles are small and evenly distributed. Stir in the egg. If the dough is crumbly, sprinkle in a tablespoon of water or milk.

3. Press the dough into an ungreased 8-inch square pan.

4. Peel, core, and slice enough apples to make 2 cups. Or, peel and slice enough peaches and/or nectarines to make 2 cups, discarding the stones. Or, cut the unpeeled prune plums in half, discarding the stones. Arrange the fruit in tightly-packed rows on top of the dough. Press in lightly. Sprinkle with the sugar and cinnamon mixture.

5. Bake on the middle rack of the oven for 25 minutes. Remove from the oven. Cut into squares to serve.

COTTAGE CHEESE STRUDEL

Makes one 28-inch roll

Strudel—an ultra-thin flaky pastry that is rolled around a sweet or savory filling and baked to golden prefection—is well known in both Ashkenazic and Sephardic Jewish cuisines. Ashkenazim know strudel as an Austrian or a Hungarian delicacy, a hand-stretched pastry; Sephardim recognize strudel as a Turkish or Greek pastry that uses thin phyllo leaves. The two strudels are closely related.

Strudel dough that is made with oil must be as thin as possible to become crisp rather than chewy. Among Ashkenazic Jews, the traditional method of preparing strudel involves a long and difficult production of stretching the dough by hand, more accurately by the knuckles. The dough is placed on a table, preferably round, that has been covered with a clean sheet. All jewelry is removed, and the hands are placed under the dough. The process of stretching strudel dough from the center outward continues until the dough is so thin that one should be able to read a newspaper through it.

I think it is unrealistic to expect most home bakers to stretch a small ball of dough to a thin sheet the size of a large kitchen table. The more manageable size here, while using the traditional method, produces a thin enough, many-layered pastry. Bread flour, which is available in national brands, makes a strong dough that helps prevent the cottage cheese from leaking out. The filling is sweet but not cloying, making it suitable not only for dessert but as a breakfast pastry or snack. To serve with soup, reduce the sugar to one tablespoon. A fine Shavuot treat any time of day.

For apple strudel, use the filling in the next recipe.

INGREDIENTS:

1¼ cups bread flour (stir the flour, spoon gently
　　into a dry-measure cup, then level with
　　the edge of a spatula)
¼ teaspoon salt (optional)
⅜ cup lukewarm water (not over 100 degrees F.)
2 tablespoons beaten egg
1 tablespoon mild-tasting vegetable oil or melted
　　unsalted butter
1 cup (8 ounces) small-curd creamed cottage cheese
½ cup (4 ounces) farmer cheese
1 egg (graded large)
¼ cup granulated white sugar
½ cup dark raisins
2 tablespoons melted unsalted butter for brushing
　　the dough
¼ cup breadcrumbs
Beaten egg for glazing

DIRECTIONS:

1. In a medium-size mixing bowl, place the flour and salt. In a small bowl or a cup, mix together the water, the 2 tablespoons of egg, and the tablespoon of oil or melted butter. Add the liquid all at once to the flour and salt. Beat with a wooden spoon until the mixture holds together. Don't worry if the dough is sticky at this point.

2. Turn out onto a clean, smooth work surface. Using a pastry scraper or a rubber spatula, scrape up the dough in one piece, lift it about a foot above the counter, and throw the dough down onto the counter. Repeat about a dozen times, until the dough becomes springy and loses its stickiness. Cover with a clean kitchen towel while preparing the filling.

3. Use a spoon to beat together the cottage cheese, farmer cheese, egg, and sugar. Mix in the raisins. Set aside.

4. Adjust an oven rack to the middle of the oven. Preheat the oven to 425 degrees F.

5. Grease a large baking sheet.

6. Lightly flour a large clean, smooth work surface at least 3 feet long and 1½ feet wide. Flatten the dough between your hands, then gently stretch to a 6-inch circle. Place the dough on the floured surface. Place your hands under the dough, palms down. Working from the center outward, stretch the dough gently over the backs of your hands. If you are not making progress, use a rolling pin from time to time to stretch and even out the dough. The goal is a rectangle 26 to 28 inches long and 14 to 16 inches wide.

7. When the dough is the correct size, trim off the thick edges. Brush the dough thoroughly with 2 tablespoons of melted butter, then sprinkle with the breadcrumbs. Spread the filling in a strip an inch in from the long edge, ½ inch in from the ends. The filling will flow to about 3 inches wide.

8. Roll the dough around the filling as tightly as possible, jelly-roll style. Pinch the long edge against the filled roll, then pinch the ends and tuck under. Carefully transfer to the greased baking sheet, making a horseshoe so you don't have to cut the dough in half. (The filling will leak out if you cut through.) Brush all exposed surfaces with well-beaten egg.

9. Bake in the middle of the oven for 20 minutes or until golden brown. Carefully transfer to a wire rack to cool. Slice into serving-size pieces just before serving. Serve warm or at room temperature.

Note: To make 2 smaller rolls, divide the dough in half. Stretch and roll the dough to make two rectangles approximately 12 x 14 inches each.

APPLE STRUDEL WITH PHYLLO

The homemade phyllo dough of the Sephardim is an olive oil pastry (see page 56) that is not used often because prepackaged phyllo dough is readily available. Even if you like to cook everything from scratch, there are times when you will want to take advantage of the prepared, thinner-than-paper phyllo pastry. Buy fresh phyllo leaves if you can, as they will be softer and easier to use than the frozen leaves available in supermarkets. Phyllo leaves dry out very quickly. Do not open the package until you are ready to use the pastry, and always keep unused leaves covered with plastic wrap or a damp but not wet kitchen towel. Treat phyllo leaves with respect, not just because they are fragile, but because they make superb, crisp, flaky strudel.

INGREDIENTS:

5 or 6 large Golden Delicious, McIntosh, Greening or
    other cooking apples (enough for 4 cups sliced)
¼ cup granulated white sugar
½ teaspoon ground cinnamon
6 tablespoons (¾ stick) unsalted butter, melted
    (substitute vegetable oil for pareve)
2 tablespoons dry breadcrumbs or crushed cornflakes
½ cup dark raisins
½ cup chopped walnuts
8 leaves phyllo (approximately 14 x 18 inches each)

DIRECTIONS:

1. Preheat the oven to 425 degrees F.

2. Grease a large baking sheet.

3. Peel, core, and slice enough apples to make 4 cups. Mix the apples with the sugar and cinnamon. Set aside. Have the remaining ingredients measured.

4. Open the package of phyllo. Peel off 1 sheet of phyllo pastry and place it on a flat surface. Immediately cover the remaining phyllo completely. Brush the first sheet of phyllo lavishly with melted butter. Repeat with 3 more layers of phyllo, brushing well each time. Sprinkle the top layer with half of the breadcrumbs or cornflakes.

5. Spread half the apples in a strip along a long end of the dough, leaving an inch margin on the long edge and half an inch on each end. Scatter half the raisins and half the nuts on top of the apples.

6. Carefully roll up the dough around the filling, making a long, thin roll. Tuck under the ends. Place flap side down on the baking sheet. Brush the top and sides all over with the melted butter.

7. Repeat with the remaining ingredients, making a second log.

8. Cut through the top of the first few layers of the pastry, marking whatever size pieces you will want, but do not cut through the apples or the filling will leak out during baking. The top layers of phyllo must be cut before baking because they will tear if you wait until after the pastry has baked.

9. Bake on the middle rack of the oven for 25 to 30 minutes, until the pastry is crisp and brown and the apples are tender. Remove the baking sheet from the oven. Run a metal spatula or pancake turner under the pastry to make sure that it will not stick. Cut the strudel into slices while still warm. Serve warm or at room temperature. To crisp cold strudel, place in a 350-degree F. oven for a few minutes.

MOHN STRUDEL

Makes two 11-inch rolls

You can imagine my pleasure at a community-wide *Oneg Shabbat* when I saw a senior citizen couple quietly packing up a plate of my mohn strudel to take home. Although somewhat embarrassed upon noticing me, they explained that "you don't see homemade mohn strudel these days. We haven't had it in years."

Mohn (Hebrew for manna; also the Yiddish and German word for poppy seeds) cakes from Germany and poppy seed strudels from Hungary (*rétes* in Hungarian) are traditional Ashkenazic pastries. Poppy seeds are significant in Judaism because they are said to resemble the "manna from heaven" that fed the Israelites when they fled Egypt with Moses and wandered in the desert for forty years. While one can still buy mohn strudel in Jewish bakeries, it is indeed rare for the home baker to make poppy seed strudel, and even more unusual to start with poppy seeds instead of using a can of filling.

To guarantee a smooth, moist filling, before cooking the filling you will need to grind the poppy seeds in a spice grinder or a coffee bean grinder. If you do not grind them, the filling will have a seedy rather than a smooth consistency. Filling prepared from ground seeds is somewhat richer; the texture is a matter of personal preference. Poppy seeds are often available in bulk at health food stores, where they are sometimes considerably less expensive than the small quantities available on supermarket shelves.

The strudel dough in this recipe calls for shortening, which melts during baking, making tiny pockets of flaky dough. The dough is somewhat easier to make than the traditional strudel dough, as it does not need to be stretched as much. Mohn strudel can also be made with the dough on page 352 or with phyllo pastry (see the previous recipe).

INGREDIENTS:

FOR THE FILLING:

> 1 cup poppy seeds
> ¼ cup honey
> ½ cup water

FOR THE DOUGH:

> 1¼ cups unbleached white flour (stir the flour,
>   spoon gently into a dry-measure cup,
>   then level with the edge of a spatula)
> Pinch of salt
> 2 tablespoons solid white vegetable shortening
> 1 egg (graded large or extra large)
> 2 teaspoons water, approximately
> Beaten egg for sealing and glazing

DIRECTIONS:

1. For a smooth filling, grind the poppy seeds in a spice grinder or a coffee grinder. The seeds can be ground to a powder or even to a paste, depending on the grinder.

2. For the filling, in a 1-quart pot bring the ground poppy seeds, honey, and water to the boil over high heat. Reduce to a gentle boil and cook uncovered for about 4 minutes, stirring frequently, until the mixture becomes very thick. Be careful of spattering as the water boils off. Reduce the heat to low, cover the pot, and cook for an additional 2 minutes. Remove from the heat and cool to room temperature before using.

   For poppy seeds that have not been ground, cook the mixture uncovered for 8 minutes, then cover and cook for an additional 2 minutes. The mixture should be the consistency of a thick porridge. If desired, purée the mixture in a blender or a food processor. While the mixture will still be seedy, it will become somewhat less granular. Cool to room temperature.

3. For the dough, in a small bowl mix together the flour and salt. Use your fingers or a fork to work in the shortening, then the egg. Sprinkle in enough water to make a pliable, slightly sticky dough. Cover and let rest for about 15 minutes.

4. Adjust an oven rack to the middle of the oven. Preheat the oven to 375 degrees F.

5. Grease a large baking sheet.

6. Divide the dough into 2 equal pieces. Place each piece on a well-floured work surface. Roll out each piece of dough to a 5 x 7-inch rectangle. The dough will be easier to roll out if you work back and forth between the two pieces, which allows the gluten to relax between handlings. Continue to work back and forth between the two pieces as you use a combination of gentle rolling and stretching until each rectangle is 9 x 12 inches.

7. Spread half the filling to within half an inch of the edges of each rectangle of dough. Beginning at one long end, roll up the dough tightly, jelly-roll style. Seal the long edge with beaten egg, then pinch and tuck under the ends to seal. Brush the top of the filled rolls with beaten egg.

8. Bake for about 30 minutes, until golden. Carefully transfer to a wire rack to cool. While still warm, cut through the top of the dough to mark the slices. Cut all the way through when cool.

BABKA

Makes one 9-inch tube cake

A buttery yeast batter made with both whole eggs and egg yolks, studded with raisins, and flavored with lemon or orange peel produces *babka,* a Polish coffeecake that found its way into Jewish bakeries and homes in the United States. The success of babka for home bakers can be attributed to its relative ease of preparation and the fact that one's individual touch can be put on the basic recipe (refer to the variations).

The method below is different from the chocolate-filled babka in the next recipe, but those familiar with traditional Jewish coffeecakes will say "Umm, babka" when presented with either. Both babka recipes use moderate amounts of butter and egg yolks, which can be increased according to personal taste.

Plain babka is not too sweet, making it a good between-meal snack with coffee or tea. It can even be sliced and toasted for breakfast. Whether plain or toasted, babka is served in the traditional Eastern European style, in thick slices. Babka can also be prepared with a sweet syrup that is poured over the cake after it is removed from the oven (see the orange-apricot variation). Expect the babka in this recipe to have the coarse texture of any batter bread that is prepared with a simplified method of mixing, no kneading, and only one rising.

Although typically made in a special *kugelhopf* mold or a fluted tube (Bundt) pan, a regular tube pan turns out a fine babka, and two medium-size loaf pans (5 cups, 8½ x 4½-inch size) can be used as well.

INGREDIENTS:

1 package (¼ ounce) active dry yeast
¼ cup warm water (105 degrees F.)

1 cup unbleached white flour (stir the flour,
    spoon gently into a dry-measure cup,
    then level with the edge of a spatula)
¼ cup granulated white sugar
¾ cup hot milk (120 degrees F.)
½ cup (1 stick) unsalted butter, at room
    temperature
1 tablespoon grated lemon or orange rind
2 eggs (graded extra large)
2 egg yolks
¼ cup granulated white sugar
2 cups unbleached white flour (measured as above)
1 cup dark raisins

DIRECTIONS:

1. In a small bowl or a cup, dissolve the yeast in the warm water.

2. In a large mixing bowl, stir together the first cup of flour, the first ¼ cup of sugar, and the dissolved yeast. Stir in the hot milk, mixing to blend. The flour can be somewhat lumpy at this point. Set aside for a few minutes while you measure the remaining ingredients. The yeast will begin its activity and the mixture will have begun to bubble when you come back to it.

3. Slice the butter into 8 or 9 pieces. Scatter the butter and the lemon or orange rind onto the yeast mixture. Add the eggs and egg yolks, the remaining ¼ cup of sugar, and the 2 cups of flour. Beat for 2 minutes with an electric mixer on high speed. Mix in the raisins.

4. Butter a 9-inch (12-cup) tube pan. Use a rubber spatula to turn the batter into the tube pan, leveling the top. Cover with plastic wrap and allow the batter to rise in a cool room (68 to 70 degrees F.) until it reaches the top of

the pan, 2½ to 3 hours. Check from time to time, and remove the plastic wrap before the batter touches the top. (You can speed up the rising time by placing the batter in a warmer area, up to 85 degrees F., but that will impart a yeasty flavor to the babka.)

5. Toward the end of the rising time, adjust an oven rack to the bottom third of the oven. Move any other racks below so the tube pan will fit. Preheat the oven to 350 degrees F.

6. Bake for 30 to 35 minutes. The top will be brown, no imprint will remain when the cake is touched lightly with the fingertips, the cake will just begin to pull away from the sides of the pan, and a cake tester inserted in the middle of the cake will come out clean.

7. Place the pan on a wire rack. Let the babka rest in the pan for 10 minutes, then run a knife around the outside of the cake and the inner tube, and carefully turn out the babka. If you are going to dust the babka with confectioners' sugar (see the first variation), cool on a wire rack. Transfer to a cake plate and cut just before serving. If you are going to use a sugar syrup (see the second variation), transfer the babka to the serving plate while it is still hot.

Wrap leftovers well. Store babka for a few days at room temperature, or wrap the cooled babka well and freeze.

Note: Thin slices of babka are too delicate for the toaster. Therefore, cut thick slices and toast under the broiler, turning once. Babka is no ordinary piece of toast and must be watched carefully to prevent burning.

VARIATIONS:

Babka with Confectioners' Sugar Topping

When the babka has cooled, sift a tablespoon of confectioners' sugar directly over the top, dusting lightly but evenly.

Babka with Orange-Apricot Flavor

As soon as the babka comes out of the oven, and while it is cooling for 10 minutes before being turned out of the pan, start the syrup. In a 1-quart pot stir together 1 cup of sugar, ½ cup of orange juice, and 2 tablespoons of freshly squeezed lemon juice. Bring to a rolling boil over high heat; boil for 1 minute to dissolve the sugar completely. Scrape down the sides and stir as necessary to keep the mixture from boiling over. Remove from the heat. Cool for 5 minutes, then stir in 2 tablespoons of apricot brandy. Place the hot babka on a serving plate that will be large enough to accommodate a small overflow of syrup. Pierce the top all over with a large kitchen fork, then slowly and evenly spoon all of the warm syrup over the top of the babka, allowing some to run off the sides.

Rich Babka

Increase the butter to 1½ sticks and add two extra egg yolks.

BABKA WITH CHOCOLATE FILLING

Makes two 8½ x 4½-inch loaves

Here, the yeast is mixed with enough flour and water to grow and bubble pro-lifically before it is mixed with remaining ingredients, giving a good boost to the dough. The flour-water-yeast mixture, called the sponge, virtually guarantees that the coffeecake will rise well. The dough is kneaded briefly, producing a finer, more even-textured cake than the babka in the previous recipe.

The loaves are filled and topped with a chocolate-and-nut mixture. If babka becomes a favorite coffeecake in your household, you'll discover yourself adding your own touches—perhaps cinnamon in place of the chocolate, or cur-rants plumped in hot water instead of the raisins, maybe even semisweet choco-late pieces. And if you prefer one big coffeecake, use a *kugelhopf* or a nine-inch tube pan in place of the two loaf pans.

INGREDIENTS:

FOR THE FILLING AND TOPPING:

⅔ **cup firmly packed dark brown sugar**

2 tablespoons unsweetened cocoa

¼ **cup finely chopped walnuts, almonds, or pecans**

¼ **cup (½ stick) unsalted butter, chilled**

FOR THE SPONGE:

1 cup unbleached white flour (stir the flour,
spoon gently into a dry-measure cup,
then level with the edge of a spatula)

1 package (¼ ounce) active dry yeast

¼ cup granulated white sugar

1 cup moderately hot milk (110 degrees F.)

FOR THE DOUGH:

½ cup (1 stick) unsalted butter, at room temperature

¼ cup granulated white sugar

2 eggs (graded extra large)

2 egg yolks

2 teaspoons vanilla extract

2 cups unbleached white flour (measured as above)

1 cup dark raisins (optional)

1 cup unbleached white flour (measured as above)

DIRECTIONS:

1. **For the filling and topping,** in a small mixing bowl use a fork to stir together the brown sugar and the cocoa. Stir in the chopped nuts. Use your fingers to break up the butter into small pieces, then work in the butter. The mixture should be crumbly, not too smooth. Set aside.

2. **For the sponge,** in a 1-quart mixing bowl use a fork to stir together the cup of flour, the yeast, and the ¼ cup sugar. Stir in the moderately hot milk, mixing to blend, then beat with the fork for about 30 seconds. Cover the bowl with plastic wrap. Allow the mixture to rise at room temperature until it reaches the top of the bowl (about 30 minutes in a 70-degree F. room). Remove the plastic wrap before the mixture rises to the top and touches it.

3. Butter two 8½ x 4½-inch loaf pans and set aside.

4. **For the dough,** in a large mixing bowl, using an electric mixer on high speed, cream the ½ cup of butter until it is soft. Beat in the sugar, creaming well, then beat in the whole eggs one at a time. Next, add the egg yolks and the vanilla

extract. Beat only until well mixed. Turn off the mixer and scrape down the sides of the bowl. Now, with the mixer on low speed (to prevent splattering), beat in the yeast mixture, then beat in 2 cups of flour a cup at a time. Stir in the optional raisins. The dough will have the consistency of a very thick batter.

5. Spread the remaining cup of flour into an 8-inch circle on a clean work surface. Turn out the dough onto the flour. Begin kneading with the aid of a pastry scraper or a metal spatula, folding the dough onto itself and pressing down lightly. Knead for 3 to 5 minutes, until all of the flour is incorporated and the dough is springy.

6. Divide the dough into 4 equal pieces. Using the pastry scraper or spatula, transfer one piece of dough into each prepared loaf pan. Wet your hands and press the dough evenly into each pan. Sprinkle ¼ of the filling and topping mixture on the surface of the dough in the pans. Top each with a second piece of dough, again leveling the dough with wet fingers. Sprinkle on the remaining filling and topping mixture.

7. Cover the pans with plastic wrap and allow the dough to rise in a draft-free area until it reaches the top of the pans. A slow rising of 1½ hours in a room about 70 degrees F. is ideal, but if you are in a hurry, the temperature can be as high as 85 degrees F. Remove the plastic wrap before the dough reaches the top.

8. Toward the end of the rising time, adjust an oven rack to the middle of the oven. Move any other racks below so that the loaves will have room to rise above the pans. Preheat the oven to 350 degrees F.

9. Bake for 30 to 35 minutes, until the loaves test done (see Step 6 of the previous recipe). Place the pans on a wire rack. Let the babkas rest in the pans for 10 minutes, then run a knife around the sides and turn out each babka onto the wire rack. Serve warm or at room temperature. Wrap well to store at room temperature for a few days, or wrap well and freeze.

CARAMEL SCHNECKEN

Makes 24 schnecken

The Jews of Germany who came to the United States brought with them some of the pastries that were part of the afternoon *kaffeeklatsch*, the informal gathering for drinking coffee and for enjoying conversation. Schnecken have remained among the most popular of these pastries. Always called by its foreign name, *schnecken* translates literally to "snails," referring to the coiled shape.

In this recipe, a yeast dough rich in butter and sour cream is refrigerated after it is mixed, enabling the cook to prepare the pastries in two stages. So while you must plan ahead, you don't need a huge block of time all at once. The dough is rolled into a rectangle and sprinkled with a raisin-and-nut filling, then it is rolled up and sliced. And as tender and delicious as the dough and its filling may be, it is the luscious caramel-nut topping that you will remember. When baked in muffin cups, the pastries will be crisp outside. When baked as a coffeecake (see the variation), the sides will be soft.

Serve schnecken for breakfast or brunch, as a snack with coffee or tea, as a lunch box treat, or for dessert. For those who like a less sweet pastry, try the schnecken in the recipe following this one.

PREPARING THE DOUGH

1 package (¼ ounce) active dry yeast

2 tablespoons lukewarm water (105 degrees F.)

1¼ cups unbleached white flour (stir the flour, spoon gently into a dry-measure cup, then level with the edge of a spatula)

¼ cup (½ stick) unsalted butter, at room temperature

1 egg (graded large or extra large)
¼ cup granulated white sugar
½ cup sour cream
¼ cup additional flour

1. In a small bowl or a cup, sprinkle the yeast over the water. Stir with a fork to combine, then set aside.

2. Place the 1¼ cups of flour in a 1-quart mixing bowl. Slice the butter into ¼-inch pieces, then use a pastry blender or your fingers to break up the butter into small, evenly distributed pieces. Use a large spoon to stir in the dissolved yeast, the egg, sugar, and sour cream. Beat vigorously for about 30 seconds.

3. Scrape down the sides, cover the bowl tightly with plastic wrap, and refrigerate for a minimum of 12 hours, up to 48 hours.

4. Remove the bowl of dough from the refrigerator, and allow the dough to stand, covered, for 2 to 3 hours, until it is at room temperature and has risen nearly to the top of the bowl.

5. On a clean, dry work surface, spread ¼ cup of flour into a 3 x 4-inch rectangle. Turn out the dough onto the flour. Using a pastry scraper or a spatula, turn the dough to coat it all over, then use the scraper or spatula to knead the dough 10 to 15 times by lifting it a few inches above the work surface and slapping it down. At the end of this brief kneading, the dough will have absorbed all the flour and will be slightly springy.

6. Return the dough to the mixing bowl, cover, then chill for a minimum of 1 hour before proceeding. Just before you are ready to continue, prepare the filling.

FILLING THE DOUGH

¼ **cup granulated white sugar**
½ **teaspoon ground cinnamon**
½ **cup raisins**
¾ **cup finely chopped pecans**
2 **tablespoons unsalted butter**

1. Mix together all ingredients except for the butter and set aside.

2. In a small pot or skillet, melt the butter over low heat. Prepare twenty-four 2½-inch diameter muffin cups (two standard 12-cup muffin tins) by brushing the bottoms and partway up the sides with some of the melted butter. Set aside. Reserve the remaining melted butter.

3. Spread a clean work surface (about 8 x 10 inches) with a thin layer of flour. Punch down the refrigerated dough, flatten it slightly between your hands, then place the dough on the floured surface. Flatten to a 5 x 8-inch rectangle. Sprinkling lightly with flour as necessary, use a rolling pin to roll out the dough to a 10 x 22-inch rectangle. From time to time, lift up the dough to make sure it is not sticking.

4. Brush the dough with more of the melted butter. (Reserve the remainder of the 2 tablespoons of melted butter for brushing the tops of the schnecken before baking.) Scatter the filling over the dough, then roll the dough very tightly, jelly-roll style, from one long side. Cover the filled and rolled dough with a clean kitchen towel for a few minutes while you prepare to bake the schnecken.

PREPARING FOR BAKING

10 tablespoons (1¼ sticks) unsalted butter
¼ cup light corn syrup
1 cup firmly packed dark brown sugar
¾ cup pecan halves, approximately

1. In a clean 1-quart pot, heat the butter over moderately low heat with the corn syrup and brown sugar, stirring to blend. Bring just to the boil. Continue cooking and stirring just enough to blend well. This caramel syrup will be used to coat the bottom of the muffin cups and will become the topping when the schnecken are turned upside down to cool.

2. Cover the bottom of each muffin cup with a teaspoon of the syrup. Place 2 or 3 pecans (depending on size) in each cup.

3. Gently roll the filled and rolled dough until it is 24 inches long. Slice the dough into twenty-four 1-inch pieces. Carefully transfer the rolled-up pieces to the muffin cups, pressing one piece into each muffin cup, cut side showing. Brush the tops with the remainder of the 2 tablespoons of melted butter from Step 4 on page 369. Cover the muffin pans lightly with plastic wrap or wax paper. Allow the schnecken to stand at room temperature (about 70 degrees F.) for 1 hour. They will rise somewhat, but because the dough was cold, they will not double in volume.

4. Toward the end of the rising time, preheat the oven to 375 degrees F. Bake in the middle of the oven for about 20 minutes, until light brown.

5. Remove the muffin pans from the oven, immediately run a knife around each pastry, then invert each muffin pan onto a large baking sheet. The schnecken will drop out. Spoon any syrup remaining in the muffin cups onto the pastries. Serve warm or at room temperature. Store leftovers in a tightly closed container, or freeze for later use.

VARIATIONS:

Caramel Schnecken Coffeecake

In place of muffin pans, use two 9-inch round cake pans. Brush the bottoms with melted butter, spread the syrup, and scatter the whole pecans over the syrup. Arrange 12 pastries evenly in each cake pan, 8 or 9 around the outside, 3 or 4 toward the middle. Let rise and bake as above. The schnecken will fill the pan during baking. Turn out as one piece, and present as one coffeecake. Gently break off individual rolls as servings.

Almond Schnecken

Substitute almonds for the pecans. Use ¾ cup slivered almonds in the filling and 1 teaspoon slivered almonds in each of the muffin cups.

CINNAMON-NUT SCHNECKEN

Makes 36 schnecken

Crisp and nutty, here are schnecken for those who prefer a less sweet pastry than the one in the previous recipe. The dough can be individually coiled for true schnecken (the German word for snails) or made into two large coffee-cakes, with crisp outside pieces and softer inside pieces that are wonderful for dunking into coffee. If you do not have young children, then borrow some when you prepare these schnecken, for I know of no better way to introduce a child to the fun of baking than to have them help shape these hands-on pastries.

INGREDIENTS:

FOR THE DOUGH:

1 package (¼ ounce) active dry yeast
¼ cup warm water (105 degrees F.)
3 tablespoons solid white vegetable shortening
2 tablespoons granulated white sugar
1½ teaspoons salt
¾ cup hot milk (120 degrees F.)
3 cups unbleached white flour (stir the flour,
    spoon gently into a dry-measure cup,
    then level with the edge of a spatula)

FOR ASSEMBLING THE SCHNECKEN:

½ cup (1 stick) unsalted butter

¾ cup granulated white sugar

¼ cup firmly packed light or dark brown sugar

1 teaspoon ground cinnamon

¾ cup finely chopped pecans

DIRECTIONS:

1. In a small bowl, dissolve the yeast in the warm water.

2. In a large mixing bowl, place the shortening, 2 tablespoons of sugar, and the salt. Pour in the hot milk. Stir to dissolve the shortening. Cool to lukewarm. You will be able to comfortably hold the bottom of the bowl in your hand.

3. Use a large wooden spoon to stir the dissolved yeast into the lukewarm milk mixture, then mix in the flour 1 cup at a time.

4. Turn out the dough onto a clean, lightly floured surface. Knead for 6 to 10 minutes, until an indentation springs back when you poke the dough with a finger. Add a little flour if necessary to keep the dough from sticking.

5. Place the dough in a clean mixing bowl large enough to accommodate it when double in volume. Cover tightly with plastic wrap, and let rise in a warm place until doubled. The length of rising time depends on the warmth of the area where the dough is rising. The dough will take about 1½ hours to rise in an 80-degree F. environment.

6. When the dough has risen, melt the butter over low heat. Transfer the butter to a small bowl.

7. In another small bowl, mix together the remaining ingredients.

8. Punch down the dough. Divide into 36 approximately equal pieces. (First divide the dough in half, then in half again. You now have 4 pieces of dough.

Divide each of the 4 pieces into thirds. You now have 12 smaller pieces of dough. Divide each into 3 small balls. Now you have 36 pieces of dough.) On a clean work surface, use your hands to shape each piece into a 6-inch log. (Children used to working with clay will know exactly how to do this.)

9. Grease two large baking sheets.

10. Dip each log into the butter, coating completely, then roll into the cinnamon-sugar-nut mixture. Shape into a flat coil as though you are making a coiled-up snake. Place on the greased baking sheet, leaving an inch between each pastry.

11. Cover lightly with plastic wrap and allow the schnecken to rise in a warm area (about 80 degrees F.) for 45 minutes. The pastries will become light and puffy, but they do not need to double in volume.

12. Toward the end of the rising time, adjust the oven racks to the middle and upper third of the oven. (The schnecken will burn on the bottom if they are baked too close to the bottom heat source.) Preheat the oven to 350 degrees F. Bake the schnecken for 16 to 18 minutes, until light brown and baked through. Midway through the baking, reverse the baking pans on the racks, and turn the baking pans front to back.

13. Immediately transfer the baked schnecken to wire racks to cool. Serve warm or at room temperature, or freeze for later use.

VARIATION:

Cinnamon Schnecken Coffeecake

The coffeecake will be round and shaped like a flat, coiled rope. However, instead of being made up of one long piece, each will consist of 18 pieces. The first piece is rolled into a flat coil. The second one begins where the first left off.

For two large coffeecakes, grease two baking sheets. Divide the dough into 36 pieces, then roll each piece into a 6-inch log, dip into the butter, and coat with the nut mixture as above. Shape the first piece of coated dough into a flat coil and place it in the center of one greased baking sheet. Begin the second piece of dough where the first left off. It is not necessary to attach the pieces or to pinch them together. Begin the next piece of dough where the second one ended. Continue until you have used half of the pieces of coated dough to make a round coffeecake consisting of 18 pieces of dough. Press down lightly with your hands to flatten the coffeecake. Repeat with the remaining pieces of dough, making a second coffeecake. Cover lightly with plastic wrap, and let the coffeecakes rise in a warm area (about 80 degrees F.) for 45 minutes. The coffeecakes will expand and rise somewhat, becoming puffy, but they do not need to double in volume.

Adjust the oven racks to the middle and upper third of the oven. Preheat the oven to 350 degrees F. Bake the coffeecakes for 25 to 35 minutes. Midway through the baking, reverse the baking pans on the racks, and turn the baking pans front to back. The coffeecakes are done when golden brown. The center coil should be firm but the outside dough should not be too crisp. Loosen the coffeecakes with a spatula but do not try to remove them from the baking sheets until they have cooled somewhat. Cool them on the baking sheets on a wire rack. While still warm (but not hot), the coffeecakes can be transferred to a serving plate. They are delicious warm or at room temperature. The coffeecakes are eaten informally as each diner pulls off pieces. The outside pieces will be crusty, the inside soft.

MANDELBROT

Makes about 40 cookies

Although it is more a cookie than a bread, crisp, toasted, twice-baked *mandelbrot* ("almond bread") is named for the German words for almond (*mandel*) and bread (*brot*). A specialty among Ashkenazic Jews, mandelbrot is eminently dunkable, a most appropriate accompaniment to coffee or tea. Closely related to other twice-baked European cookies—Germany's *zwieback* and the *biscotti* of Italy—mandelbrot is successful in Jewish homes as a not-too-sweet, easily transportable pareve cookie that stores well at room temperature. You can expect to see mandelbrot on the dessert table at family gatherings during holidays, and mandelbrot is a favorite traditional cookie to serve at synagogue functions.

The quantity of almonds varies with the cook. The proportion of almonds in the recipe below makes a rich mandelbrot textured abundantly with the nuts. Toasting the almonds first, an optional step, brings out the flavor of the almonds and makes them more crisp. When whole almonds are used in place of chopped, biting into the whole nuts will make a contrasting texture to the otherwise brittle cookie. Modern cooks like to add chocolate chips, and some like candied fruit as well. The addition of almond extract to the dough imparts a pleasant almond flavor to the entire cookie.

INGREDIENTS:

$1\frac{1}{2}$ **cups slivered or coarsely chopped blanched almonds**

2 **eggs (graded large)**

$\frac{1}{2}$ **cup granulated white sugar**

$\frac{1}{4}$ **cup mild-tasting vegetable oil**

1 teaspoon vanilla extract
1/4 teaspoon almond extract (optional)
2 cups unbleached white flour (stir the flour,
    spoon gently into a dry-measure cup,
    then level with the edge of a spatula)
1½ teaspoons baking powder

DIRECTIONS:

1. If desired, toast the almonds in a preheated 350-degree F. oven for about 10 minutes, until light brown. Immediately transfer to a cool plate or bowl.

2. Adjust an oven rack to the middle of the oven. Preheat the oven to 350 degrees F.

3. In a medium-size mixing bowl, beat the eggs and the sugar with an electric mixer on high speed for about 4 minutes, until the eggs are thickened and light in color. Beat in the oil, the vanilla, and the optional almond extract.

4. Sift together the flour and baking powder. Then, using a large metal or wooden spoon, stir the dry ingredients into the egg mixture ½ cup at a time. Stir in the almonds.

5. The dough should be stiff enough to roll into a log between wet hands. If it is too sticky, refrigerate the dough for half an hour.

6. Divide the dough in half. Wet your hands and form each half into a roll 2 inches in diameter by 11 inches long. Place on an ungreased baking sheet. Bake for 30 minutes, until light brown. Rotate the baking sheet back to front once during baking for even browning. The logs will flatten somewhat during baking.

7. Remove the baking sheet from the oven. Raise the oven temperature to 375 degrees F.

8. While they are still hot, carefully loosen the logs with a metal spatula. Let them cool on the baking sheet placed on a wire rack for about 5 minutes. Now, using a sharp knife, cut each log into ½- to ¾-inch slices, and lay each slice flat on the baking sheet.

9. Return the slices to the oven for 5 minutes, then turn over each slice and bake for another 5 minutes. The mandelbrot should be lightly toasted on both sides.

10. When cool, store at room temperature in a tightly closed container.

VARIATIONS:

Whole Almond Mandelbrot

Use untoasted blanched whole almonds. Cut the mandelbrot into 3/4- to 1-inch slices in Step 8 above.

Mandelbrot with Chocolate

Stir in ½ cup semisweet chocolate pieces with the almonds.

RUGELACH

Makes 64 rugelach

Flaky crescent-shaped pastries that are traditionally filled with a mixture of nuts, raisins, and/or jam, derive their name—*rugelach*—from a Yiddish term meaning "horn-shaped." A rich butter and cream cheese dough is rolled thin to make a marvelous melt-in-your-mouth pastry. In this recipe, as is traditional, the prepared rugelach dough is chilled in the refrigerator overnight. The next morning, the work area and rolling pin are floured, and the chilled dough is rolled, filled, shaped, and baked. To compensate for the extra flour that is worked into the dough during the rolling process, a small amount of sour cream is added to the dough as a tenderizer.

Eight rugelach are made from each round of dough. The entire batch of dough can be made at once and kept in the refrigerator for several days, allowing the home baker who only has half an hour to spare here and there to make small quantities of the rugelach at a time. Or, the quantities of dough and filling can be cut in half.

In addition to the traditional nut filling, jam and chocolate fillings are presented as variations, along with a more unusual but sensational sesame seed filling that mixes the traditional and the modern, the Sephardic and the Ashkenazic. If desired, make several different fillings for one batch of dough.

INGREDIENTS:

FOR THE DOUGH:

**2 cups unbleached white flour (stir the flour,
spoon gently into a dry-measure cup,
then level with the edge of a spatula)**

1 cup (2 sticks) unsalted butter, at room temperature

8 ounces (1 large package) cream cheese, at room
    temperature

¼ cup sour cream

Extra flour for rolling

FOR THE FILLING:

½ cup (1 stick) unsalted butter (to be melted, for
    brushing)

2 cups finely chopped walnuts

½ cup golden or dark raisins, plumped if desired by
    soaking in 1 cup boiling water for 5 minutes

½ cup granulated white sugar

1 tablespoon ground cinnamon

1 egg (graded large) for glazing

DIRECTIONS:

1. For the dough, in a large mixing bowl place the flour, 1 cup of butter, the cream cheese, and the sour cream. Mix on a low speed with an electric mixer just until the ingredients are evenly distributed and the mixture forms a dough. The dough can be mixed in two batches in a food processor using the pulse setting. Or, if you enjoy working with your hands, mix the butter, cream cheese, and sour cream into the flour with your fingers. You will end up with a smooth dough in a short time.

2. Flatten the dough into a rectangle about half an inch thick, wrap well in wax paper or plastic wrap and refrigerate for 8 hours or longer.

3. When you are ready to shape and bake the rugelach, melt the ½ cup of butter for brushing over low heat. Set aside.

4. For the filling, in a small bowl mix together the walnuts, the raisins (drain well if plumped in water), the sugar, and the cinnamon.

5. Adjust an oven rack to the middle of the oven. If you will be baking two batches at once, place the second rack above. Preheat the oven to 350 degrees F.

6. Divide the dough equally into eight pieces. Work with one piece of dough at a time, returning the remainder to the refrigerator.

7. Lightly flour a clean work surface. Place one piece of dough on the work surface. Pound the dough about a dozen times with a rolling pin. This will warm the dough a bit and will soften the butter and cream cheese, making the dough easy to roll out. Flour the rolling pin and roll the dough from the center outward to a 9-inch circle. Keep the rolling pin and the work surface lightly floured as necessary.

8. Brush the dough liberally with melted butter. Scatter about ¼ cup of filling over the dough. Using a pastry wheel or a sharp knife, cut the dough in half, then quarters, then each quarter in half again. You now have 8 elongated triangles. Roll up each triangle tightly from the broad end to the tip. Turn the ends down slightly to make a crescent shape. Transfer to an ungreased baking sheet. Repeat Steps 7 and 8 until you have used all the dough and filling (or until you have made the quantity desired for the moment).

9. Beat the egg well. Brush the rugelach well with the beaten egg. Bake for 15 to 18 minutes, until golden and sizzling. (If two batches are baked at a time, midway during baking reverse the baking sheets top to bottom and front to back. This will ensure even browning.) Immediately transfer the rugelach to a wire rack to cool. Rugelach are outstanding while still warm, but they are also outstanding when eaten after a few days at room temperature. Store in a covered container at room temperature, or wrap well and freeze for later use.

VARIATIONS:

Rugelach with Jam

In place of the melted butter, spread 1½ tablespoons (1 tablespoon plus 1½ teaspoons) of seedless raspberry jam or apricot jam on each round of dough before filling with the nut mixture.

Rugelach with Chocolate

Brush the dough either with melted butter or with jam as in the above variation. In place of the raisins, substitute 2 cups of semisweet chocolate pieces (¼ cup for each round of dough).

Rugelach with Sesame Seeds, Jam, and Chocolate

In place of the filling in the basic recipe, you will need ½ to 1 cup of sesame seeds, ¾ cup of seedless raspberry jam, and 1 to 2 cups of semisweet chocolate pieces. Toast half a cup of the sesame seeds at a time in a 7-inch cast-iron skillet over moderate heat. Shake the pan often for even toasting. As soon as the sesame seeds begin to smell delicious and when a few of them make a popping noise (both events will happen at about the same time), transfer the toasted seeds to a bowl. Toast the remainder of the sesame seeds if you are using more than half a cup.

Spread a round of dough with 1½ tablespoons of the jam. Scatter 1 to 2 tablespoons of toasted sesame seeds evenly on top of the jam, then scatter 2 to 4 tablespoons of semisweet chocolate pieces. Press the chocolate pieces lightly into the dough. Cut the dough and shape and bake the rugelach as indicated in Steps 8 and 9 in the basic recipe.

HAMANTASHEN

Makes 30 hamantashen

The link between Jewish foods and Jewish history is vividly represented by the triangular-shaped pastries known as *hamantashen*. During Purim, Jewish people symbolically devour the evil Haman when eating "Haman's pockets" (originally *mohn tashen*, "poppy seed pockets"). One explanation for the name is that Haman stuffed his pockets with bribe money. According to tradition, the triangular shape is said to resemble the type of hat worn by Haman. Hamantashen are also known as *oznay Haman*, "ears of Haman." It was once the practice to cut off the ears of criminals before hanging them, and eating Haman's ears is a reminder that Haman was eventually hanged.

Hamantashen are traditionally stuffed with poppy seeds, fruit, or jam, or sometimes with cheese. While hamantashen can be made with either a yeast or a cookie dough, a cookie dough is recommended because it is tasty, faster than a yeast dough (no rising time) and easier to work with. The cookie will be crisp at first, then it will soften when stored in a covered container.

For a smooth poppy seed filling, before cooking the filling you will need to grind the poppy seeds in a spice grinder or a coffee grinder. If you do not grind them, the filling will have a seedy consistency. Filling made from the ground seeds is somewhat richer; the texture is a matter of personal preference.

PREPARING THE FILLING

MOHN (POPPY SEED) FILLING:

> **1 cup poppy seeds**
> **½ cup honey**
> **½ cup orange juice**

1. For a smooth filling, grind the poppy seeds in a spice grinder or a coffee grinder. The seeds can be ground to a powder or even to a paste, depending on the grinder.

2. For the filling, in a 1-quart pot bring the ground poppy seeds, honey, and orange juice to the boil over high heat. Reduce to a gentle boil, and cook uncovered for about 4 minutes, stirring frequently, until the mixture becomes very thick. Be careful of spattering as the water boils off. Reduce the heat to low, cover the pot, and cook for an additional 2 minutes. Remove from the heat and cool to room temperature before using.

For poppy seeds that have not been ground, cook the mixture uncovered for 8 minutes, then cover and cook for an additional 2 minutes. The mixture should be the consistency of a thick porridge. If desired, purée the mixture in a blender or a food processor. While the mixture will still be seedy, it will become somewhat less granular. Cool to room temperature.

PRUNE, APRICOT, OR MIXED FRUIT FILLING:

1½ **cups pitted prunes, dried apricots, or mixed dried fruit**
6 tablespoons water
1 tablespoon sugar
Pinch cinnamon
1½ **teaspoons freshly squeezed lemon juice**

1. In a 1-quart pot, bring the dried fruit and water to the boil over high heat. As soon as the water boils, turn off the heat, cover the pot, and allow the fruit to stand in the pot on the turned-off burner for 30 minutes.

2. Stir in the remaining ingredients, mashing the fruit with a fork. Cool to room temperature.

PREPARING THE DOUGH

2 cups unbleached white flour (stir the flour,
spoon gently into a dry-measure cup,
then level with the edge of a spatula)
1½ teaspoons baking powder
6 tablespoons granulated white sugar
3 tablespoons unsalted butter or solid white
vegetable shortening
2 eggs (graded large)
2 tablespoons orange juice
1 teaspoon grated orange rind (optional)
1 teaspoon vanilla extract (optional)
½ teaspoon almond extract (optional)
Beaten egg for glazing the dough

1. In a medium-size mixing bowl, use a fork to stir together the flour, baking powder, and sugar. Work in the butter or shortening with the fork, a pastry blender, or your fingers. Add the eggs, orange juice, and, if desired, the optional orange rind and vanilla and almond extracts. Gather the dough into a ball with your fingers, working in any flour that remains dry.

2. Adjust an oven rack to the middle of the oven. Preheat the oven to 350 degrees F.

3. Grease 2 large baking sheets.

4. Divide the dough in half. Work with one piece of dough at a time, keeping the other half covered. Pat the dough into a 6-inch circle between 2 sheets of wax paper. From time to time, remove and replace the wax paper to prevent the dough from sticking. Use a rolling pin to roll out the dough into an 11-inch circle. Cut as many circles of dough as you can with a 2⅝-inch cookie cutter. Reroll the scraps to ⅛-inch thickness and cut more circles. You will end up with 15 circles of dough.

5. Divide half the filling among the circles of dough, placing a heaping teaspoon of filling in the center of each circle. Pat the filling to within half an inch of the edge of the circle. Using both hands, bring the edges of the dough around the filling to make a triangle. Pinch the edges together securely. The dough will not cover the filling—there will be some filling showing through at the center. Push the filling down at the center to make it level.

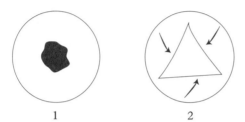

1   2   3

6. Brush the dough (but not the filling) with beaten egg.

7. Bake the hamantashen for 12 to 15 minutes, until light brown. Transfer to a wire rack to cool. While the first batch is baking, prepare the second. Store hamantashen in a covered container at room temperature, or wrap well and freeze for later use.

COCONUT MACAROONS

Makes 36 to 40 macaroons

Meringue that is mixed gently with a generous amount of grated coconut looks exactly like any meringue drop cookie when baked. But bite into the cookie and you will recognize a fresh, light version of the canned macaroons that fill grocery shelves during Passover. Homemade coconut macaroons emerge from the oven crisp on the outside and chewy on the inside, and will remain that way if stored on a plate and lightly covered with plastic wrap. When wrapped tightly or kept in a covered container, they become soft outside, remaining chewy inside. When stored completely uncovered, they become crisp throughout. Coconut macaroons can be stored at room temperature for as long as two weeks, becoming more and more chewy each day. They freeze well and thaw quickly.

INGREDIENTS:

> **2 eggs whites (from eggs graded extra large)**
> **2 teaspoons freshly squeezed lemon juice**
> **10 tablespoons granulated white sugar (scant**
>   **$^2/_3$ cup)**
> **1½ cups shredded unsweetened coconut**

DIRECTIONS:

1. Line two large baking sheets with parchment paper.

2. Preheat the oven to 300 degrees F.

3. In a medium-size clean, dry mixing bowl, with clean, dry beaters, use an electric mixer on high speed to beat the egg whites until they just begin to foam. Add the lemon juice and continue to beat until frothy but not yet white or thick. Keep the mixer at high speed and add the sugar 1 tablespoon at a time, beating a full minute after each addition. The sugar will be dissolved and the mixture will be very thick and white.

4. Turn off the mixer and use a rubber spatula to fold in the coconut ¼ cup at a time. To fold, cut through the center of the egg whites all the way down to the bottom of the bowl. Bring the spatula up against the side of the bowl, then rotate the bowl a quarter turn and cut through again. Repeat until the coconut is mixed in.

5. Drop the mixture by level tablespoons onto the parchment on the baking sheets. Or, use a cookie press or decorating bag with a large star tube. The cookies will retain their shape when baked.

6. Bake the macaroons for 20 minutes, reversing the pans from top to bottom and front to back halfway through the baking. The cookies should just barely brown. Turn off the oven, then open the oven door and allow the macaroons to cool completely before removing them from the oven. Carefully lift the macaroons off the parchment. Store at room temperature or freeze.

ALMOND MACAROONS

Makes 28 to 30 macaroons

Almond macaroons are a Passover specialty that requires no substitutions: they consist only of almonds, sugar, and egg whites. For a marvelous chewy consistency—and to prevent the macaroons from spreading during baking—bake the cookies in miniature baking cups (1½-inch diameter).

INGREDIENTS:

1 cup (packed) ground blanched almonds
1 cup granulated white sugar
2 egg whites (from eggs graded extra large)

DIRECTIONS:

1. Set out 30 miniature baking cups on a baking sheet. Preheat the oven to 350 degrees F.

2. In a small bowl, mix together the ground almonds and the sugar.

3. In a small clean, dry mixing bowl, with a clean, dry wire whisk or beaters, beat the egg whites until they just barely hold stiff peaks. They should still be moist. Fold in the almond and sugar mixture ½ cup at a time. The mixture will be like a paste. Drop by level tablespoons into the baking cups.

4. Bake in the middle of the oven for 12 minutes. Immediately remove the baking sheet from the oven and transfer the cookies in the baking cups to a wire rack. Keep the macaroons in the baking cups until ready to serve. Store at room temperature in a covered container.

TAIGLACH

Makes 1 lovely pyramid

If you think that because these little balls of dough are coated in honey they are probably served on Rosh Hashanah to usher in a sweet year, you are right. *Taiglach* pyramids, an Eastern European specialty, are displayed in bakeries for the Jewish New Year. When you follow the recipe below exactly, you will be able to produce these same pyramids in your own kitchen.

INGREDIENTS:

2¼ cups unbleached white flour (stir the flour,
　　spoon gently into a dry-measure cup,
　　then level with the edge of a spatula)
1 teaspoon baking powder
3 eggs (graded large)
2 tablespoons mild-tasting vegetable oil, approximately
1 cup honey
½ cup firmly packed dark brown sugar
½ teaspoon powdered ginger
1 cup halved or coarsely chopped walnuts or pecans

DIRECTIONS:

1. Preheat the oven to 350 degrees F.

2. In a medium-size mixing bowl, mix together the flour and baking powder. Make a well in the center. Drop in the eggs and 2 tablespoons of oil. Use a

wooden spoon to beat in the eggs and oil, making a soft dough. If the dough is crumbly, add up to a tablespoon more oil.

3. Divide the dough equally into 4 pieces. On a clean work surface, roll out each piece to a 20-inch log. Break off small pieces of dough and shape into ¾-inch balls, making 20 from each log, 80 in all.

4. Place on an ungreased baking sheet. Bake on the middle rack of the oven for 15 minutes, until light brown on the bottom.

5. Meanwhile, in a 2-quart pot stir together the honey, brown sugar, and ginger. Bring to the boil over high heat. Reduce the heat to low and cook, uncovered, for 10 minutes, stirring occasionally. Take care that the mixture does not boil over the pot.

6. Drop the baked balls of dough into the boiling honey. Cook for 15 minutes, stirring gently from time to time. Add the nuts. Continue cooking for an additional 5 minutes, stirring often.

7. Remove the pot from the heat. Let stand for 15 minutes.

8. Use a clean sponge to wet a clean, smooth kitchen surface, then turn out the mixture into a 9-inch circle to cool slightly on the wet surface.

9. Lightly grease a 6-inch circle in the center of a serving plate.

10. As soon as the mixture is cool enough to handle, wet your hands and shape the mixture into a pyramid. Place the pyramid on the center of the serving plate. Sometimes the pyramid needs a little help retaining its shape. Be prepared to reshape the mixture as it cools. If desired, before serving, spoon any honey that may drip to the bottom back over the top.

SESAME HALVAH

Makes two 4½-inch bars

Halvah, also pronounced *halavah*, is known to American Jews as a ground sesame seed mixture that is purchased in small bars or cut from huge rounds. It can be made at home by mixing pulverized toasted sesame seeds with a sugar syrup. Homemade halvah, which has a strong sesame taste, is more moist and darker in color than purchased halvah.

In the Middle East, Sephardim know halvah as a sweet preparation most often made from semolina (cream of wheat or farina). In the semolina variation, the grain is first cooked in olive oil, then mixed with the sugar syrup. Slices of sesame and semolina halvah are enjoyed as a snack or a dessert. Homemade halvah will keep at room temperature for about a week.

INGREDIENTS:

2 tablespoons granulated white sugar
2 tablespoons corn syrup
¼ cup water
1 cup sesame seeds
¼ cup toasted slivered almonds (optional)
½ teaspoon vanilla extract (optional)
Extra toasted sesame seeds for rolling (optional)

DIRECTIONS:

1. In a 1-quart pot, bring the sugar, corn syrup, and water to a rolling boil over high heat. Stir to dissolve the sugar, then remove from the heat. Set aside.

2. In a 7-inch cast-iron skillet over moderate heat, toast half the sesame seeds. Shake the pan often for even toasting. As soon as the sesame seeds begin to smell delicious and when a few of them make a popping noise (both events will happen at about the same time), transfer the toasted seeds to a bowl. Toast the remainder of the sesame seeds. Pulverize half the toasted seeds at a time in a blender until they are powdery. Place in a medium-size bowl and mix in the optional toasted almonds with a fork.

3. If vanilla flavoring is desired, stir the vanilla extract into the sugar syrup. Mix the sugar syrup with the powdered sesame seeds (and almonds).

4. Wet your hands. Form the mixture into two bars about 4½ x 1½ inches each. Roll the bars in sesame seeds if you like. Let harden at room temperature. Wrap in plastic wrap or foil.

VARIATION:

Semolina Halvah

Omit the sesame seeds, corn syrup, and vanilla. Increase the almonds to ½ cup of untoasted slivered almonds. Use 1 cup of sugar and 2 cups of water for the syrup in Step 1. In a 2-quart pot, heat ⅓ cup of olive oil until it is warm. Toast the slivered almonds in the oil, then stir in 1 cup of semolina. Cook, stirring constantly, until all the oil is absorbed. Stir in the sugar syrup, pressing out any lumps while stirring. Transfer the thick mixture to a serving platter. Use your hands to shape the mixture into a rectangle 6 x 12 inches, 1 inch high. Cut into 1-inch squares to serve. A fine little nosh.

Chocolate Egg Cream

Makes 1 large egg cream

Some things you just accept without thinking. Those of us who grew up in New York City knew that a two-cents plain was a glass of seltzer, and an egg cream was a glass of seltzer mixed with chocolate syrup and a little milk. We didn't wonder why there was neither egg nor cream in this ice cream soda without the ice cream.

In mixing up egg creams at home, we don't use standard measurements. We do it by eye. So when I had to convert eye measurements to cookbook measurements, my husband and I set out a number of different size glasses, a jar of U-bet chocolate syrup, plenty of seltzer, and a container of milk. We did a lot of measuring and testing, and we hope you will like our best egg cream.

INGREDIENTS:

3 tablespoons chocolate syrup (tested with U-bet)
⅜ cup whole milk
8 ounces seltzer

DIRECTIONS:

1. Place the chocolate syrup in a 16-ounce glass.

2. Add the milk, stirring until the chocolate is mixed in completely.

3. Add the seltzer, stirring carefully so it doesn't bubble up and over the glass.

VARIATION:

Chocolate Egg Cream—Eyeball Method

I take a 16-ounce Coke glass, the kind that's narrow at the bottom and bubbles out at the top. Pour in a little over an inch of syrup, then about 2 inches of milk. Stir rapidly until all the syrup is dissolved. Pour in the seltzer to about ½ inch from the top of the glass, stirring all the while. Two straws, please!

Index

INDEX

H

L

METRIC CONVERSION TABLES

LIQUID MEASURES

American (Standard Cup)   **Metric Equivalent**

1 cup	= ½ pint = 8 fl. oz.	2.37 dl.
1 tablespoon	= ½ fl. oz.	1.5 cl.
1 teaspoon	= ⅙ fl. oz.	0.5 cl.
1 pint	= 16 fl. oz.	4.73 dl.
1 quart	= 2 pints = 32 fl. oz.	9.46 dl.

British (Standard Cup)   **Metric Equivalent**

1 cup	= ½ pint = 10 fl. oz.	2.84 dl.
1 tablespoon	= 0.55 fl. oz.	1.7 cl.
1 teaspoon	= ⅕ fl. oz.	0.6 cl.
1 pint	= 20 fl. oz.	5.7 dl.
1 quart	= 2 pints = 40 fl. oz.	1.1 liter
1 cup	= 16 tablespoons	
1 tablespoon	= 3 teaspoons	
1.1 quart	= 1 liter = 10 deciliters = 100 centiliters	

SOLID MEASURES

American/British   **Metric Equivalent**

1 lb. = 16 oz.	= 453 grams
2.2 lbs.	= 1000 grams = 1 kilogram
1 oz.	= 28 grams
3½ oz.	= 100 grams

OVEN TEMPERATURES

Degrees Fahrenheit	Degrees Centigrade	
240-280	115-135	Very slow
280-320	135-160	Slow
320-340	160-170	Warm
340-370	170-185	Moderate
370-400	185-205	Fairly Hot
400-450	205-230	Hot
450-500	230-260	Very Hot

About the Author

Upon graduation from the College of Human Ecology at Cornell University in 1961, Betty S. Goldberg's fervent interest in cooking progressed from extensive entertaining to eventually creating wonderful dishes of her own. She was soon planning and executing banquets for as many as one hundred twenty people, and before long she was teaching classes in Jewish, Mexican, and Chinese cooking.

The success of Mrs. Goldberg's classes led to the publication of three books on Chinese cuisine, the most recent of which is the popular *Chinese Kosher Cooking*. In *International Cooking for the Kosher Home,* she continued the process she initiated with great success in *Chinese Kosher Cooking*—namely, converting nonkosher recipes into splendid kosher dishes.

Betty Goldberg is well known in the New Haven area for her culinary achievements and for having served as dining editor of the *Westside Shopper,* where her weekly food column was seen by more than 25,000 readers.

Betty S. Goldberg resides with her husband in Woodbridge, Connecticut. In addition to her passion for cooking, she enjoys theater, gardening, Irish terriers, and visiting her four grown children (all of whom are accomplished cooks).